*The Business of Lobbying in China*

# The Business of
# Lobbying in China

SCOTT KENNEDY

HARVARD UNIVERSITY PRESS

*Cambridge, Massachusetts*
*London, England*

Library of Congress Cataloging-in-Publication Data
Kennedy, Scott, 1967–
    The business of lobbyng in China / Scott Kennedy.
      p. cm.
    Includes bibliographical references.
    ISBN 0-674-01547-9 (alk. paper)
      1. Industrial policy—China.   2. Lobbying—China.   3. Business and
    politics—China.   I. Title.
HD3616.C63K46 2005
322'.3'0951—dc22                                          2004054314

For Mary Beth, Isaac, Brian, and Ed

# Contents

# List of Tables and Figure

## Tables

## Figure

# Acknowledgments

The front cover carries only my name as author, but this book would not have been completed without the generous support of numerous individuals and organizations in the United States and China.

Field research in China can be one of the most frustrating experiences of one's professional life. And it can be one of the most exhilarating. Luckily, in this project the latter outweighed the former, largely due to the good offices of the Chinese scholarly community. Peking University's Research Center for Contemporary China served as a helpful host during the early fieldwork. In addition to its director, Shen Mingming, Yan Jie provided top-notch logistical assistance. The Pudong Institute for the United States Economy (PIUSE) proved a most helpful host during the summer of 1999. I am indebted to Guo Xuetang for his persistence and patience in helping arrange several interviews during my trips to Shanghai and the surrounding area. Several other Chinese scholars offered invaluable suggestions and contacts that facilitated more productive fieldwork.

This book originated as my dissertation. It would never have taken flight without the wise counsel of my dissertation committee members: Harry Harding, Bruce Dickson, and Susan Sell. Their probing questions and insights turned what was a general curiosity into a focused research project, and they helped me mold the collected data into a clear argument. Each has been an inspiring mentor. Over the course of this project many colleagues and friends generously served as sounding boards and as sources of important suggestions and valuable pieces of information. They include, but by no means are limited to, Michael Aller, Charles Bickers, Gardner Bovingdon, Kjeld Erik Brødsgaard, Bob Crandall, Bob Eno, Sara Friedman, Ian Johnson, Anthony Kuhn, Scott Lasensky, Susan Lawrence, Keir Lieber, Ed Lincoln, Jennifer Liu, and Andrew Mertha. I would also like to thank Nick Cullather, Harvey Feigenbaum, Roger Haydon, Nick Lardy, Peter Lorentzen, Mike Mochizuki, Jean Oi, Margaret M. Pearson, and two anonymous reviewers for Harvard University Press for offering stimulating feedback on earlier versions of the manuscript. I am particularly indebted to three colleagues: Since our days in graduate school, Jason Kindopp has been an enthusiastic interlocutor on the major issues raised in these pages. Greg Kasza went through the manuscript with a fine-tooth comb, finding inconsistencies that needed to be eliminated and holes that needed to be plugged. And Ethan Michelson offered valuable feedback on several chapters and helped me resolve problems large and small as the manuscript neared publication.

*The Business of Lobbying in China* is a story about the growing policy influence of businesspeople in the People's Republic of China, a story that could not have been told without the willing participation of its protagonists. As useful as other research methods are, in-depth interviews provide irreplaceable texture and context; and in this case, no written sources, published or otherwise, could have provided the necessary data on their own. I thank the many company executives, association representatives, government officials, specialists, and journalists who shared revealing information and candid opinions with me, a stranger who typically contacted them without warning and added to their already hectic schedules. The enthusiasm and thoughtfulness with which they discussed the topics contained in the following pages were the surest sign that I had happened upon something worthy of study. To protect their identities, the names of my interview sources are replaced by codes in the notes (the appendix contains an explanation of the coding system).

While all of my interviews were memorable, I recall one association leader in particular who was initially annoyed by my presence, blithely flipping my name card onto the desk and hurrying me to get on with my questions. Before too long, though, he recognized the underlying logic of my inquiries as ones he himself had long been concerned about, and the frustrations he felt in his job came pouring out. At the end of our meeting, believing he had found a kindred spirit, he asked me to tell his story. With my gratitude, his and many others' are contained within these pages. I should stress, though, that neither he nor many of my sources may fully agree with my assessments about their situations or my conclusions about Chinese politics. The interviews are not pieces of a mosaic but ingredients to a meal of my own making. Where we do differ, I ask my sources for their understanding and, please, for one more interview.

For financial support, I would like to thank George Washington University for a generous fellowship that allowed me to carry out fieldwork in 1998 and 1999. The Brookings Institution provided a fellowship and collegial environment during the early stages of writing. And I am grateful to Indiana University's Department of East Asian Languages and Cultures and to its East Asian Studies Center for providing the financial assistance necessary to conduct fieldwork in 2002 and 2003 and to complete production of the book. A special thanks to Susan Nelson for permitting me to take leave for a semester to finish the manuscript.

At Harvard University Press, I want to express my appreciation to my editor, Kathleen McDermott, for her sound advice and regular encouragement. And I would like to thank Bette Page of NK Graphics for expertly shepherding the manuscript through the production process.

One personal reason I was drawn to the topic of government-business relations is that I come from a family of businesspeople. Whether a restauranteur, pharmacist, engineer, home builder, advertiser, or salesman, they each distinguished themselves in their professions. Not only have they been valuable role models to me, they also made it easier for me to understand the perspectives of the entrepreneurs and managers that I interviewed. My mother, Karen Kennedy, in addition to keeping me well fed with articles about the computer industry, showed over her career that enduring business success is the product of hard work and imagination. My father, Peter Kennedy, similarly demonstrated that business at its best is less about making cold calculations than about building relationships. I also have gained from the experiences of my sister, Sherry Syence, who has worked on both sides of the fence, in trade associations and the government. Lastly, I benefited enormously from conversations with my brother-in-law, Tad Diesel, a lobbyist in the telecommunications industry. He is living proof that lobbying can be a noble vocation.

Finally, there are four individuals who deserve my deepest appreciation. My wife, Mary Beth, has admirably endured numerous hardships so that I could both pursue my interests and have a rich personal life. She moved herself and our family to China, lived there under difficult circumstances, constantly provided encouragement and counsel, and read and reread proposals, letters, and chapters. I am eternally grateful for her sacrifice and support. And Isaac, Brian, and Ed, my three sons, have made this both the easiest and most difficult project to complete—easy because they have brought so much happiness to me, each day refilling my energy reserves, and difficult because this project received so much of my attention, more than it deserved. Mary Beth, Isaac, Brian, and Ed help me every day to see the world in its proper perspective, and it is to them that this book is dedicated.

The contributions of all of these people have made this book far better than it otherwise would have been. But while they deserve credit for improving this book, any remaining mistakes and shortcomings are the sole responsibility of the author.

# *Abbreviations*

| | |
|---|---|
| ABM | Accounting and Business Management Sub-Association |
| ACFIC | All-China Federation of Industry and Commerce |
| BEZ | Beijing Experimental Zone for High Technology Development |
| BMI | Bureau of Metallurgy Industry |
| BOF | Basic Oxygen Furnace |
| BSA | Business Software Alliance |
| BSIA | Beijing Software Industry Association |
| CAA | China Electronic Audio Industry Association |
| CAEFI | China Association of Enterprises with Foreign Investment |
| CCIC | China Chamber of International Commerce |
| CCP | Chinese Communist Party |
| CCPIT | China Council for the Promotion of International Trade |
| CEC | China Enterprise Confederation |
| CECC | China Electronics Chamber of Commerce |
| CEDA | China Enterprise Directors Association |
| CEMA | China Enterprise Management Association |
| CGCC | China General Chamber of Commerce |
| CIEA/F | China Industrial Economy Association/Federation |
| CISA | China Iron and Steel Association |

| CMCPF | China Materials Circulation and Purchasing Federation |
| CMEMA | China Metallurgy Enterprise Management Association |
| CMS | China Metals Society |
| CPPCC | Chinese People's Political Consultative Conference |
| CS&S | China Software and Technical Services Corporation |
| CSBTS | China State Bureau of Technical Standards |
| CSIA | China Software Industry Association |
| CSSEA | China Specialty Steel Enterprise Association |
| CTVEA | China Township and Village Enterprise Association |
| CVA | China Electronic Video Industry Association |
| CVD | China Video Disc |
| DVD | Digital Versatile Disc |
| FIE | Foreign-Invested Enterprise |
| ICP | Internet Content Provider |
| IEC | International Electrotechnical Commission |
| ISC | Internet Society of China |
| MEI | Ministry of Electronics Industry |
| MII | Ministry of Information Industry |
| MMI | Ministry of Metallurgy Industry |
| MOC | Ministry of Commerce |
| MOCA | Ministry of Civil Affairs |
| MOF | Ministry of Finance |
| MOFCOM | Ministry of Commerce |
| MOFERT | Ministry of Foreign Economic Relations and Trade |
| MOFTEC | Ministry of Foreign Trade and Economic Cooperation |
| MOST | Ministry of Science and Technology |
| NCA | National Copyright Administration |
| NPC | National People's Congress |
| OPEC | Organization of Petroleum Exporting Countries |
| PE | Private Enterprise |
| PEA | Private Enterprises Association |
| SAIC | State Administration for Industry and Commerce |
| SASAC | State-Owned Asset Supervision Administration of China |
| SDPC | State Development and Planning Commission |
| SDRC | State Development and Reform Commission |
| SEC | State Economic Commission |

| | |
|---|---|
| SELA | Self-Employed Laborers Association |
| SEPA | State Environmental Protection Administration |
| SETC | State Economic and Trade Commission |
| SOE | State-Owned Enterprise |
| SQTSB | State Quality and Technical Standards Bureau |
| SRS | Stone Rich Sight Corporation |
| SSIA | Shanghai Software Industry Association |
| STA | State Taxation Administration |
| SVCD | Super Video Compact Disc |
| TVE | Township and Village Enterprise |
| USITO | U.S. Information Technology Office |
| VCD | Video Compact Disc |
| VCR | Video Cassette Recorder |
| WTO | World Trade Organization |

*The Business of Lobbying in China*

# ~ 1

# Introduction: The Puzzle of Lobbying in China

IN LATE JULY 1998, on a typically hot and humid Beijing day, a representative from the cashmere maker, Erdos Group, visited the offices of the State Economic and Trade Commission (SETC), the government organ then responsible for overseeing much of China's industrial policy. He carried with him two letters, one by his own company's leaders, the second a joint appeal by Erdos and twelve other Chinese firms. By most measures they were a motley crew. Besides the famous wool clothing manufacturer, the group also included the brash, state-owned electronics producer Changhong from Sichuan, which had come to dominate the national color television market; the risk-prone video machine maker Idall from Guangdong, perhaps most responsible for bringing digital video into the homes of average Chinese; the Shandong-based Tsingtao Beer Group, the country's most famous and dominant brewer; and even Beijing's well-known retailer Wangfu-jing Department Store. The companies differed in their temperament, products, location, and ownership form. But they shared two things in common: they were all extremely large, and they had all suffered from tumbling prices that had been sweeping across Chinese industries since 1996. They collectively represented China's industrial elite, and they were in trouble. Overcapacity had left industry after industry producing far beyond demand, and the obvious consequence was deflation, draining the firms of profits.

The two letters requested that the government encourage trade associations to organize their members to agree to abide by minimum prices for their goods. Only through coordinated efforts, the firms argued, could "vicious competition" (*exing jingzheng*) in industry after industry be stopped and orderly market behavior restored. Although there were other factors at work, including lobbying from other companies, several weeks after Erdos and the twelve firms submitted their petitions, the SETC positively responded to their plea and encouraged associations across the industrial spectrum to help their firms institute "self-discipline prices" (*zilujia*), that is, price floors, in order to halt the slide in prices. For the firms, it represented an important political victory with major ramifications for China's entire economy.[1]

Based on common perceptions of Chinese politics, the above scenario would appear to be a rare instance of business intrusion into the otherwise state-dominated policy process. China has been engaged in wide-ranging economic reforms for the past two decades, and some argue that economic pluralization has led to increased efforts by entrepreneurs to defend their interests, including participating in business associations. But even the strongest proponents of this view have not claimed that businesspeople affect national policy. The more widely shared view is that Chinese firms are not interested in public policy because they are subject to a state-controlled associational system that effectively blocks their ability to defend their interests at the national level or because they can establish patron-client ties with bureaucrats to obtain privileged access to scarce resources and avoid onerous regulations.

By the mid-1990s neither of these pictures accurately reflected the depth of the business world's involvement in national policy making, an indication of both how much China has changed and how these impressions are largely derived by observing companies' interaction with local officialdom. The above story of lobbying for price cartels is typical of the growth of industry lobbying that has occurred in China over the past decade. Previous studies on policy making in China have largely confined themselves to the role of the Chinese Communist Party, government institutions, political elites, and intellectuals. Such an approach was most reasonable when China had a planned economy dominated by state-owned enterprises and even still is appropriate today to understanding policy making on noneconomic issues such as security policy. But market reforms have resulted in the emergence of private and foreign competitors and even state firms focused on their bottom lines. China may not yet have "rule of law," but it assuredly has rules by the thousands that touch upon every aspect of business. Companies are keenly aware of this new environment and are trying to shape it to their benefit. The consequence has been a transformation of both the process and substance of public policy. China's national economic policies can no longer be viewed as the clear intentions of a strong state or as only the product of bargaining between government agencies. Firms influence the policy process indirectly via their trade associations and other intermediaries, but even more common is direct lobbying by firms of their regulators. Surprisingly, although direct contact has fed corruption in local settings, malfeasance is not as common in national public policy.

What is just as important to realize, though, is that while there has been a secular growth of industry involvement in policy making, lobbying is not of a piece in China. The economic circumstances of companies and sectors has affected the manner in which companies, domestic and foreign, interact with the Chinese government and in which companies have relatively more influence on policy. Ownership—private or state-owned—long viewed as the dividing line of firms' economic and political activities, has been joined by other factors, such as size, industry concentration, and technological sophistication. (In the opening account, the thirteen petitioners were united by their common economic predicament and their market prominence, the latter of which was central to their lobbying success.) Firms' policy preferences are highly dependent on their business circumstances. Hence, Chinese and foreign companies regularly find themselves on the same side of issues. Industry associations serve as important voices for firms in some sectors more than others. And large firms of all ownership types have more in-depth direct access to the state than their smaller counterparts.

The systematic nature of this variation points to the conclusion that China has not just one political economy, but multiple political economies. Moreover, that economic factors have shaped government-business relations in China, a nation ruled by a pervasive authoritarian government, suggests that the same is true in capitalist countries around the globe. The economic circumstances of firms and industries often trump the pull of country-specific political institutions in determining how government and business interact.

I reached these conclusions by comparing business involvement in national policy making in China in three economically distinct sectors—the steel, consumer electronics, and software industries. The consideration of economic circumstances has led naturally to a focus on the key actors in this drama—firms. Associations, long viewed as the "canary in the mine" with regard to nonstate power, are given attention; but since influence does not necessarily occur via these groups, I also examine other intermediaries and direct company contact with government for their relative importance as avenues for firm influence and government regulation. Since firms, both Chinese and foreign, are the focus, so too are the issues that directly affect their interests—policies on taxation, competition, technical standards, and pollution, to name but a few. And because the adoption of a policy usually creates winners and losers, this study pinpoints conflict in the process and determines which firms have the greatest effect on policy outcomes. Relative influence is measured, not by examining how consonant policies are with given interests, but rather by tracing actors' actual involvement in the policy process.

The remainder of this chapter outlines the process that led to this study's research strategy and substantive conclusions. It begins by critically examining the range of patterns of government-business relations that have existed in countries around the world. That examination sets the stage for considering where China should be situated in these frameworks. Earlier scholarship has persuasively shown that China fits into more than one of them. The discussion then considers how the variation across the Chinese landscape can be understood by taking into account the role of economic factors in shaping government-business relations in the policy process. It is equally important to then explain how the Chinese case pushes forward the broader theoretical debate. Drawing on these components, the chapter concludes by outlining this project's research design, the results of which, presented in the rest of the book, can contribute to a new appreciation of the forces affecting patterns of lobbying in China and in the world more broadly.

## Alternative Patterns of Government-Business Relations

Both in China and elsewhere, firms and states have interacted in a whole host of relational patterns that are differentiated by contrasting levels of firm autonomy, varying patterns of organization, and different norms underlying interactions (see Table 1.1).

Pluralism involves members of society acting individually and in concert with others, either through informal channels or through autonomous, voluntary, and nonhierarchical formal organizations that have overlapping jurisdiction, to defend their interests on public policy issues, vis-à-vis both other members of society and the state. This definition of pluralism shares with that definition commonly used in the study of Western politics—the notion that there is relatively open access to the political system for members of society to articulate their interests. However, given the rise of direct corporate lobbying in the United States and Western Europe, conceptions of pluralism should not privilege formal groups (e.g., associations) over informal arrangements or individually based interactions with the state.[2] In sum, pluralism includes both a plurality of avenues of access to the political system and a plurality of societal participants who compete and cooperate in defending their interests.[3]

By contrast, corporatism is

> a system of interest representation in which the constituent units are organized into a limited number of singular, compulsory, non-competitive, hierarchically ordered and functionally differentiated categories, recognized or licensed (if not created) by the state and granted a deliberate representational monopoly within their respective categories in exchange for observing certain controls on their selection of leaders and articulation of demands and supports.[4]

Critical to this definition is that it leaves ambiguous the mechanisms by which such a relationship between the state and business are formed. On the one hand, corporatist arrangements may be forced upon society by a state that creates, finances, and staffs institutions that are used primarily as avenues to have society adhere to the government's policy preferences. This "state corporatist" model is clearly reflected in the experiences of Portugal and Brazil in the middle portion of the twentieth century.[5]

Table 1.1 Expectations of government-business relations under different frameworks

| | Pluralism | Societal corporatism | State corporatism | Clientelism | Monism |
|---|---|---|---|---|---|
| **Level of firm autonomy** | Firm has operational, financial autonomy | Firm has operational, financial autonomy | Formal autonomy undercut by pressures to adhere to state policies | Official patrons may influence firm operations, finance | Firm has no autonomy over personnel or operations |
| **Avenues of interaction** | | | | | |
| Indirect | Mediated via non-hierarchical, voluntary associations and other intermediaries (e.g., law firms) | Mediated via hierarchical, involuntary associations acting as arena for state-industry negotiations | Mediated via hierarchical, involuntary associations acting as transmission belts of state policy | Formal associations significant only as conduit for patron-client ties | Very limited role for associations and other intermediaries |
| From firm's perspective | Firm lobbies via associations and other intermediaries, promoting interests of firm and industry | Firm defers to association to represent their interests in negotiations | Firm follows orders of and reports to an association | Firm manipulates associations to benefit interests of itself and patron at expense of industry and state institutions | Firm does not participate in associations or rely on other intermediaries |
| Direct | Extensive direct state-firm interaction not part of clientelist relationship | Limited direct interaction | Limited direct interaction | Extensive direct interaction that is part of patron-client relationship | Extensive direct interaction on personnel and operations related to the firm, not broader policy |
| From firm's perspective | Firm lobbies directly, focusing on substantive policy issues of interest to firm and industry | Firm does not directly try to influence state policies | Firm does not try to influence state policies or receive orders directly from the state | Firm nurtures personal ties by providing material benefits to patron in exchange for preferential state policies | Firm contacts state to provide firm-related information and obtain personnel and production orders. |
| **Norms of interaction** | | | | | |
| State-firm relationship | Competitive | Cooperative | Cooperative | Cooperative | Cooperative |
| Policy process transparency | High | High | Low | Low | Low |

On the other hand, corporatist arrangements may be based on a framework that is mutually agreed upon by the components of society and the state. Rather than acting as "transmission belts," associations can also act as forums for "voluntary and informal coordination of conflicting objectives through continuous political bargaining between interest groups, state bureaucracies, and political parties."[6] Influence under societal corporatism is both top-down and bottom-up. Thus, although state and societal corporatism share structural similarities, they are driven by very different dynamics and power relations. Examples of societal corporatism have been most readily apparent in the small industrialized states of Western Europe, Scandinavia, and East Asia.

While the distinction between corporatism and pluralism is clear, corporatism itself can reasonably be used in broad or narrow contexts. It can refer to an entire system in which leading representatives of the state, business, and labor engage in tripartite negotiations over major policies that, once agreed upon, each side is responsible for implementing back down through their respective hierarchies (the state bureaucracy, labor unions, and trade associations). Alternatively, corporatism is often used to describe a partial set of associations in a system or even a single association that has a jurisdictional monopoly over a functional issue, whose membership is involuntary, and whose decisions are binding on all of its members. This latter conception, commonly referred to as "meso-corporatism," is typically applied to associations that are specific to a region or industrial sector.[7]

Next, clientelism can be defined as a sustained pattern of reciprocal (and usually illicit) exchange between a state patron and a nonstate client based on personal ties and conducted via informal networks. Central to clientelism are asymmetric power relations—either the patron or the client hold resources that the other lacks. As such, clientelism inherently involves a positive-sum, symbiotic relationship, which is what gives clientelism its apparent stability. In a pluralist system there is also direct contact between firm executives and government bureaucrats, but the process and outcome of their interaction is not premised on narrow personal loyalty but derives from the broader interests of the firm and the state institutions. In a clientelist system, patronage predominates to the extent that it becomes more important than the formal institutions that are supposed to structure relationships.

Finally, monism involves a system of representation in which the state's ruling party organizes society into groups with jurisdictional

monopolies that are hierarchically ordered and that demand ideologi-
cal obedience from their members.[8] Although in some respects similar
to state corporatism, monism envisions a more fundamental penetra-
tion of society by the ruling party such that the boundary between the
state and these groups is essentially nonexistent. In addition, in monism
relations are not mediated by associations or other intermediaries as
they are in corporatism and pluralism. The classic examples are state-
owned enterprises (SOEs), Communist Party youth groups, and other
organizations erected as part of the Leninist state's effort to remake
society in the party's image. In the economic sphere, monism is most
appropriate to the central-planning era when enterprises and the bureaucracy interacted only in so much as they needed to carry out preset
plans, not to struggle over their contents or discuss broader policy issues.

Two caveats need to be stated about the presentation of these frameworks. First, readers familiar with the debate over China will notice the
absence of civil society from the discussion here.[9] Sinologists who have
done research on state-society relations have been attracted to the concept because of its identification as a precondition of democratization
following the collapse of Communism in Eastern Europe and the former Soviet Union. Such an interest is consistent with research on other
parts of the globe.[10] Leaving aside the question of whether there is a
link between the development of civil society and democratization, civil
society, unlike the frameworks described above, does not specify a particular pattern of interaction with the state. It sets society against the
state, but exactly how the two relate is left open. Members of civil society could choose to lobby in a pluralist manner, as individuals, and via
disparate associations, but they could also join highly structured associations, akin to societal corporatism, which would authoritatively represent their interests.[11] Including civil society, thus, would "mix apples
and oranges."[12]

Second, although government-business relations in many countries
have approximated these frameworks, the frameworks do not exhaust
the categories of potential patterns, and it is quite possible that more
than one pattern exists in a single political system. As a result, these
frameworks should be seen as ideal types. While an attempt will be
made to see to what extent Chinese reality approaches these patterns,
an equally important aim is to describe how state and business interact
in China as accurately as possible. The ideal types are starting points

and not ending points.[13] By facilitating comparison with previous re-search on China and elsewhere, they are guideposts that can orient our inquiry, but they should not limit it. This is particularly relevant since the ultimate focus of this project is not to identify similarity to any one model but rather to explain how variation in economic circumstances affects how business is politically organized and how great its level of influence is.

## Previous Research on China: Fulfilling Expectations

Previous work on government-business relations in China has provided important evidence that China varyingly fits into one of the frame-works, save monism. These empirical and theoretical contributions have also identified questions for further inquiry.

Some scholars find that China has elements of a state corporatist system for managing relations between the state and businesses. They primarily point to several transsectoral associations and chambers of commerce created to strictly monitor and control enterprises of different ownership types. The first such business group was the All-China Federation of Industry and Commerce (ACFIC), which private companies were forced to join before the vast majority were socialized in the mid-1950s.[14] Since the 1970s, the ACFIC has been joined by the Chinese Enterprise Management (Directors) Association for state-owned enterprises, the Self-Employed Laborers Association for small-scale private firms, and the China Association of Enterprises with Foreign Investment for foreign firms.[15] Consistent with this framework, it has been documented that the government has not permitted overlapping jurisdiction between local chambers of commerce.[16] Relatedly, there has been some research showing that local industry associations are primarily extensions of bureaucratic authority.[17]

Alternatively, some suggest that economic development has led to a decline in the state's control over enterprises and the emergence of a civil society whose interaction with the state is emblematic of plural-ism or societal corporatism. According to proponents of this view, the party-state's attempt to spur growth through the encouragement of a nonstate economy has unintentionally resulted in entrepreneurs' au-tonomy from the state and a pluralization of power.[18] They have natu-rally coalesced into a new "private-business class" that does not see its interests in concert with those of the state, an attitude that partly explains widespread social support for the 1989 demonstrations across China.[19] Despite surviving that crisis, according to some, the Chinese party-state's power has continued to be eroded by an increasingly large nonstate sector in a manner consistent with expanding pluralism.[20]

Significant evidence from existing research consistent with the pluralist and societal-corporatist models suggests that state and nonstate entrepreneurs are increasingly involved in national and local business associations that promote their interests. Multiple studies give myriad examples of how even associations that are formally organized by the state are significant avenues by which businessmen exchange market information and articulate their interests. Much attention has been paid to the growing partisan activity of the ACFIC, but some industry-specific associations, urban and rural, are also becoming more active on behalf of their members.[21]

And lastly, while not denying the significance of an expanding market economy, a growing body of literature provides evidence that market reforms do not automatically create an independent bourgeois class that seeks to defend its interests vis-à-vis the state. Since firms cannot depend on the legal system to protect their interests, they have responded by building patron-client ties based on personal connections (*guanxi*). Officials provide entrepreneurs access to scarce goods, credit, government and overseas markets, and protection from onerous regulations. Entrepreneurs, in return, provide officials with payoffs and gifts, employment, and business partnerships. These vertical alliances far outweigh horizontal cooperation among firms.[22] Many of these entrepreneurs, in fact, are former officials who have parlayed their connections into massive fortunes. "Like barnacles on a ship," Zweig writes, "they draw their sustenance from their parastatal relationships with the ministries from which they were spun off."[23]

Consistent with the finding of clientelism, some argue that these symbiotic ties are so endemic that they have mushroomed into what Wank calls "commercial clientelism."[24] Instead of a clear distinction between government and business, there is a "single-blended class" of entrepreneurs and bureaucrats reliant on each other for key resources. Thus, "what appears as a liberation of society has actually . . . been an incorporation of society."[25] Meisner, clarifying the distinction with other frameworks, concludes that, "given its strong bureaucratic character, China's new capitalist class contributes not to 'pluralism' . . . but rather to a further blurring of the line between state and society."[26]

## (Not) Explaining Variation

Earlier scholarship has provided valuable windows into government-business relations in China, but there are two gaps in the literature that need to be addressed. The first is that despite significant evidence for the existence of multiple patterns, analysts often only emphasize a single framework. Since there appears to be some truth in each perspective, there needs to be an accounting of this variation. Some have, in fact, highlighted variation. For example, several scholars describe business associations that range from official to semiofficial to popular.[27] However, the sources of this remarkable variation among associations is not systematically studied. There has yet to be any satisfying explanation for why state corporatist arrangements have apparently been more persistent and stable in some parts of the economy but in others, have been destabilized, being supplanted by societal corporatist, pluralist, or clientelistic patterns of interaction.

The most likely reason for the inadequate attention to variation in state-business relations is an assumption that all markets are alike. The neoclassical tradition views the market as essentially an exchange between buyer and seller that occurs without government interference. From this perspective, all post-Communist states are moving from a command economy in which bureaucrats had redistributive power to a market economy in which officials have little power.[28] This dichotomy between plan and market largely explains the great deal of attention devoted to China's private economy and property rights, and it also underlies much of the research on Chinese state-business relations.[29]

But in reality, while there is a fundamental difference between planned and market economies, markets themselves vary. Not only do governments and culture affect the nature and shape of markets, but the specific economic characteristics of firms and their surrounding environment also affect markets.[30] As Table 1.2 shows, markets' economic characteristics are open to extreme variations, differences that can have dramatic political consequences.

The potential implications of economic variation in markets for government-business relations have been underexplored in the litera-

**Table 1.2** Economic variables explaining market variation

| Firm-specific characteristics | Firm-environment characteristics |
|---|---|
| 1. Ownership (state, private, corporate, foreign) | 1. Ownership share of sector or regional economy |
| 2. Size (absolute and relative to other firms) | 2. Economies of scale |
| 3. Profitability | 3. Firm concentration |
| 4. Organization of production (e.g., Fordist or post-Fordist) | 4. Production intensities (skilled and unskilled labor, capital, technology, knowledge) |
| 5. Involved in single or multiple sectors | 5. Level of pollution created in production |
| 6. Production located in single or multiple regions | 6. Product homogeneity (standardized or unstandardized) |
| | 7. Vulnerability to price fluctuations (price elasticity) |
| | 8. International role (level of foreign investment, dependence on export markets and imported inputs) |
| | 9. Sectoral share of regional economy |
| | 10. Sectoral profitability |
| | 11. Regional level of wealth |
| | 12. A country's position in the international economy |

ture on China. Those who emphasize the spread of the market in China properly identify the market as an important source of dynamism in China's political economy that did not exist under a centrally planned economy. However, their view of all markets as alike leads them to expect that the spread of markets should be accompanied by an *undifferentiated* movement toward civil society in which a clearly distinct bourgeoisie attempts to defend its interests vis-à-vis the state, either through pluralist or societal corporatist frameworks, something that has clearly not occurred.[31] Conversely, those who emphasize state corporatism or clientelism rightly point to signs of the maintenance—or even growth—of officialdom's power, but both perspectives do not consider how the various aspects of markets can define the range, effectiveness, and relative benefits of options available to local and national officials. Such factors can make clientelism or corporatism more feasible in some situations than in others.[32]

Some initial progress already has been made in recognizing the importance of economic variation. Odgaard suggests that perhaps larger enterprises are more likely to utilize their private ties with officialdom, while Unger argues that the All-China Federation of Industry and Commerce is more independent than its small-firm cousin, the Self-Employed Laborers' Association, because ACFIC members are relatively more wealthy. White, Howell, and Shang analyze associations in cities that vary according to the proportion of output created by state-owned enterprises (Shenyang and Nantong), and they find state corporatism more prevalent, though on the defensive, in the city more dominated by state-owned enterprises (Shenyang). And Guthrie finds that business managers in the most intensely competitive sectors (he cites electronics) most strongly believe that *guanxi* is of decreasing significance in business. These suggestive findings create a foundation for further systematic inquiry.[33]

## The Consequences

In addition to only rarely examining variation across markets, another feature that unites much of the literature on government-business relations in China, particularly studies on associations, is a discussion of why economic change in China has not created a powerful civil society that could impel China to democratize. Given the timing of the renewed interest in the concept of civil society and state-society relations in general—Communist regimes were collapsing in Eastern Europe and the Chinese Communist Party was faced with huge popular protests—it is not surprising that attention would revolve around China's failure to democratize and the future prospects for such change. The 1989 protests and subsequent crackdown have established a research paradigm that has infused much of the work on state-society relations in China since.[34] While the linkages among the economy, civil society, and political institutions is obviously an important issue, like all paradigms, it leads one to ask certain questions and not others.

Much of the "search for civil society" has begun and ended with a measurement of the degree to which associations are autonomous from the state. The assumption is that the greater the associations' autonomy, the more they are able to challenge or criticize the state. This assumption overlooks the possibility that an association may gain state access, and hence influence, by marginally sacrificing some autonomy. Focusing on associations also privileges organized political activity. While relevant to measuring civil society, doing so necessarily overlooks the potential influence that individual companies may have on the state, not just on issues particular to the company, but on broad public-policy issues as well. Given companies' multiple paths of influence, growing business influence is not necessarily dependent on stronger associations. In addition, since democratization is a long-term issue, scholars have tried to measure broad social trends. Hence, the bulk of research has been "at the grassroots," among small firms and local associations, while the specific issues with which the associations have grappled have been of secondary concern when choosing cases.[35] The lack of urgency of the problem itself (democratization) has allowed scholars to choose their cases in a manner that does not require them to speak to more immediate issues that have the attention of firms and the government.

The pull of the democratization issue has placed many China watchers in the unenviable position of orienting their research to an event that has not occurred, turning them in a sense into prognosticators. It has also diverted attention away from equally pressing issues, such as economic growth, the quality of governance, and the distribution of political influence. It is the last topic with which this book is interested.[36]

One useful way to tackle the question of firms' relative political influence in China is to focus on the business community's role in policy making. But to date, research on state-society relations in China has largely avoided the policy realm.[37] And, conversely, previous research on the national policy process has focused on the party-state and found only a minimal role for nonstate actors. While it is generally recognized that bargaining and compromise are central to the process, such interactions have been found to revolve around the country's political elite or Communist Party and government institutions, at the national and local levels.[38] Some studies have highlighted the role of specialists, such as economists and lawyers, but their ties to the bureaucracy, both institutional and financial, have outstripped their links to interest groups or society at large.[39] The most widely used textbook on China summed up the conventional wisdom by noting that in China, "neither in theory nor in practice is individual advocacy or interest-group activity regarded as legitimate."[40] Broader social forces have been found to have an implicit role only to the extent that they have taken private actions that the state has then legitimated or sought to curb, or during the implementation phase when members of society could abide by or obstruct policies that were already adopted inside the walls of the state without their input. Similarly, some scholars have found that market contexts shape policy options, but not that market actors specifically lobby for their preferred policies.[41] If economic change over the past two decades has had a significant effect on how politics are currently practiced, then the business community's *direct* role in policy making should be evident. And if their involvement is significant, then existing models central to our understanding of Chinese policy making need to be revised.[42]

## The Significance of Economic Factors

The two weaknesses in studies on government-business relations in China can be ameliorated by drawing on research from elsewhere that compares firms' interaction with the state within an individual sector across nations and across multiple sectors within a nation. Much of this research has been a part of the debate in political economy over whether capitalist systems, or components of them, are converging toward a common pattern. Scholars have examined the organization, beliefs, and behavior of the three primary actors within capitalist systems—government, business, and labor—and how they interact with one another.

Numerous studies have found that economic circumstances shape the extent to which firms are interested and able to cooperate with one another. In some instances, this conclusion has been reached by documenting how firms in different sectors within a country are more or less dependent on associations. For example, in Turkey the country's auto sector is dominated by a few large firms that can influence the government directly through informal networks, and as a result the auto industry's association is weak. By contrast, Turkey's ready-to-wear clothing industry, with its many small producers, has an association deeply involved in that industry's self-regulation and lobbying of the government.[43]

Others have identified similar patterns of business organization in the same industry across countries that otherwise have different political economies. Contributors to a multicountry study found that associations tend to thrive in competitive industries, in decentralized sectors, and in more mature phases of the product life cycle (such as textiles, pharmaceuticals, semiconductors).[44] Similarly, because of a standardized product and vulnerability to price fluctuations, dairy producers require a great deal of coordination. Thus, in almost every country, dairy producers are organized in a meso-corporatist framework in which the state plays a major role.[45]

Finally, some have noticed that firms in the same sector in different countries have a declining interest in trade associations and have become more politically active individually. A comparison of the chemical industries in Germany, Great Britain, and Italy found that because the chemical industry is highly concentrated and has high economies of scale and internationalized production, firms in all three countries have increasingly stepped up their direct lobbying of government and participated less directly in associations.[46] More broadly, the internationalization of production and technological change have led to an erosion of corporatist mechanisms across sectors and countries.[47]

These examples all demonstrate how the environment created by industries orients firms to interact in certain ways with both their home government and even governments in other countries. Sectoral analyses of government-business relations gain their explanatory power from the fact that sectors embody distinct constellations of more basic economic characteristics. Companies in a sector share common interests that may give them a natural affinity for cooperating, but the economic characteristics of the firms themselves and that of their sector can shape the incentives for how they interact with one another and the state, by inducing firms to act collectively in the market and in their dealings with the government; to not cooperate and act independently; or to avoid any involvement, direct or indirect, with the state. Industry concentration, the percentage of sales shared by the industry leaders (typically measured by the combined sales of the top four or eight firms), has received the most sustained attention by scholars.[48] Ownership form, company size, production methods and organization, a country's factor endowments, trade patterns, the competitiveness of markets, and price elasticity have also been used to explain variations in business-government relations.[49]

On the other hand, there is ample evidence that economics do not always dominate actors' political behavior but that it is affected by ideology, culture and norms, and political institutions. Noneconomic factors often shape actors' identities as well as their interest in and capacity for collective action.[50] Thus, many scholars are skeptical of convergence across capitalist systems and find that countries are still defined by relatively internally homogeneous and distinctive political economies.[51] With regard specifically to state-business relations, the argument is that countries have a political system whose formal institutions and informal norms apply to firms and sectors across economic settings.[52] Studies show that distinctive national patterns of state-business relations are enduring and often trump an economic logic that would suggest common patterns in economically similar sectors across countries.[53] Many scholars believe that national patterns of government-business relations are so obvious that they do not feel it necessary to systematically consider the potential effect of economic factors.[54]

Applying these insights to the Chinese case, the argument would be that China's political institutions have conditioned its bureaucrats and businessmen, regardless of their location in the government or economy, to behave in a common fashion, both among themselves and vis-à-vis each other. This argument would be most consistent with those who find that clientelism or state corporatism are the dominant patterns of business-government relations in China, because both frameworks stress the overriding significance of state actors.

As sobering as these latter findings are, what appears most likely—and is found in the current study—is that no one independent variable is all-powerful and that both economic and political circumstances shape government-business relations. Those studies that give regard only to economics overstate their case. Sometimes a firm's or sector's various economic characteristics work at cross purposes or do not inherently induce a certain type of behavior (multisectoral conglomerates are an obvious case in point). Moreover, states are not passive; rather, they regularly attempt to shape their societies, though not always productively or successfully.[55]

Those that solely stress the importance of political institutions in structuring government-business relations are vulnerable from at least two directions. First, even if there is one formal system of government-business relations in a state, the stability and significance of these arrangements may vary within the country due to economic circumstances. For example, state-sponsored associations may operate smoothly in some sectors but because of different economic circumstances be dysfunctional in others. Relatedly, economic factors may point to forces that undercut the country's entire system. For example, the rise of big business in Korea and economic liberalization in Taiwan have undermined much of their state corporatist association systems.[56]

Second, the lack of convergence is not in itself adequate proof of the dominance of political factors over economic ones. Countries typically have different economic endowments and circumstances. Similarly, a sector is composed of economic conditions that prevail in the industry generally as well as those that are particular to a given country. For example, the steel industry has high economies of scale globally but varying levels of concentration in different countries. Such country-specific economic contexts can induce contrasting behavior by state and business alike.[57] Conversely, economics is not the only force supposedly pushing convergence. For example, in negotiations over membership in the World Trade Organization international political pressure has also caused countries to modify their local political arrangements to conform with practices elsewhere.[58]

Thus, there is good reason to give attention to both economic and political factors in studying China's political economy. Because one can systematically compare patterns of business-government relations in sectors whose economic circumstances are clearly specified, sectoral analyses provide the opportunity to disentangle and identify the independent influence of economic circumstances and political institutions and examine the tensions between them.

Besides helping to explain the variation in how business and the state in China interact, research that focuses on economic variables' role in this relationship also can assist in better understanding how economic factors and patterns of interaction affect relative levels of influence on public policy. Studies concerned with corporate influence often treat business as a homogeneous group.[59] The studies on government-business relations reviewed above have been ultimately concerned about how patterns of government-business relations affect the quality of governance and economic development. While not explicitly focused on relative influence, it is an issue that naturally arises from a focus on factors that affect firms' relative capacity and interest in collective action, because there is a concern for how industry's behavior, economic and political, promotes or inhibits good governance and development. This concern leads these studies to consider the various factors, economic and political, that affect relations. Consequently, they expand our vision beyond the single measure of autonomy that is the most common focus of attention in research oriented toward measuring the emergence of civil society.

## China as a Critical Case

The discussion of comparative research suggests that economically sensitive studies can enlighten us about the variable patterns of government-business relations that coexist in China's political economy.[60] In addition, China can serve as a critical case that can enrich our understanding of these broader theoretical issues. Those specialists stressing the relative importance of economic and political factors in shaping government-business relations have raised enough doubts about one another's findings that the discussion requires further exploration and can profit from using a fresh perspective. More specifically, most of the empirical evidence has been drawn from advanced capitalist states and to some extent from newly developed countries. Less-developed countries like China have been absent from the discussion.[61]

The Chinese case distinguishes itself even further from previous ones by its economic history and current political institutions. For almost thirty years, China had a centrally planned economy in which market forces played a minimal role. Since the late 1970s China has shifted from a planned to a capitalist economy. However, unlike European post-Communist states, which quickly instituted privatization schemes, China has attempted to revitalize and reform state-owned enterprises. Private enterprises have been encouraged to form, but state-invested enterprises still accounted for 47 percent of industrial output in 2000.[62] At the same time, China has maintained an authoritarian regime that formally reserves to itself the right to make policy and that is not accountable through standard and transparent procedures to nonstate actors.

Several consequences flow from China's situation. First, this study is able to consider the importance of the economic factor of ownership form to an extent difficult in studies of other capitalist countries. Second, if economic factors do matter, two decades of reforms should have provided enough time for them to display their effect on government-business relations.[63] On the other hand, the continued existence of an authoritarian regime makes it more difficult for economic factors to affect government-business relations than in democracies that have been the site of most studies. If economic factors can be shown to matter in China, then they likely matter elsewhere. Finally, not only is the study's timing significant for how far beyond the initiation of reforms it occurred, but it is also auspicious that research primarily was conducted just prior to China's entry into the World Trade Organization. Membership in WTO is causing changes to China's regulatory system and economy. For these reasons, this study serves as a useful baseline from which to compare future circumstances, a situation that should both enrich our understanding of China and facilitate future analysis of relevant political theories.

## The Research Design

This book takes the opportunity for the Chinese case and political economy theory to mutually enlighten each other by analyzing two interrelated questions: First, how do economic factors, like those in Table 1.2, affect the pattern of business-government interaction, like those in Table 1.1? And second, to what extent do these patterns, in turn, affect the relative influence of firms on the policy-making process? The study identifies the formal patterns of interaction that exist as well as determining their stability and significance on firms' relative influence in various economic contexts.

The approach taken to answer these questions is straightforward. The heart of the book consists of comparative case studies of firms, both Chinese and foreign, their interaction with their counterpart associations (at the subsector, sector and transsector levels) and other intermediaries (such as lobbying firms), and their direct contact with local and national government bodies (ministries and legislative organs). The project examines their relationships in general and on specific policy issues in order to identify variation both in patterns of interaction and in firms' relative influence on policy matters.

In order to explain the links between economic contexts and patterns of interaction, I analyze firms from three economically distinct industrial sectors—steel, consumer electronics, and software. As suggested above, the sectors themselves are not variables in their own right; they are proxies that are composites of multiple, more basic economic variables. The three industries differ in several ways, including their economies of scale, capital intensity, output share of state-owned and foreign-invested enterprises, and firm concentration. The software industry tends to be extremely knowledge intensive, requires highly educated professionals, yet has few economies of scale. Hence, software firms tend to be relatively small. Firm concentration, as measured by the top four dominant firms' share of total sales, is quite low. Also, in China domestic private and foreign firms control the market. By contrast, the steel industry is capital and labor intensive, and thus has very high economies of scale. The production of steel in China is more concentrated than is the production of software, and state-owned enterprises account for the lion's share of steel output. Finally, except for having higher concentration levels, the economic circumstances of the consumer electronics industry sit roughly in between those of software and steel.

Besides meeting the burden of selecting economically distinct sectors, these industries also have their own inherent significance. Steel has consistently been central to the PRC's development drive. And although the industry lags behind global standards of quality, China has been the world's largest steel producer since 1996. The consumer electronics industry has been growing even faster to meet the demands of China's expanding numbers of urban and rural consumers as well as markets overseas. The software industry is of much more recent vintage—which is immediately apparent when one meets the young entrepreneurs who run most of the firms—but it has been hailed by political and industry leaders as a crucial component for the creation of an information economy in the twenty-first century. In some ways, the steel, consumer electronics, and software industries are metaphors, respectively, for China's past, present, and future.

In addition to choosing three economically distinct sectors on which to focus, I have also taken care to address the variation that exists within each sector. Specifically, firms of contrasting sizes (large and small) and ownership forms (state-owned and private) were selected from each sector. Moreover, both large and small foreign firms from each sector are included. Since nationality is a political distinction, including foreign firms provides an additional basis to measure the relative impact of economic and political factors. That is, if the political distinction is irrelevant, then foreign and domestic firms of a similar size and ownership form in the same sector should interact with the Chinese government in a similar fashion. Many of the firms whose political behavior is analyzed are household names either globally (for example, Sony, Microsoft, and Pohang Steel) or in China (for example, Baoshan Iron and Steel, Changhong, and Founder), while others are quite obscure.[64]

Determining business influence is not as straightforward as identifying the economic characteristics of firms and sectors or forms of government-business interaction. It is inadequate to look at which companies are most economically successful. Profitability or market share may be the result of many factors, of which political influence is but one. It is also not enough to identify certain policies as consistent with the interests of a particular company or group of companies, because this approach does not reveal how those policies came into being. Government officials may have anticipated which policy suits a segment of companies without having actually been directly influenced by them. Political influence can most accurately be measured by tracing the connection between the views of companies and their representatives, their actual input into the policy process, and the substance of policies once they are issued.[65] In doing such process tracing, it is also important to take into account the effect of other potential sources of influence, including government agencies, experts, and other parts of society. Business is only one participant in a game with many players.

The primary mode of inquiry involved interviews with senior executives from the firms, leaders of the business associations and other intermediaries, and junior and midlevel officials from relevant parts of the national and local bureaucracy conducted during three extended trips to China between 1998 and 2003. Interviews with the core firms and their counterparts in associations and government were supplemented in two ways, by additional interviews with other firms, industry analysts, journalists, scholars, and government officials; and by primary and secondary written material from the Western and Chinese sources.

In addition to information on the general nature of interaction, a great deal of attention was paid to specific important issues around which interaction revolved, including policies regarding taxation, intellectual property, technical standards, pricing and competition, pollution control, and tendering for government contracts. Since general attitudes might not match actions, emphasis was placed on learning about all three sides' actual behavior and the path and outcomes of relevant policy proposals. Most questions concerned very recent and ongoing behavior and issues, but when possible inquiry was also directed toward events from the 1980s and early 1990s.

This front-row-seat approach facilitates going beyond gauging firms' and associations' autonomy to examining how companies' economic circumstances push them toward one of the various frameworks—pluralism, societal or state corporatism, clientelism, or monism. We can identify the extent to which firms employ associations and deal with officialdom directly. We can go even further to see how companies vary in the depth of their direct contact with the government, including: (1) companies' attention to policy; (2) the regularity of interaction; (3) the range and rank of officials contacted; (4) the forums of interaction; (5) the range of policy issues; and (6) the degree of company proactiveness. And whether lobbying is via associations or direct contact, we can look to see if interaction is rooted in patron-client ties.

The case studies also provide the chance to determine to what extent industry is able to influence policy outcomes and how variation in influence is related to firms' and sectors' differing economic circumstances and patterns of organization. Moreover, we can also identify where relations are stable and where there are significant strains and pressure for change. For example, we will be able to examine whether firms in different sectors that are in associations with similar levels of government intervention display different levels of frustration with such intervention. The information about how firms interact with the state provides the basis for determining the level of industry's relative influence on public policy. Finally, by comparing the most recent events with earlier periods, the project can speak directly to trends over time.

## Outline of the Book

The book is composed of six chapters. The second is a primer on how government-business relations related to public policy are organized in general in China. It looks at the evolution of associations, other intermediaries, and direct contact between business and government over the past two decades. The main point of the chapter is that government-business relations in China are not fully consistent with any of the ideal types presented in Chapter 1 and that within China there is a great deal of variation.

Chapters 3, 4, and 5 grapple with this variation by analyzing business-government relations in each of the three sectors. The chapters are divided into three parts. The first places the sectors in their economic contexts and suggests how these contexts might affect the ways in which the companies interact with the government and the policy issues that arise. The next portion of each chapter analyzes the firms' actual pattern of interaction with associations and the government from a general perspective. It considers the development of associations in the sectors, firms' involvement in and level of satisfaction with associations, and the extensiveness of direct contact with officialdom.

Each chapter then explores business-government relations through the lens of specific policy issues that have been the substance around which interaction has revolved. This focus will clarify broader theories of business-government relations, opening a window into how lobbying occurs in actual practice. An attempt was made to follow similar policy areas across the three sectors (such as taxation, standards, competition, etc.), but to a large degree those policy areas that are of highest priority to companies, associations, and government agencies, were also those on which this researcher's inquiry focused. Following policies that are contentious and important from the point of view of the participants not only is useful in measuring the level of business influence on policy but also enables one to address the policy-formulation aspects of these sectors, which are directly relevant to the prosperity of China and other "transition economies" and developing countries. Thus, the study speaks both to the transformation of politics caused by the introduction of markets as well as to the consequences of politics for economic development.

The concluding chapter synthesizes the findings derived from the empirical cases by first considering them in the context of the broader political economy literature related to the issue of the relative impact of economic and political factors on business-government relations. The chapter then addresses the implications of this study's conclusions for our understanding of China, including its state-society relations, policy-making process, and chances for democratization. The discussion concludes by considering the implications this study has for various options the Chinese government has been considering for reorganizing its association system. Particular attention is paid to the costs and benefits of moving toward a more hierarchically structured system that tightly contains influence versus a more liberal regime that reduces barriers to society's policy influence.

# ~ 2

# *Organizing Business in China*

THROUGHOUT THE People's Republic of China's history, determining the shape of the party-state's institutions and defining their relationships with society have been the enduring issues of organizational policy. While the myriad failed attempts at bureaucratic reform and destructive efforts at social mobilization during the Mao era proved the futility of governance under the planned economy, market reforms enacted since the late 1970s have exponentially complicated the issue, particularly with regard to the state's relationship with society.[1] Because of the central role that industry—both state-owned and private, domestic and foreign—inevitably assumes in China's development efforts, a disproportionate concern has been directed toward how companies are organized among themselves and vis-à-vis the state. Since 1989 dozens of regulations on nongovernmental organizations, many of which have been specifically directed at business associations, have been issued.[2] Over the same period, a call for improving China's industry associations has been a staple of senior leaders' statements and party and government resolutions and reports.[3] There have been several national conferences on the subject, including at least one at Beidaihe, the Chinese Communist Party's (CCP) long-time coastal summer retreat. A panoply of chambers of commerce and trade associations exist in every sector of the economy and in every part of the country.[4] Concern over associations has taken on added urgency following China's admission to the World

Trade Organization (WTO), as Chinese companies need to better coordinate their activities to respond to more intense global competition.[5]

In order to understand how this general concern has manifested itself in particular parts of the economy (the subject of the next three chapters), we must first determine from a macro perspective the general character of business-government relations on public policy matters in China at the start of the twenty-first century. In the introductory chapter, five conceptions—pluralism, societal corporatism, state corporatism, clientelism, and monism—were raised as alternative frameworks based on variation in firm autonomy, patterns of business organization, and underlying norms of firms' interaction with government. The theme of this chapter is that from an orbital view none of these models neatly encompasses the complex reality of China today. To help understand why, the discussion begins with a look at how economic reforms have recast government-business relations. This is followed by a detailed description of China's association system. With that foundation, the focus turns to determining to what extent China fits the societal corporatist, state corporatist, pluralist, and clientelist models by comparing China's reality to the organizational and normative aspects of these frameworks.

Much of the scholarship on the Reform era has found a strong resemblance with corporatism.[6] The validity of this conclusion depends heavily on one's focus. The more broadly one conceives of government-business relations, the less corporatist China is. Many (though far from all) associations have little autonomy. Stepping back, the association system's overall structure appears more corporatist on paper than in practice. And stepping back further, associations are far from the only avenue by which business interacts with the government or, for that matter, with the CCP. There are other intermediaries and regular opportunities for direct interaction unmediated by organizations such as associations. A corporatist system not only is internally organized in a certain manner but also dominates government-business interaction, a situation which is not the case in China.

The evidence for other patterns is also mixed. While this variety of routes appears more consistent with pluralism, the limited autonomy of many associations, the business community's typically nonconfrontational approach to influencing the government, and the limited degree of transparency in the policy process suggest not making such a blanket characterization. And although direct interaction is the most common avenue of policy influence, it is far from certain that most interactions on national policy issues are part of patron-client networks associated with clientelism. In short, China does not fit any one model.

## The New Basis for Government-Business Interaction

During the Mao era, business-government relations were decidedly monist. The hundreds of industry guilds (*tongye gonghui*) and chambers of commerce for business owners that had existed and multiplied since the late Qing were closed down in the 1950s.[7] The All-China Federation of Industry and Commerce (ACFIC, *quanguo gongshang lianhehui*), which had been created in October 1953 to organize and control private companies, expanded quite dramatically but then soon ceased operations as its member firms were nationalized or closed down.[8] At the same time, the size and responsibilities of the government expanded correspondingly. With the focus on coordinated planning, direct interaction with firms was extensive and revolved around personnel, financial, and operational issues. A small minority of state-owned enterprise (SOE) managers and other elements of society were also recruited into the National People's Congress (NPC) and Chinese People's Political Consultative Conference (CPPCC) systems, but their only role was to provide a veil of legitimacy by rubber-stamping policies determined behind closed doors by the Communist Party and the ministries.[9]

In the late 1970s, China's national leadership began the process of shifting from a centrally planned economy toward a market economy. One key element of reform has been the decrease of the government's direct involvement in the micromanagement of enterprises. For SOEs, this change has involved obtaining greater autonomy over their internal affairs. Although the government has remained deeply involved in appointing senior SOE executives, most have risen to the top internally through their companies' own ranks. SOEs' sense of identity has been reinforced by the formal separation since the 1980s of their finances from that of the government's. Another crucial aspect of the reform package has been the entry of new firms—domestic and foreign—into the market.

The withering of planning and micromanagement did not mean, however, that the government has been satisfied with passively standing on the sidelines as the market has operated. To the contrary, the Chinese economy has been heavily regulated. From 1980 to early 2002, the National People's Congress adopted over 420 laws and regulations; the State Council, 920; and local people's congresses, 7,000, a majority of which pertain to the economy.[10] This is just the tip of the iceberg, for it does not include the thousands of more narrowly targeted regulations, measures, rules, notices, decisions, orders, and ideas issued by ministries, bureaus, and offices at the national and local levels that cover every aspect of business, including market entry and exit, property rights, labor, accounting, credit provision, investment, production, distribution, commerce, and taxation.

The move from planning to regulation has inevitably been accompanied by a shift in the locus of government-business relations. It is these mountains of regulations and not the details of the input-output tables in planning guidelines that have come to most directly affect the life chances of firms that do business in China. The novel importance of public policy in the context of a market economy has introduced new sources of potential cooperation and tension between government and firms. The bureaucracy may have policy positions that are in concert with the interests of industry, but the two just as often may disagree, or government may not even recognize an issue that is important to industry. Thus, there are incentives for firms and those who might act on their behalf to pay attention to and try to influence the formulation of public policy.

Not only has the move to a market regulatory regime led firms to have an interest in policy influence (and given government a reason to listen), it has also meant that the government and businesses could very well have conflicts over the *ways* they should interact, especially if the form of interaction affects the *results* of interaction, that is, which firms have relatively more policy influence. This is the subject to which we now turn.

## Mapping China's Association System

Some believe that associations are a natural accompaniment to the adoption of market-oriented reforms and the relaxation of political control over most aspects of the lives of ordinary Chinese. Chinese scholars write that Western business associations, which they date back to the early seventeenth century, were the inevitable product of the capitalist economy.[11] Although enterprises have initiated individual associations, most of the impetus for China's post-Mao associational system lays with the government, which ordered its creation in *anticipation* of a market economy, not as its consequence.[12] The government believed it needed to augment its administrative and regulatory links to existing state-owned enterprises and create new regulatory links to privately run businesses. However, the Chinese government has never had a fully articulated and coordinated strategy. So the various associations and chambers of commerce operating at the turn of the twenty-first century are more a conglomeration of organizations than a planned system (see Table 2.1).

**Table 2.1** Business associations in China* (2003)

| Business Associations Based on Members' Ownership Form | | | |
| --- | --- | --- | --- |
| State-owned | Collective | Domestic private | Foreign |
| China Enterprise Confederation–China Enterprise Directors Association (CEC–CEDA) (1979) | China Township and Village Enterprise Association (CTVEA) (1990) | All-China Federation of Industry and Commerce (ACFIC) (1953, 1984) Self-Employed Laborers Association (SELA) (1986) Private Enterprises Association (PEA) (1988) | China Association of Enterprises with Foreign Investment (CAEFI) (1987) Foreign-based chambers of commerce |

| Business Associations Based on Product Type | |
| --- | --- |
| Domestic industry and commerce | International business |
| Industry associations (and their sub-associations) Sector-specific enterprise management associations Industry guilds China Industrial Economy Federation (CIEF) (1988/1998) China General Chamber of Commerce (CGCC) (1994/1999) | China Council for the Promotion of International Trade (CCPIT) (1952, 1986) Industry-specific import-export chambers of commerce (1988) Foreign-based industry associations |

* Founding dates are in parentheses; two dates mean an association was closed and later reopened or reorganized.

One prominent feature that immediately stands out is the sheer breadth and variety of associations, something not fully conveyed in previous studies, which have tended to either analyze a limited number of associations or focus on a few localities.[13] In order to put Chinese associations in the greater context of policy making, it is necessary to first provide an introduction to their respective backgrounds, structures, members, and activities. The broadest distinction can be made between those organizations that *initially* recruited members who shared a similar form of ownership form and those whose members produce similar products.

Among those categorized by ownership, the first to be launched was the China Enterprise Management Association (CEMA, *zhongguo qiye guanli xiehui*), an organization originally for medium and large state-owned industrial enterprises. In 1979, the State Economic Commission (SEC) sent delegations to Japan and Western Europe to learn about their association systems. The delegations were led by an SEC vice minister, Yuan Baohua, a first-generation senior economic affairs official who became the driving force in the government behind associations.[14] Upon returning to China, he met with Deng Xiaoping and other leaders and raised the need for associations. Soon after, the SEC received approval from the State Council to establish associations.[15] Founded in March 1979, CEMA, which in 1999 changed its name to the China Enterprise Confederation (CEC, *zhongguo qiye lianhehui*), has a national office and branches in every province and many major cities, some of which were initiated by local enterprises.[16] Its primary members have been large state-owned industrial enterprises, but by the 1990s it counted some larger privately run companies and joint ventures among its 120,000 members. As its original name implied, CEC has focused primarily on improving the internal management of enterprises by holding seminars, providing consulting advice, and publishing magazines and books on business management. But at the government's request, it has also given its views on various draft regulations and laws, including those on bankruptcy, trade unions, and labor rights.[17]

The most well-known association originally created for private firms, the All-China Federation of Industry and Commerce (ACFIC), began its revival in 1979. That year, Deng Xiaoping openly met with some of its old leaders and affirmed that they were patriotic allies of the Communist Party and that their business would be an important contribution to the economy.[18] However, it would be 1984 before the ACFIC was allowed to accept new members and, in essence, operate. The delay seems to have occurred because there simply were not very many private companies in operation yet; domestic private enterprises with more than seven employees were not formally legalized until 1988.

The ACFIC has an even more extensive network than CEC–CEDA. It is organized in every province down to the township level. By 2003, it had over three thousand branches at and above the county level and over sixteen thousand branches below the county level, some of which had been initiated by local private companies.[19] Its membership had swelled in 2003 to 1.64 million. The ACFIC has three types of members: individuals, organizations, and enterprises. The 1.16 million individual members included 150,000 "old" capitalists who initially joined the ACFIC during the Mao era, 800,000 owners of small private companies (*getihu*), and 110,000 owners and managers from larger private enterprises as well as some lawyers and ACFIC officials. Groups (*tuanti huiyuan*), including both transsector and sector-specific industry associations, account for only 15,000 members, but their participation creates a direct link between these institutions.

Companies account for the rest of the membership. Although the ACFIC was created to organize private firms, it passed a new charter in 1988 that opened the organization to enterprises of all ownership types. Thousands of state-owned firms quickly joined.[20] As of mid-2003, among the 460,000 enterprise members, almost 72 percent (330,000) were private companies, while another 9 percent (40,000) were collective enterprises, which on paper are owned by local governments but often are actually private companies.[21] However, 20,000 state-owned enterprises and 15,000 foreign-investment companies were members as well. While a small percent of ACFIC's total membership, they likely are among the most successful companies of their type.[22]

The ACFIC distinguishes itself from all other associations by being a section of the advisory group the Chinese People's Political Consultative Conference, and like other sections, is supervised by the Chinese Communist Party Central Committee's United Front Department. Thus, the ACFIC has an explicitly political background, and hence it is defined in its charter as a "people's organization" (*renmin tuanti*), not a "social organization" (*shehui tuanti*). As a consequence, the ACFIC is not subject to the various regulations adopted in the past two decades to govern industry associations.[23]

Despite its unique circumstances, ACFIC acts as an all-purpose chamber of commerce for its member companies.[24] ACFIC sponsors a variety of market-promotion activities, such as exhibitions, seminars, and workshops. It has set up loan guarantee funds (*danbaojin*) and assisted nonstate firms to list on the domestic stock markets. Through its newsletters, newspaper (*China Business Times*), and other publications, it provides market and policy information to its members. Finally, ACFIC represents the interests of its members. Its legal affairs office at the national and local levels have defended members in lawsuits. More importantly, the ACFIC regularly participates at the national and local levels in the policy process on laws and regulations that affect the non-state economy, both taking institutional positions on issues as well as providing support to individual ACFIC members who propose resolutions to the national and local branches of the advisory People's Political Consultative Conference.[25]

The other associations specifically targeted at private enterprises are the Self-Employed Laborers Association (SELA, *geti laodongzhe xiehui*) and the Private Enterprises Association (PEA, *siying qiye xiehui*).[26] Both are run by the State Administration for Industry and Commerce (SAIC), a primary regulator of businesses, and its local branches. At the SAIC's initiative, local SELA branches began to be set up in 1982; and in 1986, after branches existed in over 90 percent of China's counties, the national SELA was formally established. All Chinese individually run businesses (*getihu*), private companies with less than eight employees, are automatically made members of SELA upon obtaining business licenses.[27] Local branches of the Private Enterprises Association began to be created in 1988 when private enterprises too large to be registered as *getihu* were formally legalized.[28] However, no national PEA was ever established. Unlike ACFIC, the main mission of SELA and the PEA in most localities appears to be to assist the State Administration of Industry and Commerce regulate their members. This assistance includes ensuring that members fully pay their taxes, adhere to relevant regulations, and are aware of ongoing political campaigns.

The China Township and Village Enterprise Association (CTVEA, *zhongguo xiangzhen qiye xiehui*) was created in 1990 by the Ministry of Agriculture to help regulate collective enterprises registered with the lowest administrative levels of government. CTVEA has branches in most provinces, but its presence at the county and township levels is surprisingly spotty, with a total of only one thousand member companies.[29]

The final type of general associations categorized by ownership are those directed at foreign firms operating in China. With the ranks of joint ventures and wholly foreign-owned firms growing, the Ministry of Foreign Economic Relations and Trade (MOFERT) in November 1987 set up the China Association of Enterprises with Foreign Investment (CAEFI, *zhongguo waishang touzi qiye xiehui*).[30] It began with just five hundred large firms, but it soon set up a national network in every province and in some lower-level jurisdictions where there were numerous foreign-invested firms. At the end 1997, the latest date reliable figures are available, CAEFI had over ninety thousand members nationwide, which was 62 percent of all foreign-invested firms operating in China at the time, up from 40 percent in 1991.[31] Like the chamber representing private business, CAEFI engages in market promotion, assists members caught up in specific disputes, and contributes to policy discussions.

Another set of all-purpose associations specifically for multinationals operating in China are those chambers of commerce that have been founded by foreign governments or foreign companies themselves. Unlike CAEFI, foreign chambers of commerce are organized by nationality, and each country is supposed to have only one chamber of commerce with one office.[32] However, in practice, several countries have multiple branches around the country (such as Germany and Britain) or even have entirely separate organizations in different cities (the United States).[33] By 1999 there were are already forty-four foreign chambers of commerce operating in China.[34] Some chambers, such as Germany's, make all firms from their country with investment in China automatic members.[35] Those whose membership is voluntary may have several hundred individual and firm members. The largest, the American Chamber of Commerce in the PRC, located in Beijing, had 750 company and 1,550 individual members as of 2003. Chambers' members are not restricted by location and often have facilities throughout China. All foreign chambers are involved in market promotion activities of some sort, but their involvement in policy discussions varies. Some proactively defend their members' interests by making representations to local and national government agencies, while others routinely refer regulatory disputes to the commercial section of their respective embassies.

The other broad category of associations operating in China are those whose members produce a similar product. When the State Economic Commission received approval to establish the China Enterprise Management Association in 1979, it was also given permission to set up a limited number of industry-specific associations, the first two being the Packaging Association and the Feed Association. In the mid-1980s the SEC and various ministries were encouraged to set up associations as part of the effort to streamline the bureaucracy and reduce official intervention in enterprises, such that by 1988 there were already sixty-eight national industry associations.[36] In 1993, the ministries of light industry and textiles were turned into general associations and their product divisions turned into trade associations (eleven in textiles, forty-three in light industry).[37] The same tactic was applied between 1998 and 2001 when several industrial ministries were first turned into state bureaus of the State Economic and Trade Commission and then replaced entirely by associations.[38]

As a consequence, the number of national industry associations rose severalfold, from 160 in 1993 to 482 in 1997. Their ranks dropped to 362 by 2002, as some were closed as part of the government's effort to tighten regulation of social organizations following the 1999 protests by the Falun Gong spiritual group.[39] On top of this overall growth, many sectoral associations also have more narrowly focused sub-associations (*fenhui*) attached to them. Many national sub-associations, which totaled sixteen hundred in 2002, were not created at the associations' initiation but are affiliated with the association to avoid the appearance (if not the reality) that the general and sub-associations compete with each other.[40] Thousands of sectoral associations have also been created at the provincial level and below, often not in concert with national ones and usually only in provinces where the industries are relatively developed. National trade associations' members typically include companies of diverse ownership forms from across the country.

In addition to the standard industry associations, there are several other types of sectoral associations in China. CEMA (now CEC–CEDA) established twenty-eight national-level sectoral management associations (for example, for railways, metallurgy, and construction), and many of these sectoral management associations have provincial branches. Moreover, at the initiative of companies, there has been a dramatic reemergence of industry guilds (*tongye gonghui*) at the national and local levels. As of 2003, there were eleven national industry guilds affiliated with the All-China Federation of Industry and Commerce and almost thirty-eight hundred regional ones under the aegis of branch Federations of Industry and Commerce around the country, a quadrupling of their numbers in five years.[41] Most guild members belong to the ACFIC, though their ranks include all types of firms, domestic and foreign.

Just as the government was setting up sector-specific associations, in 1986 it also established the China Industrial Economy Association (CIEA). The national body's members include its 26 provincial branches, 150 national-level domestic industry associations, and 300 companies. Although in the late 1990s it started attracting a few private companies, the vast majority of the group's members are state-owned enterprises. From its inception, it has conducted research, informed its members about government policies, and provided policy proposals to the bureaucracy. Since being renamed the China Industrial Economy Federation (CIEF, *zhongguo gongye jingji lianhehui*) in 1998, CIEF is also supposed to provide some degree of guidance and coordination of activities of its association members.[42]

Beyond the myriad sectoral associations focused on the domestic economy, there are also three types of associations focused primarily on international business. The first, the China Council for the Promotion of International Trade (CCPIT, *zhongguo guoji maoyi cujin weiyuanhui*), founded in 1952 and then reopened in 1986, has tried to obtain foreign trade and investment opportunities for Chinese companies as well as to be attentive to relevant policy debates.[43] Led by the Ministry of Commerce, CCPIT has a national network of 650 local branches and 18 sector-specific trade councils in a variety of industries (for example, machinery, textiles, and electronics). As of 2003, CCPIT had over sixty thousand member companies throughout the country. Most were state-owned enterprises, but a growing share were domestic private and foreign-invested companies.[44]

The second group of associations focused on international commerce are six sector-specific chambers of commerce for Chinese importers and exporters set up beginning in 1988. Involved in many of the same industries as the CCPIT trade councils, the import-export chambers collectively have over sixty subassociations and likely over twenty thousand company members.[45] In addition to providing overseas market information as CCPIT does, these chambers also assist trade authorities in the provision of trade and quota permits and help Chinese companies defend themselves against antidumping and safeguard actions brought by foreign companies.

Finally, foreign sectoral associations have opened in China, either as branches of associations founded elsewhere or as fully independent new organizations. There are likely several hundred foreign trade associations operating in China, but it is difficult to be sure because they are still not allowed to register.[46] Foreign associations typically engage in market-promotion activities, but they vary in their level of self-regulation and lobbying on behalf of their members.

## The Limited Autonomy of Business Associations

Mapping China's business associations reveals a panoply of organizations that spans the country and virtually every sector and involves companies of every ownership type. This is a necessary first step in comparing government-business relations in China to the corporatist, pluralist, and clientist frameworks.

Based on the descriptions presented in Chapter 1, if China's system were state corporatist, one would expect that: (1) associations lack autonomy; (2) that membership in associations is compulsory; (3) that associations are hierarchically ordered; and (4) that individual associations have jurisdictional monopolies. (Since, in societal corporatist systems, associations are typically independent, it requires fulfillment of only the latter three criteria.) The first two aspects involve individual associations; the latter two concern the relationships between associations. These criteria of corporatism would be supported by a norm of government-business cooperation based on an assumption of shared interests between the two sides, which would provide a rationale for a government role in associations. Despite the breadth and depth of China's association system, based on an assessment of the associations described above and the relevant regulations, it only partially meets some of these criteria.

The aspect of state corporatism most prominent in China—and one that relates to both the normative and organizational features of government-business ties—is that of limited autonomy. If one were to consider only official intent, associations in China would have very little independence. The government has conceived of associations primarily in economic, not political, terms. The hope has been to make associations "bridges and belts" (*qiaoliang he niudai*) to all types of firms (not just SOEs) in an industry so that ministries could shift from directly regulating firms under their auspices to regulating the sectors as a whole.[47] And so associations are expected to be "advisors and assistants for the government's regulation of the economy."[48] To the extent that associations protect their members' legitimate rights and interests, these interests are seen as fundamentally consistent with those of the state. This official perception of harmony between business and government interests legitimates the latter's involvement in associations.

However, businesses' increasing sense of self-interest and rights that are distinct from and potentially in conflict with those of the state's has led to a greater questioning of an official role in associations.[49] Many people in and out of government believe associations should be predicated on defending the interests of their members, not on being impartial intermediaries that also help the government.[50] To be able to do so, these observers believe associations need to be autonomous from official control; otherwise they inevitably become "second governments." Official involvement is, thus, perceived as a detrimental intrusion, not as a helpful hand.[51]

Partly because of the weakening consensus over official goals and the norms which sustain them, the reality of association autonomy is somewhat more complex. In general, associations' independence can be compromised if they are: (1) initiated by the state; (2) required to register and be affiliated with a government agency; (3) staffed by government officials; and (4) dependent on government financing (see Table 2.2).

As noted above, the government has initiated a large portion of associations in China, including the vast majority of national-level associations categorized by ownership, CIEF, most industry associations, China Council for the Promotoin of International Trade (CCPIT), and the import-export chambers of commerce. Those launched without Chinese government initiative include some branches of CEC–CEDA, ACFIC, and China Association of Enterprises with Foreign Investment (CAEFI), the foreign-based chambers of commerce and industry associations, some industry associations, most industry sub-associations, and all industry guilds. Even when the government does so in concert with companies, the former's involvement may affect how the association defines the scope of its membership, mission, and specific activities.

**Table 2.2** Autonomy of business associations in China (Y=yes; N=no; darker shading signifies greater autonomy)

| Business association | Chinese govt initiative? | Affiliation | Staffed with (former) govt officials? | Financially dependent on govt? |
|---|---|---|---|---|
| **Based on ownership form** | | | | |
| China Enterprise Confederation-China Enterprise Directors Association (CEC-CEDA) | varies | SASAC | Y | varies |
| China Township and Village Enterprise Association (CTVEA) | Y | Ministry of Agriculture | Y | Y |
| All-China Federation of Industry and Commerce (ACFIC) | varies | CCP United Front Dept | Y | N |
| Self-Employed Laborers Association (SELA) | Y | SAIC | Y | Y |
| Private Enterprises Association (PEA) | Y | SAIC | Y | varies |
| China Association of Enterprises with Foreign Investment (CAEFI) | varies | MOFTEC | Y | N |
| Foreign-based chambers of commerce | N | CCPIT | N | N |
| **Based on product type** | | | | |
| Industry associations | varies | SASAC and ministries | varies | varies |
| Sectoral management associations | Y | SASAC | Y | Y |
| Industry guilds | N | ACFIC | N | N |
| China Industrial Economy Federation (CIEF) | Y | SASAC | Y | Y |
| China General Chamber of Commerce (CGCC) | Y | SASAC | Y | Y |
| China Council for Promotion of International Trade (CCPIT) | Y | MOFCOM | Y | N |
| Import-export associations | Y | MOFCOM | Y | varies |
| Foreign-based industry associations | N | — | N | N |

Associations in China also are formally required to register with the Ministry of Civil Affairs (MOCA) to legally exist and operate. Given that the government has rejected applications for new associations and canceled the licenses of existing ones, this is not a pro forma exercise.

In addition, associations must be affiliated with a "responsible business department" (*yewu zhuguan bumen*), typically the part of the government that most directly regulates their industry.[52] As such, the sector-specific industry associations are affiliated with the appropriate line ministries or equivalent industry bureaus at the regional level. When ministries have been eliminated, oversight has shifted to other more general government agencies.[53] Three exceptions to the requirement of having a government overseer are industry guilds, which are affiliated with the ACFIC; foreign-based chambers of commerce, which are supervised by the China Council for the Promotion of International Trade; and foreign industry associations, which are not allowed to register and so are not formally regulated by any government agency.[54]

Staffing is another way autonomy can be compromised. Despite rules against doing so, it is common for an association's chairman and some of the vice chairmen to be former or current government officials and the secretary-general (who actually runs the day-to-day affairs of the association) to be a retired official.[55] Official staff is most prevalent in those associations categorized by ownership, CIEF, China General Chamber of Commerce (CGCC), the sectoral management associations, CCPIT, and the import-export chambers of commerce. It is absent among the foreign-based associations and industry guilds, while official presence in industry associations varies considerably. However, even when some association leaders are (former) bureaucrats, there is wide variance in the degree to which both the government is actually involved in the association and company members hold influential positions in the association.

Lastly, the government can also influence an association's behavior to the degree it controls its finances. When domestic associations were initially founded in the 1980s, the great majority relied on government appropriations. Alternative sources—membership dues and fee-for-service activities (for example, exhibitions and consulting)—were minimal. Through the 1990s, SELA, CTVEA, CIEF, CGCC, and the sectoral management associations still depended primarily on government outlays. However, all other associations have diversified their financial resources. Although the 1989 and 1998 social organizations regulations (Article 4 in each) have banned "for-profit activities," these regulations have nevertheless been interpreted to allow associations under varying formulas to obtain income by providing services to both members and nonmembers.[56] Pushed by the government's own budget shortfalls and pulled by the opportunity to increase their income, the financial umbilical cord that tied most associations to the government is in the process of being severed.

Comparing the four dimensions of autonomy, affiliation with a "responsible business department" is the most consistent bond between associations and government, followed by the government's hand in their creation, and the presence and influence of officials as association staff. The financial resources of associations are increasingly obtained from members and business activities. In sum, while autonomy varies considerably among associations, the general atmosphere of close government oversight is still widespread.

## The Missing Organizational Components of Corporatism

Limited autonomy, while a cornerstone of state corporatism, is just one facet of corporatist systems. The other three components—associations that are compulsory, are hierarchically ordered, and have jurisdictional monopolies—are less prominent in China.[57] Associations in China are voluntary in law, and the vast majority appear to be voluntary in practice. Article 1 in both the 1989 and 1998 regulations state that social organizations are directed at protecting "freedom of association," and the 1998 regulations (in Article 2) specifically state that social organizations, including associations, are "voluntarily formed." All associations in China are required to have charters, and as a matter of course they state that membership is voluntary. In practice, SELA is the only mandatory association for *all* firms in its area of interest. None of the other associations approach full membership for firms of a certain ownership form or in a certain sector. The CAEFI comes closest, with over 62 percent of foreign-invested firms as members, but foreign firm executives concur that CAEFI is not mandatory.[58] The ACFIC's 1.64 million members account for only a small minority of entrepreneurs and companies eligible to join. The various sectoral associations typically have a minority of their industry's firms as members. In some sectors, while no conclusive evidence was uncovered, it does appear that the government informally requires certain firms, usually the largest companies in the industry, to join an association. However, this seems to be the exception rather than the rule.

The next criterion of corporatism—hierarchy among associations—is extremely weak in China. The most common geometric metaphor used to describe corporatism is a pyramid, in which "peak" transsectoral and national associations, respectively, have authority over sector-specific and local associations and also act as the main intermediary between the government and the lower-level associations. China instead has an extremely "flat" association structure, which is visible along three dimensions. First, China has several transsectoral associations, but no one of them has authority over any of the others, nor do they represent others in meetings with the government. There is simply no one "peak" association, like those found in Japan or Germany, that serves such a role. The ACFIC, perhaps the most likely candidate, has no influence over the China Industrial Economy Federation or the China Association of Enterprises with Foreign Investment. Each is affiliated with different government or party agencies, none of which has authority over the other.

Second, transsectoral associations do not have authority over sector-specific associations. The latter are often members of the former, but in interviews, representatives from both types of associations consistently said that there was no "subordinate relationship" between them. And while the transsectoral associations occasionally pass on policy information to their sector-specific association members, the latter more frequently interact with a full range of government agencies.[59] This equally applies to sub-associations; even though they are officially under the guidance of more general associations, they often operate as entirely separate organizations.

Lastly, national-level associations do not have authority over local associations. Their powers are circumscribed by guidelines issued in both the 1989 and 1998 regulations (Article 7 in each), which state that national-level and transregional associations are regulated by national government agencies, and local associations are regulated by local governments.[60] In late 1989 the Ministry of Civil Affairs issued a notice prohibiting national-level associations from setting up regional branches, a ban extended in the 1998 regulation on social organizations. Instead, local branches should be set up by local officials or firms. This applies to both transsectoral associations, like SELA and CIEF, as well as sector-specific associations. So, even when a local association is staffed and financed with government resources, those are *local* resources.[61] Such rules are an attempt to hinder the ability of associations to mobilize nationally, but they may also be a concession made by the national government to local authorities fearful of losing control over how their jurisdictions are regulated.[62] Similarly, when a local association needs to interact with a national government agency, it sometimes goes through its national association, but it may also contact the national government directly. Hierarchy between the national association and local branches is further diluted by the fact that when companies join a local branch of an association, they are not necessarily members of the national association. This is particularly true among industry associations, but it is also increasingly the case among associations categorized by ownership.[63] This situation raises the likelihood that national associations do not fully represent local ones.

In each of the three dimensions just cited, authority to regulate an association is granted to the appropriate national or local government agency to which it is affiliated, not the association "above" it. The result is that whether the relationship is between different transsectoral associations, transsectoral and sector-specific associations, or a national association and its local branches, authority is highly fragmented. Hence, it is a misnomer to speak of transsectoral or national-level associations in China as "peak" associations.

Finally, in corporatist systems, associations have a jurisdictional monopoly over the representation of their respective interest groups, both at the national and local levels. The pyramid metaphor, which connotes top-down hierarchical relations among associations, also implies a horizontal division among associations so that they do not overlap or compete with one another. China's 1989 and 1998 regulations both discourage the formation of "identical" (xiangtong) associations in the same jurisdiction.[64] In practice, however, China's associations do not generally enjoy such monopolies.

The jurisdictional boundaries distinguishing associations categorized by ownership have been gradually falling. As originally configured, most of the associations' jurisdiction could be clearly demarcated. Among those initially established for private enterprises, there have been efforts to limit competition. With no national-level Private Enterprises Association and a relatively inactive national-level Self-Employed Laborers Association, ACFIC has dominated the organized representation of nonstate interests on policy matters. And in some localities, ACFIC and PEA have not been allowed to coexist.[65] However, representational monopolies have been limited by several trends. All three associations that cater to private businesses have similar networks, and throughout China smaller private ventures can be in both SELA and ACFIC. Foreign companies have greater choice. Their interests can be represented by the China Association of Enterprises with Foreign Investment, the China Council for the Promotion of International Trade, and the many foreign chambers of commerce that operate in China. Although foreign chambers do not have regional branches, foreign companies across the country can join their national chamber, which can represent its members in discussions with the national and regional governments. In addition, the growing diversity of members' ownership form in many of these associations has reduced the salience of whatever monopolies the associations as organizations may have. State-owned and foreign-invested firms have joined the ACFIC, while associations that previously catered to state-owned enterprises have courted larger private and foreign-invested companies. As associations' memberships diversify across ownership forms, they are increasingly in competition with each other.

There is much more overlap among sectoral associations. The large number of industry associations, sub-associations, industry guilds, sectoral management associations, sectoral import-export chambers of commerce, and foreign-based associations makes this inevitable. Such overlap has partly occurred because of fragmented authority over the establishment of associations. Different ministries and regional bureaus can have a stake in the same industry, or the definition of what actually constitutes an industry is open to interpretation (for example, plastic-bag makers may be seen as part of both the packaging industry and the plastics industry). Thus, associations with similar foci may be established by or (if initiated by firms) affiliated with different government agencies.[66] Or an industry can be subdivided into quite narrow segments, and there may be associations (or sub-associations) for each, all under one or under multiple agencies. Often, to avoid the appearance of overlap, associations with basically the same interest adopt different names or one is made the sub-association of the other. Overlapping jurisdiction occurs between national associations, between national and regional associations, and between regional associations.[67]

When viewed from the perspective of firms, associations' monopolies of interest representation dwindle further. That is because firms often join multiple associations. Consider a hypothetical large, profitable company involved in several industries based in Hebei province. It possibly could join the national, provincial, and city branches of the All-China Federation of Industry and Commerce, the China Enterprise Confederation, the China Industrial Economics Federation, and the national and regional industry associations and industry guilds for each product it produces. In addition, it might join regional chambers of commerce and trade associations outside Hebei if it has production or sales activities elsewhere or simply if it prefers those associations to those in Hebei.[68] And if any of its subsidiaries are joint ventures with a foreign partner, the subsidiary most likely would join the national or local China Association of Enterprises with Foreign Investment, with its foreign partner also being a member of foreign-based chamber of commerce and industry associations with offices in Beijing or Shanghai. The multiplicity of memberships, which is not as uncommon as one might expect, means that this firm's interests are represented in numerous organizations, further undermining whatever supposed jurisdictional monopoly might have been intended for each association.[69]

In sum, China's association system, whether seen from the perspective of associations or firms, does not neatly fit the state or societal corporatist frameworks. Associations are primarily voluntary, increasingly financially independent, not ordered hierarchically, and not unchallenged representatives of certain interests. The limited autonomy of business associations—due to a government role in their creation, affiliation with government agencies and the frequent presence of government officials on the staff, and limited overlap among some associations originally organized by ownership—is still commonplace, but these organizational aspects of limited autonomy have been eroded by growing discord over official norms that justified government intervention in associations.[70]

## Pluralism: A Mixed Picture

If corporatism is a poor description of government-business relations in China, the question then arises as to whether pluralism is any more appropriate. In a pluralist system, one would expect to find: (1) an association system whose characteristics are opposite those of a corporatist one—autonomous and voluntary associations not hierarchically ordered or maintaining jurisdictional monopolies; (2) alternative paths besides associations that business may use to interact with the state; (3) interaction with the state on public policy issues; (4) values that permit the vigorous articulation and defense of interests that may be in conflict with those of the state and other members of society; and (5) a transparent policy-making process.

The first two criteria involve patterns of organization and parallel the discussion of corporatism. The third, the issues that bring government and business together, is important in order to distinguish interactions emblematic of pluralism from those identified with monism or clientelism (in the latter two, relations revolve only around issues specific to the firm). The final two issues are normative factors; though not explicit in the definition of pluralism (or corporatism), they may be important in providing an environment in which members of society can effectively defend their interests. The degree to which open conflict is legitimate distinguishes pluralism from all the other frameworks. An examination of current government-business relations in China reveals enough variation on each of these five criteria so that pluralism does not appear to be an appropriate moniker either.

First, as mentioned above, while China's associations are not entirely corporatist, neither are they completely pluralist. They are increasingly financially independent, they are generally voluntary and nonhierarchically ordered, and there are few jurisdictional monopolies, particularly among industry associations. However, there are still constraints on the autonomy of many business associations with regard to their affiliation to a government agency and staffing by officials. These obstacles to independence, though uneven in specific dimensions and in areas of the economy, can inhibit the ability of businesses to collectively defend their interests.

An area in which China appears more pluralist involves the variety of avenues, indirect and direct, by which businesses interact with government. In corporatist systems elsewhere, associations dominate government-business relations. In pluralist (or clientelist) ones, this is not necessarily the case. If associations are organized in a corporatist manner yet are not important intermediaries between business and government, it would be misleading to identify a country's government-business relations in toto as corporatist.[71]

Besides associations, there are other indirect routes of contact between the Chinese state and businesses operating in China. China's economic transformation has seen the emergence of a wide variety of professional service industries. At the beginning of the Reform era, China had only 212 lawyers working in seventy-nine law firms. Almost a quarter century later, it had 122,000 lawyers employed in ten thousand firms. Many corporations also have their own legal staff. And by 2002, foreign law firms had 160 offices in China.[72] Similarly, China's first domestic public relations firm opened in 1986, and a decade later their number had mushroomed to twelve hundred. At the same time, many of the world's largest public relations firms also established China operations.[73] In addition, lobbying companies, domestic and foreign, have also emerged in the last decade.

Not surprisingly, commercial law firms offer conventional legal counsel to companies, and public relations firms assist in publicizing companies and their products and services through the media and other fora.[74] But some of these companies, along with lobbying firms (discussed more fully below), also engage in public affairs (*gonggong shiwu*) activities, representing their clients' interests vis-à-vis the national and local governments. They interact with officialdom to inform lawmakers about their clients and industry, to obtain authoritative interpretations of laws and regulations, and to make suggestions about those same laws. The main difference between foreign and domestic firms appears to be in their level of sophistication. Foreign law and public relations firms have a more comprehensive strategy to promote their clients' policy agendas.[75]

Beyond these other intermediaries, the most important potential alternative to associations is direct interaction between the government and firms. There are several reasons why direct contact is potentially so prominent. Perhaps the most important is the legacy of the command economy.[76] Although planning was not as centralized in China as in the Soviet Union, it still involved every aspect of enterprises' existence, including personnel, provision of capital, supply of inputs, and production of outputs. The five-year and annual plans created inextricable vertical links between enterprises and the government, while they created disincentives for horizontal ties among enterprises.

During the Reform era, the scope and role of planning substantially changed. The mandatory plans of the Mao era were replaced in the

1980s by guidance plans, in which the government used particularistic sanctions and benefits to induce state-owned firms to comply with their contents. At same time, the plan moved from being the entirety of an enterprise's attention to being just a part of it, as they were allowed to sell production above the plan on the market.[77] In the 1990s, guidance plans were replaced by indicative plans that set general goals and suggestions as opposed to enterprise-specific requirements. The importance of planning dropped, but the Mao era left a legacy that stressed direct interaction between government and businesses. Although originally only involving state-owned enterprises, the legitimacy of direct interaction has extended to domestic and foreign private firms.

Second, there are signs that associations are a low priority for much of the bureaucracy. Despite the end of traditional planning, the size and the responsibilities of China's government have *grown* in the post-Mao era. On the other hand, market-oriented reforms also represent a challenge to bureaucrats' ability to directly determine economic outcomes. Stingy about their already modified powers, many officials are inclined to see associations as a threat to their raison d'etre. As a result, many officials appointed to run government-created associations have been low-level cadres near retirement age who have not had much authority over the bureaucracies they left. Assigning such figures to head associations is a way to formally reduce an organization's staff and at the same time make it more likely that the association will not usurp the bureaucracy's original powers. To the extent associations are a low priority, officials show that they want to continue the planning-era practice of directly interacting with businesses.[78]

Just as important as the existence of multiple routes of contact between business and government is the degree to which the government is open to being influenced by business on public policy issues. This aspect of pluralism has grown remarkably during the last decade. During the planning era, there was more give and take than is usually recognized. On the one hand, the government tried to ensure conformity with its plans by nationalizing enterprises, controlling appointment decisions of their senior managers, and establishing Chinese Communist Party branches within the enterprises. On the other hand, even mandatory planning involved some degree of consultation between enterprises and the government agency to which they were affiliated, either a national ministry or a local government. Before plans were disseminated, enterprises made requests for various resources, some of which had to be met to ensure their compliance with the rest of the plan. Thus, negotiation was built into planning. In fact, the details of plans were negotiated between enterprises and the government even after plans were announced, leading one former official to remark that China's planned economy was really a "negotiated economy" (*tanpan jingji*).[79] China's experience in this regard mirrors that of other centrally planned economies.[80]

Because of the issues involved, negotiation under the planning era was consistent with monism. However, such activity provided a precedent for government-business dialogue in the Reform era when the breadth of interaction has grown. The substance of government-business relations has broadened far beyond operational questions that devolved from setting and implementing plans to issues of public policy that affect industry. As a result, firms' interaction with the government has expanded beyond the one government department to which they are affiliated or registered to encompass whatever agencies, national and local, adopt policies that affect their business and industry. Industry attention is primarily focused on State Council ministries and offices, as opposed to the National People's Congress, since the former adopt a much greater number of regulations that more specifically affect their interests.[81] The breadth of interaction applies to all types of companies, from state-owned enterprises and collectives to domestic and foreign private firms. They are all similarly affected by laws and regulations adopted by different parts of the government, and so potentially interact with an equally wide array of government bodies.

Relatedly, the timing, initiative, and arenas for direct government-business interaction have also evolved. It is clear that the two sides have regular contact *before* policies are adopted. Sources in people's congresses, the State Council, industrial ministries, and local governments concurred that it is common practice to obtain the opinions of industry as part of their attempts to regulate the economy.[82] Such exchanges of opinions are initiated by both sides and occur during the consideration of specific laws and regulations and as part of the regular process of regulatory oversight, which then might then prompt a new policy initiative. The government may call a meeting with industry (specific firms and/or associations) over a policy issue, industry may ask the government to do so, or industry may be the host and invite officials to attend.

At one extreme, ministries at the national and regional levels have held formal hearings as one way to obtain industry's opinions, a rapidly expanding practice that has recently been officially encouraged for people's congresses.[83] At the other extreme, companies and associations regularly invite officials to press conferences and product announcements and use these occasions to mention policy issues or at least to heighten the officials' sense of the industry's importance. A company does not need to be based in Beijing to become involved in the national policy process. Executives can travel to the capital to meet officials in person. Besides, many larger companies, domestic and foreign, have branch offices in Beijing whose primary purpose is to keep in touch with their regulators. In addition, national agencies often send delegations to meet with local governments, experts, companies, and associations in other cities as a part of their regulatory duties. But regardless of a company's or association's location, it can write reports and letters or make telephone calls to substitute for or complement face-to-face meetings.

The stress here on firms' interaction with government—as opposed to the Chinese Communist Party—on policy matters is intentional. From one perspective, the party has to be involved. Most senior local and national government officials are CCP members, and party committees parallel the state bureaucracy. This overlap of people and offices led more than one business executive to tell this researcher that the government and the party may be "a distinction without a difference."[84] Despite that, the great majority of businesses that interact with officialdom on national public policy do so as if the distinction does matter. That is, they lobby the government as if it has its own independent authority. When attempting to learn about or influence a national policy, companies primarily go to government agencies. And although officials may wear a second party hat, companies usually determine which official to contact based on their "[government] business title" (*yewu zhicheng*), not their party post.

The central government likely has become the locus of attention in national public policy issues for several reasons. First, as others have found, the party as an institution has withdrawn from day-to-day involvement in the consideration of most national regulations outside of domestic and international security issues.[85] Although the party regularly forms leading groups on a variety of economic issues and has schools that double as research institutes on public policy, these bodies focus on broad issues, not detailed regulatory matters. (Moreover, they tend to operate in secrecy, making them difficult to contact in any case.) Only the government has the breadth and depth of institutions to attempt to regulate what has become an extremely complicated economy. Government bureaucracies are assigned these roles and have official decision-making authority.[86] And second, while it is possible to coax a senior party official to push a government agency to make a policy decision favorable to a company or industry, firms tend to avoid attempting this because such efforts can backfire. Government bureaucrats fiercely prize their turf and do not appreciate intervention from external sources, even senior party officials. In addition, CCP officials can become involved in elite factional politics, which may make them a useful ally at one moment and a dangerous liability the next.[87] Thus, to avoid offending bureaucrats with whom one has to interact over a sustained period or being associated with a political loser, industry interests have strong disincentives to going outside standard government channels. You may win the battle of the moment but lose the longer regulatory lobbying war.

There are two exceptions to this focus on the government. First, national party leaders regularly make tours of companies around the country or host leaders or representatives of foreign companies visiting China. Although the official may be wearing his or her government hat, the companies are aware of the official's position in the party leadership and his or her primary responsibilities. Whether participants meet on a factory floor in the heartland or in oversized lace-draped chairs in Beijing, these gatherings typically are public relations events, hence the extensive media coverage they are given. If there is a substantive exchange, companies are most likely to raise issues specific to their operations, though it is possible they will broach broader policy issues.[88] The other exception occurs when an economic policy directly touches upon domestic or international security issues, in which case there is likely more focused party attention. A good example would be aspects of policies for the Internet, where the CCP Propaganda Department, among other government and party agencies, is involved in the policy process concerning the content and distribution of information to the public. Internet content providers can benefit from discussing these issues with the Propaganda Department, even if in the end the formal policy is announced by a government bureau.[89]

As significant as the existence of multiple paths of interaction and a growth in contact on policy matters that may result in policy influence are in relation to the existence of pluralism in China, businesses could be inhibited in their ability to influence the government because of official norms that have stressed cooperation between the two sides because of shared interests and secrecy during the policy-making process. Both were prominent aspects of politics during the Mao era and have been seen as consistent with traditional Chinese political values as well as common among Communist regimes.[90] A look at China today shows a mixed record on the norms concerning the degree of cooperation and the level of transparency that makes a firm conclusion on their consequences difficult.

Government officials generally expect that attempts to affect the policy process should outwardly be conducted in a nonconfrontational manner. It is rare for businesspeople and their representatives to be described as part of "interest groups" (*liyi jituan*) or their activities as "lobbying" (*youshui*, or *yuanwai huodong*) or even "influence" (*yingxiang*), all terms that connote social pressure on and inherent conflicts with the state.[91] References to interest groups and lobbying are primarily used in discussions of business-government relations in other countries.[92] Instead, business involvement in policy making in China is typically couched in less confrontational and more neutral terms, such as "participating in politics" (*canzheng*), "exchanging views" (*jiaohuan kanfa*), or "providing ideas" (*tigong jianyi*). Relatedly, policy ideas are best presented as benefiting not only the lobbying party but also broader Chinese society and the government. It is appropriate to take issue with government policies, but such disagreements should be aired and resolved behind closed doors. These norms apply equally to Chinese and foreign businesses.[93]

On the other hand, there are also signs that these norms have weakened. As noted in the discussion on association autonomy above, because they see their interests in potential conflict with the state's, many companies are increasingly disillusioned by associations with significant official involvement. The need to be cautious in how to frame their views has not stopped businesspeople from presenting many of their ideas. And despite issues being cloaked in more neutral terms, officials admit they understand that businesses' views and proposals reflect their particular interests and that this is a natural part of interacting with them.[94] One official even said, without prompting, that associations should be "lobbying the government."[95] A comparative perspective also potentially lessens the weight of this factor. American lobbyists regularly face difficulties operating in Western Europe because they are perceived to be heavy handed and not adequately deferential to officials. But by modifying their behavior or, as often is the case, hiring a local lobbyist who knows the unwritten "rules of the game," Americans still manage to exert some influence on public policies.[96] In that context, the norm of cooperation may be mostly a matter of style.

The norm concerning the degree of transparency in policy making has similarly been in flux. The party-state has maintained a mammoth document system with various levels of confidentiality, thereby compartmentalizing information flows.[97] In addition to the existence of "internal" (*neibu*) regulations, the system has limited dissemination of draft laws and regulations that are later published. There has been some progress in transparency over the past decade, mostly due to foreign pressure. In a 1992 memorandum of understanding on market access signed with the United States, China pledged that all laws and regulations related to trade would be published and that those that remained unpublished could not be enforced. Since then, China has established an official register in which it publishes foreign trade and investment laws. In the late 1990s, many national and local government offices began setting up their own Web sites, where they provided the texts of major laws and regulations, statistics, and statements and speeches by senior officials.[98] The commitment to enforce only publicized regulations was reaffirmed in China's accession agreement to the World Trade Organization. Finally, the government has begun to publish more draft laws in major newspapers and ask for public comment on them.[99]

However, in absolute terms, China's policy-making process is still far from transparent. There are some exceptions, but the texts of most laws and regulations are published only after being passed by the government. There have also been complaints that many government Web sites do not contain adequate useful information.[100] In addition, the media, both electronic and print, popular and industry-specific, have had an unending flow of stories announcing new policies, but there are far fewer stories published detailing the process by which those policies and laws came into existence. As a result, businesses, foreign and domestic, have had to spend a great deal of energy determining not only the substance of draft policies but also which agencies and officials are involved in their consideration. Even when members of business have access to the policy process, they are often discouraged from sharing their information more broadly.[101]

In sum, there are several aspects of government-business relations that distinguish China from a corporatist system (state or societal) and point in the direction of pluralism. Several of the association system's characteristics are not consistent with corporatism, there are multiple indirect and direct avenues of contact between business and the state, and the two sides regularly interact over policy issues at each side's initiative before policies are enacted. (This last aspect also conflicts with key expectations of monism and clientelism.) However, the constraints on association independence, the limited transparency of policy making, and the norms stressing cooperative tone in government-business relations can restrict the ability of the business community and others in society to defend their interests. Limits on associations and transparency likely have a more definitive effect on efforts at influence than norms of cooperation. Regardless, the combination of these factors suggest that from a macro perspective China does not fully fit a pluralist framework.

## Beyond Clientelism

Finally, it also appears that government-business relations on national policy making do not fit the clientelism pattern either. This is surprising given the consensus that corruption is so widespread. Although there is no reliable data, the impression of foreign and domestic observers is that corruption has risen dramatically since the early 1990s.[102] Analysts have found corruption to be endemic, a natural by-product of government's intrusive hand in regulating the economy.[103] While it is certainly possible for businesses, either directly or through associations, to rely on patrons in government for help on issues of concern, there is good reason why we should not a priori view this as the dominant modus operandi for lobbying at the national level.

Most important, national public policy does not lend itself easily to clientelism. The great majority of documented cases of clientelist relations between a business and an official revolve around problems specific to that firm that can be resolved by the intervention of one or two officials. These include approval for business licenses, investment plans, permits, bank loans, and the sale of certain products; reduction of tax payments; access to land and other resources; and favorable verdicts on court cases. These issues are primarily regulated at the local level, and, thus, that is where corruption is most rampant.[104] By contrast, a national public-policy issue typically affects a wide swath of firms, and the process involves numerous officials, often from multiple bureaucracies. Consequently, patronage commonly observed in local settings does not easily translate to national economic policy. Granted, the national government is responsible for a variety of company-specific issues, from approving large investment projects to permitting specific drugs to go on the market. And it is more than conceivable that clientelism pays off on these issues. Such problems are a smaller subset of the national government's regulatory ambit.[105]

Consequently, there are two types of lobbying firms in China. Some are best characterized as PR firms, where "PR" stands not for "public relations" but "private relations." Staffed by former officials or relatives of current officials, they use their connections to solve specific, narrow-gauged problems for individual companies. While some of these outfits have contacts with national politicians, they primarily deal with provincial and lower level government and party officials.[106] By contrast, lobbying firms focused on national policy employ former officials but use them not as "influence peddlers" but as part of their strategy to push broader policy issues. One foreign lobbying company, with a record of successful influence on national policy, employed seven former Chinese officials. According to an interview source, these staffers helped the firm through the bureaucratic maze so the company could present its policy positions to decision makers. He insisted they never traded cash for influence but instead shaped the policy debate in a way that provided a "win-win outcome" for all interested parties.[107]

A skeptic could point out that since China is not a democracy and its leaders are not accountable through elections, offering material incentives appears to be the only motivation for officials to follow the demands of business or other interest groups, regardless of the issue. Such a view, though, overly highlights the "electoral connection" that empowers lobbyists in democracies and overlooks other reasons why the Chinese government has become more susceptible to industry lobbying beyond patronage.[108] As a prodevelopment regime, the Chinese state is ideologically oriented toward business. The two are in some sense partners seeking to use the other to achieve their own goals. While the government is in a position to influence business, firms have gained policy leverage because they are central to accomplishing government objectives such as a growing economy, stable prices, high employment, and expanding tax receipts. Without industry's cooperation, these and other goals cannot be achieved, either for a specific bureaucracy or for the government as a whole. Relatedly, because of their involvement in the economy, businesses are a critical source of knowledge on issues that affect their success. Such information may be neutral in tone, concerning, for example, market trends and production techniques. But just as often a business "educates" officials to viewing problems from the company's perspective, all the while showing how the firm's preferred outcome can also benefit the government and the country as a whole. In sum, its central place in achieving government objectives and its authoritative knowledge give industry, Chinese and foreign, a "privileged position" at the policy table.[109]

This analysis does not mean that national-level corruption involving business does not occur, only that it is more likely to happen at the local level. Nor does it mean that connections (*guanxi*) are irrelevant in national policy making, only that connections are not equivalent to clientelism or corruption.[110] Companies or their representatives can develop new connections or rely on old ones to build trust with their regulators, learn about government policies, and push their own agenda, all without being required to offer material incentives in return.[111] As such, using connections can be consistent not only with clientelism but with the pluralist or corporatist frameworks as well.[112]

## Conclusion: Explaining Variation

This overview of business-government relations paints a complex picture, one that is not neatly captured in any single model. It is hard, if not impossible, to put reality in stark, definitive terms. China is not only a shade of gray, but a gray that is mixed with different hues and tints. Associations' autonomy is generally highly constrained, but there are gradations of control based on the relative involvement of government in the associations' creation, staff, and financing. Associations are

usually voluntary and arranged nonhierarchically and without jurisdictional monopolies, but there are exceptions. There has been tremen-
dous growth in the rise of other indirect routes and direct contact over
substantive policy matters. However, attempts at influence may be constrained by norms to appear not to be doing so and by continued efforts
at secrecy. National policy issues are less vulnerable, but not immune,
to patron-client ties compared to issues around which government-
business ties revolve at the local level. Almost every affirmation of a
pattern is accompanied by hedges and qualifications.

As difficult as it may be to parsimoniously sum up Chinese reality,
this need not be a frustrating conclusion. The models against which
China has been compared are just ideal types, ones that very few countries fully fit. They do not exhaust the possible patterns of government-
business relations that exist in the world. They have been helpful in
orienting the analysis and providing a basis of comparison with earlier
research, but the ultimate goal is not to say to what extent China fits
one or the other models, since to the degree that China differs, the
models may obscure as much as they illuminate.

China is in a period of flux in which there is a great deal of internal
variation. In such a situation, determining the *sources* of dynamism and
variation that exist is more important than trying to attach a label to describe China at any one moment in time. As such, outlining the present
overall system as a whole is only the starting line, not the finish line, of
analysis. That is why the remainder of this study analyzes China
through the context of three industries—steel, consumer electronics,
and software—that have contrasting economic circumstances, and
through the context of firms that are of different forms of ownership,
sizes, and nationalities. The central thesis of this study is that much of
the variation both in the ways government and business interact and in
the outcome of their interaction (that is, which firms are most influential) are related to the varying economic circumstances of individual
firms and the sectors of which they are a part.

# ~ 3

# The Steel Industry:
# Walking on One Leg

*W*HEN THINKING of heavy industry in China, one invari-
ably conjures up images of a smoky steel mill. Following the founding
of the PRC, developing the steel industry became the hallmark of
China's attempt at rapid industrialization, as the saying went, to "pass
England and catch America" (*chao ying gan mei*). Investment in the
1950s was weighted toward heavy industry and steel in particular, as enterprises like Beijing's Capital Iron and Steel (*Shougang*) and Anshan
Iron and Steel (*Angang*) in Liaoning province were dramatically expanded. During the Great Leap Forward, backyard furnaces mushroomed, and in the 1960s, the Third Front strategy led to the spread of
steel mills in western China, such as the Panzhihua factory that sits in a
remote corner of Sichuan province. Such mammoth steel enterprises
became the hub of encompassing minisocieties, with their own housing, hospitals, canteens, and schools. Despite twists and turns in a general strategy for economic development, an overriding concern for
steel has been a constant.[1] Steel output rose from 1.4 million tons in
1952 to 32 million tons in 1978 and 182 million tons in 2002, making
China the world's largest producer of steel for the seventh year in a row.
The industry's thirty-two hundred enterprises employ over two million
workers.[2] And steel complexes still dominate many of the economies of
some cities, both large and small.[3] In short, one cannot overstate the
importance of steel to China's economy. The irony is that while China

has become a "big steel country," as many sources for this research concurred, China is far from being a "strong steel country." By international standards, China's steel industry is extremely inefficient and produces poor-quality steel. China's steel mills are thought of as anachronistic dinosaurs, windows into an earlier era.[4] In China's brand of "market socialism," the steel industry is viewed as less market and more socialism.

Though not directly addressed in journalistic or academic accounts of the steel sector's woes, there is an impression that not much has changed since the Mao era in how the steel industry interacts with the government. Since state-owned steel factory general managers and their Chinese Communist Party (CCP) secretaries are still appointed by the party-state, one would expect them to be relatively compliant and not interested in influencing public policy. In this context, ministries ought to speak on behalf of the firms under their jurisdiction, and, conversely, potential intermediaries such as associations would be undeveloped and irrelevant to the policy-making process.

An examination of China's steel industry reveals a more complex picture, one that confirms some of these impressions but challenges others. One that largely holds—and sets steel apart from the consumer electronics industry and especially the software industry—is the paucity of associational activity. Steel-related associations exist, but they are largely government controlled and ineffective either at regulating business or at representing business's views to the state. The exceptions, in the stainless steel subsector, are more independent and score occasional victories for their members, but they are weak and live a marginal existence. The dearth of reliable associations has not meant, though, that steel companies do not attempt to defend their interests or influence policy. Instead, enterprises use direct contact with government to forward their interests. Despite the obvious distinction that state-owned enterprises (SOEs) have direct access (and often overlap in personnel) with their immediate superior government bodies—state-owned, private domestic, and private foreign steel companies all tend to interact directly with government regulators. The commonality of a hyperreliance on direct ties masks differences in ties among companies of different sizes. Larger firms, primarily SOEs but even foreign firms to some extent, have more regular and senior access to government on a wider array of policy issues than smaller firms.

This skewing of relations toward only direct contact, what might be called "walking on one leg," means that relations have not fit either the corporatist or pluralist models. Although the two models have different expectations for the organization and activities of associations, both see associations as playing critical roles in mediating ties. That has not been the case in China's steel industry. But since patron-client ties were not found to be prominent, clientelism is an inappropriate characterization of relations as well.

The almost complete dependence on direct ties has been of most benefit to large SOEs. The relative access they have compared to smaller firms of any ownership form has translated into greater relative influence in several policy areas.

To explain how these conclusions were reached, this chapter will first provide an overview of the steel industry's economic circumstances in order to highlight how these conditions affect the pattern of government-business relations and to identify the main issues around which interaction has revolved. It then goes on to contrast the state of industry associations with the growth of companies' direct involvement in policy making. Finally, these trends will be fleshed out by examining government-business relations on three policy issues: pricing, international competitiveness, and environmental protection.

## The Economics of Steel

No one sector in China is "typical" of all of Chinese industry, hence the need for and utility of comparison. The steel industry's economic characteristics are distinct compared to the other two sectors in this study, but there is also some heterogeneity within the industry. Conversely, the industry's economic difficulties share some similarities to that of other sectors, but they are deeper than most.

First, China's steel industry is predominantly state-owned. In 2001, SOEs accounted for 72 percent of the sector's output, 88 percent of its total assets, and 74 percent of its sales revenue. This is quite a contrast to the consumer electronics and software industries, where SOEs account for 33 percent and under 10 percent of output of those sectors' output, respectively.[5]

On the other hand, over the past decade SOEs have been joined in significant numbers by collectives, domestic private enterprises, and foreign companies. Although SOEs dominate the industry in terms of output, they only accounted for 20 percent of the country's thirty-two hundred steel companies in 2001, which is up five percentage points from 1997. There are no reliable data on the numbers of domestic private enterprises, but they likely number over one thousand.[6] There are a few private integrated steel factories, but they are puny compared to the country's largest firms. One of the largest domestic private producers, Nantong Specialty Steel, located a few hours upriver from Shanghai, has an annual capacity of thirty thousand tons. But most private enterprises are engaged in processing raw steel smelted elsewhere. A significant growth area for such firms has been the stainless steel market, a category in which China has traditionally lacked productive capacity. For example, there are over seventy private stainless steel pipe makers in Wenzhou, a coastal region of Zhejiang province historically known for both private enterprises and metals processing.[7]

Foreign companies have also expanded their presence. Through the 1980s, foreign steelmakers only exported to China, but in the 1990s they formed numerous joint ventures with Chinese partners.[8] Like domestic private enterprises, foreign presence has grown in areas in which SOEs have not excelled. NKK, one of Japan's "big five" steel manufacturers, has a steel-drill plant with China Petroleum along the Bohai Gulf and a tin-plate factory in Fujian. Timken, a U.S.-based producer of tapered ball bearings, has a joint venture in Shandong.[9]

Second, China's steel industry has very high economies of scale. This is common to steel globally, but China's steel industry is distinctive in its reliance on outdated technologies and production processes. While the global industry has radically changed over the past thirty years, China has struggled to keep pace. Traditionally, the steel industry was dominated by vertically integrated producers who smelted iron ore into pig iron, then oxidized pig iron into raw steel, and finally shaped raw steel into finished products. Integrated producers have extremely high economies of scale because of large, fixed costs in plant and equipment; but after this initial investment, marginal costs of increased output decline.[10] According to a leading steel industry expert, an efficient integrated mill can produce 6–7 million tons annually.[11] Beyond China, this standard has been successfully challenged by "mini-mills," a title that should not be equated with small size. First emerging in the 1960s, mini-mills replace the use of iron ore and pig iron with scrap metal as their chief input, first melting it in electric furnaces and then reshaping it into products. With improvements in continuous casting technology (which can be used in both types of plants), mini-mills are competing with integrated mills in all product categories and can produce more than three hundred thousand tons annually. These changes in the industry have left integrated producers with diseconomies of scale.[12]

China has been dominated by integrated steel factories that have used open-hearth and basic oxygen furnaces (BOF). Beginning in the 1980s, China phased in more BOFs and began introducing electric furnaces. In 1997, BOF-made steel accounted for 73 percent of all steel made in China; only 18 percent was made in electric furnaces. Similarly, the continuous casting process, standard in the steel sectors of industrial countries, was a late arrival in China. In 1980, only 6 percent of steel in China was made through continuous casting; that figure had risen to 61 percent in 1997 and 87 percent in 2001. This was a significant improvement, but it still left China behind world leaders, who use continuous casting for over 95 percent of their steel.[13]

Because of their outdated equipment and processes, Chinese steel enterprises often hire a large number of employees. Many integrated mills have tens of thousands of workers, but there are also hundreds with between five hundred and two thousand workers, and processing plants that have between one hundred and five hundred employees.[14] It is tempting to conclude that the industry is bifurcated between large SOEs and small nonstate firms, but there are so many smaller state-owned steel factories that this distinction does not hold up.

Third, this reliance on outmoded technology and labor makes Chinese steel enterprises large relative to other domestic industries, but also quite inefficient in comparison to other countries. The amount of steel produced per enterprise and per worker in China is quite low by world standards. In 1997 the average Chinese firm produced only eighteen thousand tons.[15] China has only a handful of plants like Shougang and Angang that can produce several million tons annually. They are joined by hundreds of factories, some integrated producers and others that just engage in processing semifinished steel into finished products, that make far less. A 1993 report found that Japan's blast furnaces in 1988 were thirty times the size of those in China.[16] In 1996, there were eighty-three steel factories under construction, and even the largest among them averaged only 170,000 tons' capacity.[17]

In addition, regardless of enterprises' absolute size, the vast majority produce a low amount of steel per worker. Labor productivity has risen severalfold, but China is still far below world standards.[18] Put another way, in 1997 Japan produced about the same amount of steel as China but with only one-twentieth the number of workers. Chinese steel remains competitive domestically, not to mention internationally, only because of China's low labor costs.

The consequence of outmoded technology and low efficiency is low-grade steel products. The vast majority of domestic output goes into construction, railways, bridges, trucking, and shipping. According to China's own statistics, even with the recent improvements in eliminating open-hearth furnaces and moving to continuous casting, "advanced-quality" steel still accounted for only 28 percent of total output in 2001, just four percentage points higher than in 1980. As a result, China has been reliant on imports for high-grade iron ore and finished steel products, including stainless steel and various alloys, that go into producing passenger automobiles, appliances, and scientific instruments. Thin sheets and iron ore remain the top two largest imports for the sector.[19]

There are some exceptions to this gloomy picture, the most important being Baoshan Iron and Steel (*Baogang*), located in Shanghai's northeast corner. Initially planned as a medium-sized facility in the late 1970s, Baogang began production in 1985 and since has expanded in three phases to become China's largest and most efficient producer. By all accounts, the company produces high-quality steel for a variety of markets. Baogang supplies most of the steel sheet for China's major automakers, and it alone accounts for almost 40 percent of China's total steel exports.[20] Baogang has had the advantage of history—or rather lack of one—on its side. From its inception, it has installed the most advanced furnaces and other technology from Japan and Germany, and it has been allowed to maintain a relatively slim labor force. The greatest threat to its regal status occurred in late 1998, when Baogang was merged with two much more inefficient producers, the Shanghai Metallurgy Group and Meishan Iron and Steel.[21]

The fourth characteristic is a direct consequence of having numerous firms with low output—low market concentration. In 2001, China's top four enterprises combined to produce only 28 percent of the country's finished steel, down from 33 percent in 1990.[22] By contrast, in

Japan, the top five makers typically account for 80 percent of that country's steel capacity. There is a great range in concentration among product categories; those that can be easily produced by smaller enterprises have extremely low concentration levels. In addition, because of the encouragement of local productive capacity during the Mao era and the entrance of small, private producers in the 1990s, China's steel industry is also regionally dispersed.

The final economic factor relevant to the steel industry's interaction with the government is steel's vulnerability to price fluctuations. As an intermediate material used in a whole range of industries, from construction to many durable goods, demand for steel often follows business cycles. Because long lead times are needed for production runs and furnaces cannot be easily turned on and off like an assembly line, it is quite common for steel to be in short supply at the beginning of an expansion but in oversupply in the middle of an economic cycle, sending prices first up and then down. Moreover, given the growth in the importance of international trade to China's steel industry and reductions in tariffs, changes in demand and supply elsewhere also affect prices in China.

These five factors—the predominance of SOEs, high economies of scale, low efficiency, low market concentration, and vulnerability to price shocks—have all been central to the industry's mounting crisis in the 1990s. Oversupply, caused by both surging imports and a rapid expansion of domestic production, has resulted in price deflation. The consequence has been lower profits (or high losses), which has meant less capital available for investment in efficiency-improving technologies and lower tax receipts.

The steel industry's economic circumstances have also affected the way in which government and business have interacted to address the sector's dilemmas. The predominance of large SOEs creates a low expectation for the development of associations. Given the ease of access to government, direct interaction for such firms would seem more appropriate. Low market concentration also increases the difficulty for firms to cooperate with one another. On the other hand, the industry's vulnerability to price fluctuations, which raises the dangers of spikes in unemployment and falls in taxes, makes concerted action by firms and government to jointly manipulate prices and production an appealing strategy. Such circumstances—which came to prominence in China in the 1990s—can be an impetus to associations. This was the case in

Japan's steel industry throughout the twentieth century, and it was not uncommon in the United States prior to the 1950s.[23] Thus, China's steel industry has been pulled toward cooperation by its susceptibility to price fluctuations but has been pushed away from it by the presence of large SOEs and the low concentration of output. The pattern of government-business relations on policy issues over the last decade has been a reflection of this tension.

## The Weakness of China's Steel Associations

In his detailed study of China's steel industry, Steinfeld never once refers to industry associations, either in regard to government regulation of enterprises or the latter's attempts to defend their interests.[24] And for good reason. Consistent with the expectation given the predominance of SOEs, most steel associations in China have been state-controlled, ineffectual, and insignificant avenues for government-business relations.

Compared to the other sectors in this study, steel-related associations emerged belatedly. In fact, there was no national industry-wide association that dealt with significant policy matters until 1999. Prior to that year, there were a handful of narrowly focused associations, only a few of which directly dealt with policy issues (see Table 3.1). The China Metallurgy Enterprise Management Association (CMEMA, *zhongguo yejin qiye guanli xiehui*) was created in 1989, three years after most other management associations. From its founding in 1989 to its closure a decade later, CMEMA never had any autonomy. It was established at the initiative of a government agency, the Ministry of Metallurgy Industry (MMI), by which it was also fully staffed and financed. CMEMA met infrequently and kept its agenda limited to improving internal management within large state-owned metallurgy enterprises. For example, it held meetings to promote the management practices of Baogang and Handan Iron and Steel (*Hangang*). In short, its late founding, infrequent meetings, and narrow agenda suggest CMEMA was clearly not central to MMI's regulation of the industry.[25]

Another national association with broad-based membership prior to 1999 was the China Metals Society (CMS, *zhongguo jinshu xuehui*). First created in 1956, it was dormant during the Cultural Revolution and only was revived in 1991. In the late 1990s, the group held regular meetings with engineers and technicians from various state-owned

**Table 3.1** Autonomy of selected steel-related associations in China (Y=yes; N=no; darker shading signifies greater autonomy)

| Business association | Chinese govt initiative? | Affiliation | Staffed with (former) govt officials? | Financially dependent on govt? |
|---|---|---|---|---|
| China Metallurgy Enterprise Management Association (CMEMA) (1989–1999) | Y | MMI | Y | Y |
| China Metals Society (CMS) (1956, 1991) | Y | MMI, CISA | Y | Y |
| China Specialty Steel Enterprise Association (CSSEA) (1986) | Y | MMI, CISA | Limited | N |
| China Iron and Steel Association (CISA) (1999) | Y | SASAC | Y | Y |
| CSSEA Stainless Steel Sub-Association (1998) | N | CISA | N | N |
| China Metal Materials Circulation Association Stainless Steel Department (1997) | N | CMCPF | N | N |
| Ouhai (Wenzhou) Stainless Steel Chamber of Commerce (1997) | N | Wenzhou Economic Office | Limited | N |
| Japan Iron and Steel Import-Export Association (1998) | N | — | N | N |

steel companies to discuss how to improve efficiency from a technical point of view. Given its focus and its participants, the society was not a channel for government-business dialogue on policy matters.[26]

The one steel association that had any history of attention to policy issues in the 1990s is the China Specialty Steel Enterprise Association (CSSEA, *zhongguo teshu gangtie qiye xiehui*). Founded in 1986, CSSEA at first glance appears more independent than either CMEMA or CMS. Since its inception, it has been staffed by retired leaders from state-owned steel companies. Its office is not in a government building, and it collects RMB 20,000 in annual dues from each of its thirty-one members. But despite these outward signs of independence, CSSEA has largely been controlled from behind the scenes by the national metallurgy bureaucracy. Its senior staff has been appointed by the government, and steel officials serve in honorary posts. Its members have joined voluntarily, but include only SOEs (the one exception is an SOE–Hong Kong joint venture) despite the fact that there are private enterprises in the subsector.[27]

CSSEA has been more active than CMEMA and CMS. Members meet regularly to discuss issues that affect the industry, including finance, management, producer-supplier relations, and pricing. The association collects and distributes production and sales data among its members. It has also encouraged its members to coordinate prices to halt deflation. And it has obtained some preferential policies for its members, such as low-interest loans, special access to raw materials, and lower electricity rates. Still, most of the associations' activities and policy positions have been in consultation with the metallurgy bureaucracy and not of its own initiative or at the behest of its members. More often than not, the government calls its leaders to meetings to instruct them on policy, not to obtain policy input. In short, CSSEA has been largely government-controlled and supplemental to bureaucratic regulation.[28]

The above descriptions reflect the limited development and autonomy of associations, which is a product of the steel industry's dominance by SOEs. The low priority given to associations changed in the late 1990s, propelled on the one hand by a government effort to create a state corporatist system and on the other by firms in a subsector of industry with a greater proportion of small private companies.

In January 1999, CMEMA was replaced by the China Iron and Steel Association (CISA, *zhongguo gangtie gongye xiehui*). But that was not due to the demands of its members (all SOEs) for a new collective advocate; rather, the initiative came from the steel bureaucracy, which was itself in the process of being dismantled. It began in March 1998, as part of the government restructuring plan, when the Ministry of Metallurgy Industry was downgraded to a bureau and subsumed under the authority of the State Economic and Trade Commission (SETC). The new Bureau of Metallurgy Industry's (BMI) staff of over five hundred was then sliced to under one hundred, and in early 2001 it was completely eliminated along with eight other industrial bureaus within the SETC.[29] To complete the transition, in March 2003 the SETC itself was eliminated. Oversight of key national state-owned enterprises' personnel and operations was given to the State-Owned Assets Supervision Administration of China (SASAC), while responsibility for industrial policy, albeit at a broader level, shifted to the State Development and Reform Commission (SDRC).

In state corporatist fashion, the goal was to radically reduce the bureaucracy and have CISA take over as the industry's chief regulator on all major policy issues, including enterprise restructuring, standard setting, the oversight and coordination of prices and production, and international trade disputes.[30] CISA is run by former senior metallurgy bureaucrats out of the ministry's old compound and is financed by the government. Unlike the other steel associations, membership in CISA is required for any company that produces over five hundred thousand tons of steel annually. Moreover, CISA was placed in charge of supervising on the government's behalf ten more specialized steel associations, including the aforementioned China Specialty Steel Enterprise Association, and eleven other steel-related research and engineering organizations. (CISA officials, though, maintain they have an "equal" relationship with those associations.)[31]

While CISA clearly did not emerge out of company interest, some more popular associations recently have formed in the stainless steel segment of the market. Because of the limited capabilities to produce high-quality stainless steel, new domestic private companies and foreign joint ventures have sprung up in this subsector. In response, several popularly initiated stainless steel associations have been created since 1997. In fact, there are five national stainless steel associations, each of which is a sub-association of a larger association affiliated with different parts of the national bureaucracy. There are also several local independent stainless steel associations, including those in Hangzhou, Wuxi, and Wenzhou.

Though there is some variance among them, stainless steel associations are distinguished in several ways from the other steel associations described above. First, they have been initiated, run, and financed by stainless steel companies, not bureaucrats. The first, the China Metal Materials Circulation Association's Stainless Steel Department (*zhongguo jinshu cailiao liutong xiehui buxiugang bu*), was founded by a small, private Beijing company at the end of 1997. Despite the subordinate-sounding name, it is a full-fledged association.[32] The CSSEA's China Stainless Steel Sub-Association (*zhongguo buxiugang fenhui*) was founded two months later by a former chairman of the state-owned Taiyuan Steel, the country's largest stainless steel maker.

Second, the various stainless steel associations' members are diverse in a number of respects. Firms of all ownership types are well represented, from private producers in Wenzhou and Wuxi to larger, state-owned firms like Taiyuan Steel to joint ventures such as those between Baogang and Nishin of Japan and between Shagang of Jiangsu Province and South Korea's Pohang Steel. There are also domestic company members from outside the metallurgy system. For example, Shanghai's Dalong Forging and Casting Factory (*dalong zhuduan chang*), which had been regulated by the recently eliminated machinery bureaucracy, is a member of the China Stainless Steel Sub-Association. In addition, the associations have both producers and traders as members, which facilitates greater communication between the two segments of the industry that traditionally have been isolated from one another by bureaucratic hurdles.

And third, stainless steel associations are not part of the government's regulatory regime. Their chief missions are to assist their firms in the market and vis-à-vis the government. They all have publications. The Stainless Steel Department is the most active. In addition to its widely read magazine, *China Stainless Steel Market*, it publishes a newspaper, has issued several books, and runs a Web site. In the policy realm, these associations have achieved some gains for their members. To help local producers, the government has set quotas on steel imports. But these quotas impinge on some firms' ability to import the unfinished stainless steel they need to produce final goods. More than one of the associations have persuaded the government to raise the quotas or obtain special exemptions for their members. In the government's attempts to reduce overproduction, it had ordered the closing of all furnaces below a certain capacity. After discussions with one association, the order was revised to exclude firms with electric furnaces, which are used by several smaller stainless steel producers.[33]

Despite stainless steel associations' divergence from the old norm, it is important to recognize their limitations. Stainless steel is still a very small portion of the domestic industry and is not central to the overall steel industry's direction, making it difficult for associations to have much policy influence.[34] In addition, these associations live a somewhat precarious existence because of their independence. As one industry insider said, "The government does not need social organizations. They do not want to give up their own power." Some in the bureaucracy see such associations as threats. At least one stainless steel association has had to rely on protection from a senior-level official to register and grow.[35] Perhaps as a result of their vulnerabilities, stainless steel makers cannot depend on associations to effectively carry their messages to the government. They have to first and foremost rely on themselves.

When seen from the point of view of steel firms themselves, it is clear that associations, including those in stainless steel, have not been central to mediating government-business relations. Steel firms are often in multiple associations, but that is not a sound indicator of firms' evaluation of or interest in associations. There is no clear pattern based on firms' sizes; that is, smaller firms were not any more likely to be interested in associations than larger ones. Based on cases analyzed for this study, there is, however, some difference between firms of different ownership. All but one of the SOEs interviewed had very low evaluations of associations. They called the associations "academic" and not policy-oriented, saying they have been of little use.[36] Another bluntly concluded that associations "are absolutely meaningless" (*meiyou renhe yisi*).[37] CISA was singled out for outwardly appearing like an industry association but in reality operating like the old metallurgy ministry, leading one critic to hope that its aging leaders would yield to younger talent.[38] The one SOE that affirmed associations' utility did so in regard to an association outside the steel industry. Dalong, a Shanghai SOE that makes stainless steel tools, praised the forging and casting associations for their help in qualifying Dalong for tax breaks and helping it and other inefficient producers in Shanghai avoid closure.[39]

Private firms had a somewhat greater interest in associations, but like Dalong they directed this interest primarily at associations *outside* the sector. Even the stainless steel associations were praised primarily for being new sources of policy information; their efforts at organizing firms for collective action were less important to firms, and hence, less successful. By contrast, the Huadi Group (*huadi jituan*) and the Jiangnan Steel Pipe Manufacturing Company (*jiangnan gangguan zhizao youxian gongsi*), two private producers from Wenzhou, were heavily involved in the local Federation of Industry and Commerce and through it regularly met with local officials to obtain policy information and give policy suggestions.[40] Shengdiya, a small, private producer in Shanghai, joined the Shanghai Stock Company Federation (*shanghai gufen gongsi lianhehui*) because the company had issued shares to its workers and needed to keep up with related policy changes.[41] However, some private firms from Jiangsu gave equally negative assessments of their local FIC branches, claiming they could not possibly be of help.[42]

Foreign companies were not particularly more interested in associations than their Chinese counterparts. Only one had joined the government-backed China Association of Enterprises with Foreign Investment (CAEFI), and the company found CAEFI of no use. South Korea giant Pohang's stainless steel joint venture is a member of both the China Stainless Steel Sub-Association and the Stainless Steel Department, but its membership is of only marginal utility. A large Japanese firm operating in China that is a leader of the Japan Iron and Steel Association has not depended much on the China branch of the Japan Iron and Steel Import-Export Association, which only set up an office in China in 1998. Only Timken, which has had a small foreign staff in Beijing and has relied heavily on the American Chamber of Commerce and the U.S.-China Business Council for policy information, lent much weight to associations.[43]

In sum, most steel associations have been extensions of government regulation. Those that are not, for example, in stainless steel are relatively weak and have yet to become a key tool for how their members interact with the government. Importantly, those firms that have relied to some extent on associations have done so not because of these associations' complete independence. The local branch of the ACFIC, the stock federation, and the forging and casting associations, not to mention the CSSEA, all have significant government involvement. It is because of, not despite, such official attention that these associations have been able to have the access necessary to have the limited influence they have displayed. Even the stainless steel associations avoid offending officialdom in their dealings. Thus, there is an inverted-U-shape relationship between utility and independence: associations that are simple extensions of the government offer firms nothing, while overly independent associations have difficulty gaining the access to government needed to be effective advocates. Associations at the top of the inverted-U curve sacrifice some autonomy for access.[44] However, to date the height of that inverted-U curve (the amount of influence) for steel associations has been quite low. Thus, by default firms usually have one alternative left to them to influence the government: direct interaction.

## The Dominance of Direct Interaction

In the steel industry, the legacy of planning is deeper and more recent than in the other sectors analyzed in this study. The government has a history of intervention in individual enterprises and of heavily regulating the sector as a whole. Thus, direct contact between the state and business is standard for both private and state-owned companies alike. Nevertheless, one would think that there would still be differences between state-owned and private enterprises. Since the former's leaders are appointed by the state, SOEs should be subservient and defer to government authorities who act as their surrogates in policy debates. Conversely, private companies should have more initiative in defending their interests. Direct interaction in China's steel industry departs significantly from these expectations. There are differences in the way state-owned and private steel enterprises interact directly with the government in terms of the depth of interaction, but the basic nature of interaction for SOEs and private companies is less pronounced than it used to be.

To understand the changes in interaction, we must recognize that steel SOEs have developed a sense of identity distinct from the state for several reasons. Although the government has formal appointment authority over SOE leaders, most company leaders are promoted from within the firm, not appointed from the outside. Long tenure breeds loyalty. In addition, with the transition away from fiscal layouts and profit return to loans and tax payments, the distinct economic interests of steelmakers have been clarified. Steel firms' success is measured by, at worst, keeping afloat and, at best, by having a large income and being recognized as an industry leader. Finally, in the years before being eliminated, the steel bureaucracy's powers were steadily eroded. In the early 1990s, several years before the metallurgy ministry's downgrading to a bureau in 1998, it lost the power to set most steel prices or to order firms to produce specific products. In March 1998, it lost project-approval power for Shougang, Baogang, and other large steel enterprises to the new State Development and Planning Commission (SDPC). Although the bureau could still issue pleas and try to cajole steel enterprises, to quote one source, "It has no wings." One Chinese steel industry analyst concluded that what were once "mother-in-law relations" (*popo guanxi*) had become relations between two "independent entities" (*duli shiti*), in which genuine dialogue was common.[45]

While these factors theoretically affect all steel SOEs, it is only the larger ones that have had the economic muscle to take advantage of them. Zhou Guanwu, Shougang's infamous leader from 1979 to 1995, first joined the steelmaker in 1950. His appointment as vice minister of metallurgy in the 1980s was honorary and did not divide his allegiance. He engineered the company's prosperity in the 1980s, including promoting its preferential profit-retention plan, but he also was largely responsible for questionable investments in a bank, an iron mine, and a new factory, which left the company on the edge of insolvency. The only way to stop him was removal, which occurred in 1995.[46] Zhou was replaced by Bi Qun, an MMI vice minister, whose loyalties were supposedly with the government, not Shougang. However, he is not all-powerful and must share authority with others who have lengthy tenures at Shougang.

Baogang has shown a similar independent streak. Several years after it began production, Baogang demonstrated it was much more efficient than any other Chinese steel factory. From the early 1990s, MMI and senior Chinese leaders, particularly Wu Bangguo, encouraged Baogang to merge with other steel companies as a way of "the strong supporting the weak." Li Ming, Baogang's longtime chairman, whom some credit with orchestrating its success, fiercely opposed any mergers that would saddle Baogang with the burdens of others. He even took his opposition public in an interview with a foreign journalist in 1997.[47] When the merger did finally occur in late 1998, Li Ming was forced to resign and was replaced by Xu Daquan, who like Bi Qun was a senior metallurgy bureaucrat sent from Beijing. Despite Li's sacrifice, the resulting board of directors of Baogang was still dominated by people with long tenures at the company.[48] But one industry source stressed that even Xu and other recent arrivals quickly reoriented themselves toward placing Baogang's interest above all others, wittily applying the standard description of bureaucratic politics: "Your brain is in your butt."[49] Given that the company and the State Council continued to negotiate over what responsibility the new Baogang would have for the absorbed firms' debts, employees, and factory equipment, the shake-up has far from eliminated Baogang's willingness to defend its interests even when they conflict with government orders.[50]

A more complicated situation arises when there is significant overlap in personnel between a state-owned company and the local government with which it is registered. In such instances, there may be greater unity of interests at that level, but that company's identity and interests still diverge from those of more senior government levels. One such case is the Yonggang Group, which was founded in 1984 by Wu Dong-cai, then party secretary of Yonglian Village. With funds from the village and the surrounding township, Wu built Yonggang into a 2,400-employee company that produces over one million tons of construction steel annually. As the company grew, the village's borders expanded and absorbed neighboring ones.[51] The economic entity, the company, and the political entity, the village, became one and the same. Wu has been the village's party secretary and committee leader, all the while remaining Yonggang's party secretary and chairman. The other village cadres also hold senior positions in the company. On top of this, a daughter of Zhangjiagang city's party secretary is one of Yonggang's vice presidents.[52]

Despite what appears to be a clear case of clientelism at the local level, Yonggang's sense of distinct identity vis-à-vis more senior levels of government, especially the provincial and national levels, is still apparent. Government officials lack any appointment power and cannot directly affect Yonggang's business decisions; and Yonggang's economic interests are distinct from those of the provincial and central government. According to a well-placed source, Wu highly values the freedom to run the company without outside intervention.[53] Thus, the company's sense of identity vis-à-vis every level above the village is probably even more clearly defined than that of Shougang and Baogang.

That direct interaction is dominant throughout the industry is important, but when direct contact is broken down into its constituent elements, significant variation is found. These key elements are: (1) companies' attention to policy; (2) the regularity of interaction; (3) the range and rank of officials and departments contacted; (4) the fora of interaction; (5) range of policy issues; and (6) the degree of company proactiveness.

Ownership and size affect each of these aspects of direct government-business relations somewhat differently. SOEs of all sizes generally meet much more regularly with the government than domestic or foreign private firms. But large SOEs and FIEs are more similar in their greater attention to policy, the broader range and higher rank of officialdom with which they interact, and their level of proactiveness in pushing their policy preferences. Large SOEs are distinguished from large FIEs, though, in that they have a greater number of private meetings with officials, submit policy reports to the government, and interact with government over a wider range of issues. The result of this combination of differences is a *hierarchy of interaction* in which large SOEs are the most active company participants in policy making. They are followed by large foreign companies, while small enterprises of all types have a modest level of involvement on policy issues.

Large SOEs devote significant resources to keep abreast of policy trends. Both Shougang and Baogang have departments dedicated to policy making, and many large SOEs, including Baogang, have representative offices in Beijing to help them track policy. Large SOEs meet regularly with the national bureaucracy. MMI (and later BMI) held anywhere from twenty to fifty meetings each year, and most of the participants were large SOEs. However, many of these "large meetings" (*da huiyi*) were geared just to announce policy. Prior to some of these meetings, officials held private "small meetings" (*xiao huiyi*) with the largest five to ten producers. For example, Shougang and the other top producers annually met with metallurgy officials in mid-December prior to each January's national metallurgy work conference.[54] In addition, national steel officials and even more-senior political leaders most often have made investigation trips to larger state-owned steel factories, where they have discussed the situation of the company and the industry.[55] Large steel SOEs have met with senior officials in the metallurgy bureaucracy and almost every other part of the government that regulates their businesses, including the State Economic and Trade Commission, Ministry of Finance, State Taxation Administration, Ministry of Commerce, and the State Development and Reform Commission. (The exception appears to be the State Environmental Protection Agency. See "The Exception: Environmental Protection," page 89.) As one large SOE representative said, regardless of which bureaucracy is involved, "If we need to understand a policy, it is easy to find out."[56] The largest SOEs are also proactive in making criticisms of existing policies and offering suggestions for policy changes. Such discordant views are rarely made in larger public meetings, but rather occur in private off-the-record gatherings as well as in detailed reports SOEs submit to government agencies.

Large foreign steel companies are the only other class of firms that regularly interact with the national government on policy issues. They are generally just as attentive to broad policy issues as their large SOE counterparts. Even though they do not meet with government as often, it is clear that on issues that affect their interests—and even many that do not—they are often as well informed as anyone. When the government told a few large SOEs of its plan to require output decline of 10 percent in 1999, large foreign firms obtained this information soon after, over a month before it was publicly announced and a month before smaller firms of any ownership form found out.[57] Because most foreign companies are among the world's leaders and provide products that are in short supply domestically, they have little trouble meeting with senior officials in any of the bureaucracies that affect their interests, particularly in the steel bureaucracy and the Ministry of Commerce. Foreign firms' involvement shows that the quality of meetings is more relevant than their quantity in regard to how involved firms are in policy making. Foreign steel companies write formal reports less often than large SOEs do, but in their formal and informal meetings they actively try to persuade the government to modify policies to suit their interests. Because of their particular product niche, foreign firms have not been significant participants in discussions of how to control price drops or reduce capacity; their main area of interest has involved debates over export promotion and market access.[58]

At the bottom of the policy ladder sit smaller state-owned, domestic private, and foreign private companies. Small SOEs do meet with their primary regulatory department more often than small domestic or foreign private companies. For example, before being privatized in 1995, the Haimen Specialty Formed Steel Pipe Factory met with the township industrial bureau and economic commission monthly. But since then Haimen has been invited to these offices only once per year for general briefings, a situation typical of other small private steel companies.[59] Despite this difference, all small steel companies' interaction with officials is usually restricted to narrow issues of their companies' performance and local economic conditions. One small SOE decried such meetings as simply "formalism," held to give the appearance of the government's concern for its enterprises. These companies have never been asked for or offered policy views. Small private producers actually said that their more limited contact with local government did not matter very much because of the latter's limited policy-making powers.[60]

The variation in the degree of interaction with the government translates into distinct differences in levels of influence. Access to policy-making circles does not guarantee influence, but it is a prerequisite. In contrast to the planning era, when they could only affect their own plans, large steel SOEs have the ear of government on policy matters, and they believe they are able to influence policy debates.[61] The only other firms at the table are large FIEs, but they are less numerous, meet less often with government, and seek to influence a narrower range of policies than SOEs. Smaller firms of all types are completely locked out of the policy-making process. Associations do little to tip the balance to smaller firms. The primary government-led associations, the China Specialty Steel Enterprise Association and the China Iron and Steel Association, have only large SOEs as members and thus are not an avenue for small firms to amplify their voices. And given SOEs' disdain for associations, they are not significant avenues for large SOEs either. The stainless steel associations, which have large and small members, are still relatively weak and have limited influence. Typical of the small firms' position, one smaller SOE manager summed up their perspective: "The government sets policy to influence enterprises; enterprises cannot influence policy."[62]

## The Gap Between Connections and Clientelism

Despite the intensity of direct government-business contact, research did not reveal an overall pattern of patron-client ties. Company officials believe that having good relations (*guanxi*) with officials is important to obtain policy information and avoid bureaucratic red tape, but it rarely is part of an exchange relationship or rises to the level of corruption.

The most celebrated case of patron-client ties in the industry, between Shougang's Zhou Guanwu and former paramount leader Deng Xiaoping, has been revealed to have less substance than originally assumed. Shougang's profit contract was just one of many experiments tried to revitalize SOEs and was not the result of Zhou's supposed connections. In addition, the company has regularly been publicly under attack from the Ministry of Finance for its low tax burden and from the Beijing municipal government, which has attempted to obtain a share of the company's profits.[63] In the strongest case of patronage, the Zhangjiagang-based Yonggang, it is unclear what material benefits the company received from hiring the party official's relative.[64] In one other case, a domestic private steelmaker received a license to expand his factory more quickly than normal because a friend happened to work in the authorizing agency, but the friend received no benefit himself.[65] The one case concerning associations, as mentioned earlier, involved a senior official's protection of one of the stainless steel associations, but even there the patron received no material benefit and actually put himself at risk of censure by his colleagues. The irony is that this instance of patronage was used to assist one of the industry's more independent organizations.[66]

The above examples all involved narrow benefits for a single organization or official and not industry-wide policies. Patron-client ties were not found to be significant in firms' efforts to influence the national policy-making process. Large foreign companies try to maintain close contact with officials in many agencies, and this occasionally involves meeting informally to discuss policy issues. This discussion is not perceived as clientelism but as part of the normal efforts to obtain information about policy trends.[67] One large SOE official stressed that steel policies cannot be decided by one person and hence are not as susceptible to patronage.[68] On policy matters, company leaders and government officials' interaction is primarily defined by their positions in their respective institutions.

To BETTER EXPLAIN the ways in which steel companies interact with the Chinese government and their influence on policy making—the predominance of direct contact and relatively greater influence of large companies, particularly SOEs—the remainder of this chapter examines three policy areas: price controls, international competitiveness, and environmental protection. The first two are typical of companies' growing voice and influence on public policy. The last case, environmental protection, probably represents conventional conceptions of firms' limited interest in the policy process, but the discussion will suggest why this area has become the exception to the rule of greater activism.

## Cartel Calamities

Oversupply has been by far the most significant problem facing China's steel industry since the mid-1990s. In the era of fixed prices, overproduction may have led to growing stockpiles, but enterprises could still safely assume purchasers would not quibble over cost. That bygone era, though, has long since passed, leaving the industry vulnerable to the same price fluctuations that affect steelmakers everywhere. Although steel lagged behind other sectors in price reforms in the first decade of reforms, it quickly closed the gap in the second decade. In 1988 some steel prices were freed, though not to the extent of other goods. But in 1992, following Deng's "southern tour," meant to kickstart radical economic reforms, the prices for most steel products were freed. The following year, an investment boom in many industries increased the demand for steel. At the same time, some traders hoarded steel, resulting in price jumps of over 50 percent in 1993. In response to these price hikes, SOEs (encouraged by local governments) and private businessmen sensed an opportunity and invested heavily in expanding steel plants or setting up new ones around the country. Steel investment in the five-year period from 1991 to 1995 was three times greater than during the previous five years, financed not by central-government expenditures but by bank loans and enterprises' own funds.[69] Over the latter five-year period, finished steel output expanded almost 60 percent. In addition, with the jump in domestic prices, steel imports rose suddenly in 1993; though they fell off afterward, the devaluations throughout the region in the wake of the Asian financial crisis kept foreign steel competitive enough so that imports have remained at more than double their pre-1993 levels.

To the chagrin of those who invested in greater capacity, increased domestic steel production and imports outstripped the growth in demand. In 1995, stockpiles of unsold finished steel reached over 30 million tons and were still at 20.1 million tons at the end of 1998.[70] To make matters worse, factories were only operating at 60 percent capacity, leaving much of their investments sitting idle.[71] The historical seller's market had become a buyer's market, and prices fell steadily over the next several years. By 1997, finished steel cost 21 percent less than it did at its peak in 1993.[72] Prices dropped another 6 percent during the first eight months of 1998.[73] Deflation eroded the industry's already meager profits and left it with enormous liabilities. Perhaps most alarming from the government's point of view, tax receipts from the industry fell by almost 40 percent over the same period.[74]

Mired in such dire straits, many steel companies began to complain to the metallurgy bureaucracy and to steel associations about what the companies perceived as dumping by foreign and domestic firms.[75] Critically, steel companies were not alone. Many other sectors were also experiencing price deflation in the late 1990s for precisely the same reasons, leading them to complain and call for action to halt the price slides. In many industries, support coalesced around price cartels in which firms would agree not to sell their products below a certain price. Advocates of cartels cited Chinese laws that forbade dumping and permitted "industry organizations" to help firms "strengthen price self-discipline."[76] Advocates also drew on the experiences of industry associations in Western Europe and Japan to buttress their claims as to the legitimacy and effectiveness of limiting competition.[77]

Although there were reports of cartels in China from the early 1990s, interest in them reached a new level in the latter half of 1998.[78] In late July, firms from multiple industries issued joint written appeals to the State Economic and Trade Commission to "standardize market order" by encouraging trade associations to organize "self-discipline prices" (*zilujia*), that is, price cartels, thereby eliminating what they alternatively called "vicious competition" (*exing jingzheng*) and "disorderly competition" (*wuxu jingzheng*). Propelled by this external pressure as well as its own interest in staving off unemployment and a drop in taxes, the SETC responded two weeks later, in mid-August, with a policy statement that adhered to the companies' wishes. The "Idea on Instituting Industry Self-Discipline Prices for Some Industrial Products" called on industrial bureaus and associations to help coordinate prices for twenty-one products, using the products' average costs as the basis for the price floors. Some industry associations had already begun to organize price cartels by then, but the pace of activity picked up significantly after the SETC's decision. Self-discipline prices, though, faced strong opposition from efficient firms who could afford to sell their goods cheaply. They argued that instead of price controls inefficient firms be allowed to go under, thereby reducing oversupply through market mechanisms.

Falling prices in the steel industry engendered the same complaints and lobbying as elsewhere, but what distinguished steel were the ways in which associations were—and were not—utilized. Overall, steel associations were less involved in transmitting company complaints to the government about dumping and setting price floors than associations in other industries. As Table 3.2 shows, this was particularly true for price floors involving the largest state-owned makers of standard steel products, when companies either attempted to form cartels by themselves or the government orchestrated floor prices.[79] The earliest attempt was carried out independently in early 1997 by the heads of three of the most inefficient steel companies in northern China— Taiyuan, Anshan, and Benxi. Other producers, including Shougang and Angang, also met during 1997, independently and with metallurgy ministry officials, to coordinate prices.[80] But with prices and profits still

**Table 3.2** Price floor attempts in China's steel industry, 1997–2000

| Date initiated | Company participants | Organizers | Products covered | Result |
|---|---|---|---|---|
| Jan. 1997 | 3 large SOEs (Taiyuan, Anshan, and Benxi) | Firms alone | Hot-rolled strips | Failed |
| Sept. 1997 | 8 small private and state-owned enterprises | Sichuan Cold-Rolled Steel Strips & Welded Pipe Association | Strips and pipes | Succeeded |
| May 1998 | All association members (30 SOEs) | CSSEA | Stainless steel billet | Failed |
| Sept. 1998 | Applied industry-wide | BMI and SDPC | Wire rod, debar, hot-rolled coils (construction steel) | Failed |
| Oct. 1998 | Applied industry-wide | CSSEA and BMI | Stainless steel billet | Failed |
| Dec. 1998 | All association members (70+ private companies) | Ouhai (Wenzhou) Stainless Steel Chamber of Commerce | Stainless steel pipes | Failed |
| Mar. 2000 | 9 SOEs located in northern China | BMI, Shougang and Tanggang | Wire rod and debar (construction steel) | Failed |
| Mar. 2000 | 4 large SOEs | Firms alone | Large sections | Unclear |

falling a year later, large SOEs intensified their complaints to the met-allurgy bureaucracy. Through a report and visits to Beijing, they argued to the SETC that a steel cartel similar to the Organization of the Petroleum Exporting Countries (OPEC) would be in the industry's best interests. They identified three steel products used primarily in the construction industry whose prices were most in need of propping up.[81]

Industry support, though, was far from universal. The debate pitted the inefficient versus the efficient. Large SOEs, such as Baogang, who could still profitably sell steel below the industry's average production costs (the standard by which price floors would be set) opposed intervention of any sorts.[82] Left out of this debate were smaller producers of construction steel. Though inefficient by world standards, these private and state-owned companies could survive at selling steel more cheaply than large, inefficient SOEs because of their lower welfare burden. In interviews, smaller companies, state-owned and private, charged their large counterparts with dumping and said cartels violated market principles.[83] (But, as will be discussed below, this criticism did not prevent some smaller private and state-owned companies in other segments of the steel industry from supporting local cartels.)

Seeing the need to maintain employment, profits, and tax revenues, the government was won over by those in favor of "self-discipline prices," and the firms' suggestions for which products' prices to control were accepted. The SETC was in principle strongly in favor of associations organizing the cartels, but because there was no appropriate industry-wide steel association, the task of organizing the price cartel fell to BMI and the State Development and Planning Commission. In September 1998, BMI announced the price controls in a meeting with thirty-five of the country's largest steel producers, all of whom signed a pledge committing to the price floors. In contrast to industries in which cartels were organized by associations, prices floors for these steel products were mandatory and applied to firms throughout the industry.[84]

Over a year later, in March 2000, with prices still falling, large state-owned steel companies renewed their efforts to prop up the prices of construction steel, again not through an association, but either through coordination with BMI or privately among themselves. Led by Shougang and Tangshan Iron and Steel (*Tanggang*), nine makers of construction steel held the Huabei Regional Finished Steel Price Coordination Meeting with BMI. At the same time, four SOE makers of steel sections proudly proclaimed they were setting up an OPEC-like cartel on their own.

Propelled by company complaints, large SOE makers of specialty steel began their efforts to institute price cartels through the China Specialty Steel Enterprise Association. But after its May 1998 attempt failed miserably, CSSEA's role was reduced drastically, and, as with construction steel, BMI intervened to directly coordinate price floors with the specialty steel makers.[85]

Only a few steel associations composed of small private companies or a mixture of small private and state-owned companies assumed and maintained significant roles in organizing self-discipline prices.[86] In the case of steel, that meant local associations. In Sichuan, several private and state-owned steelmakers persuaded the provincial metallurgy bureau to allow them to set up an association to coordinate prices and establish privileged longterm sales contracts with large purchasers. And in Wenzhou, a local stainless steel association attempted to follow the path of other local associations and organize its seventy member producers in a cartel for stainless steel pipes.[87] These instances of association activism in steel were the exception to the rule.[88]

Although steel is noted for the limited role of associations in organizing price cartels, the success rate of such efforts closely mirrored that of other industries. As hinted above, the majority collapsed soon after being initiated.[89] The much-ballyhooed price floors for construction steel held for barely a month before prices resumed their slide. By the end of 1999, prices for construction steel were down almost 10 percent from their levels when price floors were announced fifteen months earlier.[90] The price floors met similar fates, not because of poor associations or dissatisfaction with the government, but because like so many industries in China, steel production is spread out among so many producers. Low concentration raises the difficulty of monitoring compliance, making cheating easier. The lack of airtight control over imports also did not help, since importers were certainly not part of the bargain. The attempted cartel in Wenzhou failed because of the difficulties coordinating so many producers that were exposed to national and international markets. Although China's steelmakers thought they could copy their counterparts in Japanese steel and Middle East oil, the latter two are distinguished by the small number of producers that collectively hold a high market share.[91] The one attempt in steel that clearly succeeded did so because of the limited number of producers that made monitoring easier and their isolation from the rest of the country.[92]

To summarize, the case of price cartels in the steel industry demonstrates several points. First, steel companies have a growing concern on policy issues that affect their interests. Firms, not the government, identified both the problem (deflation) and the possible solution (cartels). Second, in comparison to other industries, price floors in steel were implemented primarily through direct government-business interaction or informally by firms and not through established associations. Because of the predominance of large SOEs, direct interaction had been the norm prior to 1998, meaning no national associations had been seen as useful to either the companies or the metallurgy bureaucracy. When the issue of the price controls emerged, direct interaction was used by default. The creation of the China Iron and Steel Association, which has coordinating prices among its mandate, was supposed to redress this deficiency.[93] Associations were only significant in those segments of the industry populated by smaller private and state-owned companies. This pattern was reinforced by the policy's outcome. Although the culprit for the widespread failure of price floors was low firm concentration, many blamed the associations as inherently flawed, reinforcing the widespread impression that direct interaction with government was more useful than associations. And third, large state-owned companies had much greater influence over national policy than smaller companies of any ownership form. Greater access facilitated large state-owned firms' ability to persuade the metallurgy bureaucracy and the SETC to support price controls despite the existence of opposition among their industry peers. Although the policy ultimately was an economic failure, it still was a *political* victory for large, inefficient SOEs.

## Steel Trade Warriors

China's steel industry has aggressively sought to influence trade policy in order to increase their exports and limit imports from overseas competitors. This would have the dual effect of reducing foreign pressure on domestic prices and increasing China's capacity to produce steel products it has traditionally had to import. Despite its huge domestic capacity, China has consistently been a net importer of steel because of the predominance of low-grade steel produced at home. Most of this output has not been internationally competitive, keeping exports down. At the same time, China has had to import the high-grade steel it cannot produce itself.

Over the past decade, trade policy for steel has been pushed and pulled in attempts to satisfy the demands of China's steel producers, foreign producers, and downstream industries in China that use steel in their products (for example, automobiles). The 1992 memorandum of understanding (MOU) on market access signed with the United States that committed China to increase policy transparency (referred to in Chapter 2) also committed it to reduce tariffs and eliminate quotas and other non-tariff barriers in various industries, including steel.[94] To formally meet these requirements, the average tariffs for finished steel were reduced from 16 percent in 1992 to 10.6 percent in 1996.[95] But more importantly, China also began to eliminate non-tariff barriers. In the early 1990s, China required all steel imports to be licensed, that is, administratively approved by customs officials. To formally meet the requirements of the pledge under the MOU as well as make progress on GATT/WTO negotiations, in August 1994 the State Council issued a circular that replaced that licensing system with an "automatic registration" system. However, because it established conditions by which registration would be approved and gave discretion to customs authorities to determine if those conditions had been met, the registration system was in effect a licensing system by another name. The reforms also left in place a system of canalization in which a limited number of Chinese companies were authorized to engage in the trade of specific steel products. Upon joining WTO, China fully eliminated the registration system.[96]

The effect of the trade reforms has been a significant rise in imports. The expansion in domestic infrastructure spending led to a ballooning of steel imports from 6 million tons in 1992 to 30 million tons a year later. Although imports dropped in the next two years, imports have climbed annually since 1996, surpassing 24 million tons in 2002.[97] Imports rose despite a continuation of the protectionist licensing system, in part because the rules that allowed government discretion to curtail imports also created loopholes that allowed importers to avoid paying nominal tariff levels if the steel was to be used for certain purposes (such as export reprocessing) or in a certain locations. In the two years following the 1994 reforms, the share of steel imports admitted for processing more than doubled.[98] While a bane to domestic producers of standardized steel, such imports were a boon to Chinese steel trading companies and downstream users who needed high quality steel to manufacture their products. This situation was exacerbated by the Asian financial crisis. Through a mix of real price cuts and currency devaluations, steel from China's East Asian neighbors and countries of the former Soviet Union became much less expensive and more competitive on the Chinese market.[99] On the other side of the ledger, China's steel exports remained weak, fluctuating between 4 and 6 million tons since 1995. The Asian financial crisis, because of the devaluations and reduced demand in China's primary markets in Asia, also depressed exports.[100]

In light of these pressures, there were a variety of initiatives taken in the late 1990s and early 2000s to promote exports and reduce imports. Some of these policies appear to have been taken by the government on its own initiative, but more often domestic steel companies, usually not via an association, pressed the government for support. Large SOEs were by far the most prominent firms involved, but large foreign steel producers also lobbied on their own behalf.

The primary tool used to expand sales abroad has been to offer rebates on the 17 percent value-added tax (VAT) assessed for exported steel. The government first set the VAT rebate for exported finished steel at 11 percent in June 1998, and then raised it to 13 percent in January 1999 and once more to 15 percent in August 1999 (meaning steel exporters would pay only 2 percent VAT). The changes in rebates for steel were done in conjunction with a wide range of other products.[101] While steel firms welcomed these steps, the companies did not affect the timing or amount of the changes. Steel firms, though, were more involved in setting up an import substitution scheme directed at promoting high-end steel products. In March 1998, the government exempted twenty-three producers from paying any VAT for the steel they sold to processing enterprises in specified duty-free zones who then exported finished steel products. However, only three hundred thousand tons of such steel was sold that year.[102] So, in early 1999, ten of the largest steel producers, including Baogang and Shougang, wrote a joint letter to Premier Zhu Rongji, arguing that the initial policy was too constraining and needed to be relaxed. As a result, Zhu ordered the SETC, Ministry of Finance, the State Taxation Administration, and the General Administration of Customs to modify the policy in several ways: the number of companies that could participate was expanded from twenty-three to twenty-seven; the firms did not have to sell their steel to processors in duty-free zones; and the VAT refunds would be instituted at the time of sale, eliminating the lengthy process of applying for and receiving the rebate.[103] The policy change quickly led to increased exports of a couple of million tons. Twelve of the twenty-seven companies in the program, including Baogang, exceeded their export targets.[104]

There has been an even more aggressive effort to slow imports. Chinese steel companies have continuously complained about imports at least since the mid-1990s, demanding that the import regime's loopholes be closed or imports of certain products be halted altogether.[105] The approaching WTO accession only increased their demands for action, as companies warned that the challenges of entry are greater than the benefits.[106] However, while joining the WTO meant reduction of some old barriers, the WTO permits governments to temporarily protect local industry when it is threatened by "unfair" practices of foreign competitors, such as dumping. In anticipation of joining WTO, China first adopted an antidumping statute in 1997 and then revised it in 2001.[107] Until 2003, the Ministry of Foreign Trade and Economic Cooperation (MOFTEC) investigated the dumping charge, and the SETC the injury claim. With government restructuring, responsibility for the entire process shifted to the new Ministry of Commerce (MOFCOM).

Although steel firms likely were not part of the drafting process of these laws, they have been their second leading user, initiating three dumping cases against eight countries between 1999 and 2002.[108] In the first steel case, Wuhan Iron and Steel (*Wugang*) charged Russian firms for dumping cold-rolled silicon steel sections.[109] In the second, Taiyuan Iron and Steel, Shaanxi Precision Group, and Pudong Iron and Steel accused Japanese and South Korean producers of dumping cold-rolled stainless steel sheets on the Chinese market.[110] Interview sources revealed that Baogang quietly lobbied on behalf of the applicants because of its own emerging stainless steel capacity, which gave it an interest in limiting competition. In 1997 Baogang started a stainless steel joint venture with Japan's Nishin Steel, and soon after the application was filed in mid-1999, Baogang absorbed one of the applicants, Pudong Iron and Steel.[111] And in March 2002, based on an application from the country's three leading steel producers—Baogang, Angang, and Wugang—the government initiated an investigation into the dumping of cold-rolled steel coils and strips by firms from Russia, South Korea, Ukraine, Kazakhstan, and Taiwan.

On top of the three dumping cases, China's steel industry also persuaded the government in the spring of 2002 to respond to the United States's institution of "safeguard" tariffs of up to 30 percent against foreign steel, including products from China, with safeguard duties and quotas of its own. CISA and the China Chamber of Commerce for Exports of Metals, Minerals and Chemicals complained vociferously to MOFTEC, but more importantly, the individual heads of powerhouses such as Baogang and Angang called on the government to defend Chinese producers.[112]

It is clear that the firms took the initiative on dumping. When they complained to the metallurgy bureaucracy about the first two cases, it refused to support them, arguing that China needed to import these products, which were still in short supply domestically. Undeterred, the companies went over their heads and complained directly to the SETC and MOFTEC. (By the third case, the steel bureaucracy had been eliminated.) MOFTEC was particularly receptive to their charges, since it saw the cases as opportunities to test China's antidumping regime on the eve of its accession to the World Trade Organization.

While the steel industry has successfully prodded the government to launch inquiries, it has not always achieved complete victories. In all the cases, the government announced tariffs of over 50 percent.[113] However, in the antidumping case against Japan and South Korea and in the safeguards case, many of the products were exempted from the duties, stripping the penalties of any teeth. And in the antidumping case against producers from five countries announced in September 2003, implementation of all tariffs was suspended for several months.

The mixed final results illustrate the new importance of lobbying to China's trade policy. On paper, for applicant companies to win relief, they must prove both that imported steel was dumped into China (sold at prices below that in the home market) and that those sales injured China's own steel producers. In practice, cases often turn on the relative economic and political clout of the interested parties.[114] The applicants have been some of China's most prominent steel firms, which should easily outmatch their foreign competitors in cases administered by the Chinese government. However, in addition to participating in hearings, complaining to their own governments, and lobbying themselves, the foreign respondents also energized their Chinese customers—including large state-owned enterprises from the automobile and home appliance industries—to become involved. The foreign producers argued that Chinese companies did not manufacture these specific products and so could not have harmed China's steel industry. And the foreigners' Chinese customers, in public and in private, held that they required the foreign-made steel as inputs into their own products. At a dramatic public hearing in September 2002 the massive oil company Sinopec even went so far as to claim that it needed to continue importing steel drilling pipes because the domestic ones it had previously used resulted in the deaths of several workers. Multiple sources in industry and the Chinese government confirmed that industry advocacy was the crucial determinant in the outcome of these cases.[115]

The patterns found in pricing were amplified in trade. Large SOEs had the most prominent voice, with foreign companies playing a reactive and less prominent role. Small companies of all ownership forms have had no voice in trade policy, and associations' role was limited, at least until the trade disputes of 2002. The Stainless Steel Sub-Association would have become involved in the dumping case, but it was torn between its members' interests: Taiyuan Iron and Steel, a company that brought the charge, and POSCO and Nishin, two companies charged with dumping, all were its members. Thus, the association remained neutral in the case. This stance is made more remarkable given that the association's secretary-general was the former chairman of the board for Taiyuan Iron and Steel.[116] However, its lack of involvement in no way limited any of these companies' ability to air their opinions with the Chinese government.

Lobbying also has had a greater effect on actual trade flows than on price trends. Overall exports would have been lower had the industry not received the VAT rebates, and imports likely would have risen faster in some product segments without the registration system and antidumping duties. Even in cases where partial exemptions or delayed implementation was announced, the looming threat of trade sanctions is a strong signal to domestic downstream users to consider more fully the option of buying from local producers (or at least different foreign sources). China's steel industry has signaled that it will continue to be an active user of "fair trade" rules and has more recently lobbied the government to modify domestic laws to make antidumping cases easier to initiate, to speed up the investigation process, and to lower the standard of evidence needed to prove dumping.[117] Although the steel industry has not won all its trade battles, its growing policy activism is part of a long-term war it intends to win.

## The Exception: Environmental Protection

Conflict over price controls and attempts to make Chinese steel more competitive internationally represent the new standard of growing assertiveness among large steel companies in the policy process. There is, though, one exception to this trend: environmental protection policy. It is already well known that China's environment has been severely damaged over the past fifty years and that much of that destruction has occurred since 1978.[118] The consequences are enormous. In simple economic terms, air and water pollution annually cost the country 4 to 8 percent of its GDP.[119] The primary contributors to pollution have been industrial enterprises, including steel mills. In 1995, Shougang was responsible for 51 percent of the sulfur dioxide, 61 percent of the nitrous oxide, 75 percent of the carbon dioxide, and 50 percent of the dust emitted into Beijing's atmosphere.[120]

In the face of these conditions, China's government has not stood still. Over the past twenty years it has created a nationwide environmental bureaucracy, led by the State Environmental Protection Administration (SEPA). Working with the National People's Congress's (NPC) Environment and Resources Protection Committee and the State Council Legislative Affairs Office's Environment and Resources Protection Section, the government has passed a dozen national laws and hundreds of regulations regarding particular pollution mediums and industries, including air, water, noise, solid waste, and construction. The laws speak to steps companies should take to limit pollution before, during, and after production and the consequences for not meeting these guidelines. Together these laws have created a basic legal framework for environmental protection that is generally more complete than in most developing countries.[121]

Given the activism of large state-owned enterprises in weighing in on competition and trade policies, one would expect to see similar levels of involvement on environmental-protection policy. However, that has not been the case. Larger SOEs have had a limited role in this area. They usually have a department responsible for environment, health, and safety that tracks the legal requirements the companies have to meet.[122] And occasionally SEPA and the NPC have visited some large state-owned companies, including steel mills, during the drafting process of some of these laws to hear companies' views.[123]

However, the more prominent aspect of environmental policy making is the lack of company involvement compared to other issue areas. Whether at the national or provincial level, the key participants are the environmental and industrial bureaucracies, which are supplemented by environmental experts in a few universities and research institutes. SEPA drafts all regulations, while it or the NPC's Environment and Resources Protection Committee are the lead drafters for laws. In the process, they solicit opinions from industrial ministries and lower-level EPAs. The State Council Legislative Affairs Office's Environment and Resources Protection Section helps balance the conflicting interests among these bureaucracies. SEPA and the NPC have visited and obtained views from firms, but such consultation is not as common as in other policy areas. Similarly, the State Council's environmental office rarely, if ever, has met with producers.[124] The Shanghai EPA, the most prolific generator of local environmental statutes, has never consulted companies while drafting regulations. Even Baogang, not to mention private enterprises, has not been party to these deliberations. Instead, the Shanghai EPA gets input from industrial bureaus and experts.[125] In addition to the firms, steel associations have not been involved in environmental policy making either. Except for CISA's proposed environment- and energy-conservation working committee, none of the others has had any expertise or involvement on matters involving pollution control and abatement.

Environmental policy making is by no means monolithic, but debate is largely confined within government and some experts. The question then becomes what circumstances have made this area an exception to the trend of greater firm involvement. Several reasons stand out. First, the interests of the industrial bureaucracy are entirely consonant with producers on this issue. The industrial bureaucracy and steel enterprises are unified in the view that stringent environmental controls are too expensive and would result in slower growth and greater unemployment. For both, growth and employment are higher priorities than environmental protection. Second, industrial ministries have been politically stronger than the environmental bureaucracy. Until March 1998, SEPA did not have full ministerial rank, which put it at an disadvantageous position in negotiations over the authority it had to pass and implement tough antipollution measures. The government's progrowth agenda still leaves SEPA on the defensive. Consequently, the industrial bureaucracies have been able to water down most environmental policies. Enterprises have largely been able to hitchhike (*da bianche*) on the power of industrial ministries' bargaining power.[126] Third, because of industrial ministries and local governments' power relative to the environmental bureaucracy, polluters have been able to avoid severe penalties once they do violate laws. The vast majority of polluters pay fines, which they perceive as a necessary tax, but very are closed. Those that have been shut down have been the smallest producers, with environmental rules being manipulated to achieve industrial-policy goals. Shougang, which has chronically polluted above standards, is simply fined annually.[127] In sum, because of the unified interests of firms and their primary regulators, the power of industrial ministries during the drafting process, and the power of local governments during implementation, industrial firms, including those in steel, usually can afford to ignore the law-making process.

And last, the environmental bureaucracies have not been as welcoming of enterprise involvement in policy making as other bureaucracies have on other issues. They know what companies' positions are without even without hearing from them. On the few occasions they have been involved, companies have simply complained about environmental rules and been obstructionist. If firms participated more, the regulations would be even less stringent or might not be passed at all.[128] The industrial bureaucracy, which shares the same predilections as the firms, has a guaranteed seat at the negotiating table, and thus SEPA has no choice but to interact with them.

The Atmosphere Anti-Pollution Law is a good example of the limited role of enterprises in environmental law making. First passed in 1987, revised versions were issued in August 1995 and again in April 2000. The 1987 law was more a statement of goals than specific guidelines, and SEPA and the NPC's Environment and Resources Protection Committee wanted a revised version to include pollution permits, pollution-release fees, requirements to clean up pollution in a limited period or to face mandatory fines from SEPA, and greater controls over acid rain. The NPC committee did visit a few companies, including Tianjin Steel, at one point during drafting, but their views carried little weight.[129] No steel associations were consulted or offered any opinions on the draft. Much more important to the process were the industrial ministries and the State Council's Legislative Affairs Office's Environment and Resources Protection Section, both of which strongly opposed tighter guidelines and were unwilling to cede authority from local governments to the SEPA bureaucracy. As a result, except for improvements on the issue of acid rain, the 1995 version was similar to the law it replaced.[130]

Temporarily defeated, SEPA and the NPC did not wait long to ask for and obtain authority to begin another round of drafting. Again, companies were only sparingly consulted. The Beijing EPA office in 1998 met with four to five firms from the Shijingshan district. As expected, they complained about the difficulty of implementing a pollution-discharge permit system. Most significantly, the key enterprise from the district, Shougang, boycotted the meeting and instead sent a written report to SEPA.[131] The key battleground in the revisions were again between the environmental and industrial bureaucracies. On this occasion, the former did make some progress. The State Council and industrial ministries were prepared to give SEPA authority to institute a permit system with specific standards and a limited-period remediation requirement, but the SETC and industrial ministries held out for the right to (not) stop production or close firms that exceeded pollution-discharge standards. If history is any guide, this last compromise will lead to the continued protection of heavy polluters, including steel mills, limiting the costs to firms for not participating in the law-making process.

Two trends may lead to greater company involvement in environmental policy. Changes in the bureaucracy—the raising of SEPA's rank, the swallowing of the heavy-industry ministries into the SETC, and the SETC's elimination—may make those in charge of industrial policy less dependable agents for enterprises. In addition, new environmental NGOs may gain a foothold in the policy-making process, further threatening industrial firms. To date, they have been excluded from policy deliberations.[132] If large polluters face more than fines, they will likely take a more aggressive stance on their own *before* regulations are enacted.

## Conclusion

The general overview of government-business relations and the more focused consideration of specific policy arenas in the steel industry demonstrate how relations are slanted both in their organization and in whom they benefit most. Though the replacement of the government's metallurgy bureaucracy with the China Iron and Steel Association may signal a transformation of ties, so far associations have been largely irrelevant to government-business relations in the steel industry. Even in the stainless steel segment associations are still struggling to reach viability. Such a context has been of relative benefit to large SOEs. All companies rely on direct ties with the government, but SOEs regularly meet more senior-level officials more often, in a wider range of fora, and on a broader scope of issues than any other type of company. And large SOEs often do so at their own initiative and prior to adoption of policies. The consequence is that their relative influence on public-policy issues dwarfs that of smaller companies of any ownership form and large foreign companies.

This pattern of ties does not match any ideal type. There appears to be an intent to create a state corporatist regime for the industry, but it has gone unrealized. Although most associations have lacked autonomy, membership is usually voluntary (CISA being an exception). CISA has recently been given authority over several other associations, but there is still no evidence that this authority exists in practice. There are also multiple stainless steel associations that compete with each other. And just as important, associations are still minor players in the larger game of influence in the industry. While large companies still have direct access to the policy process and often vigorously make use of this channel to defend their interests, the dearth of association activism and limited transparency of the policy process distinguish government-business relations in steel from pluralism as well. And finally, the lack of patron-client ties in the national policy process suggests clientelism is not an appropriate fit either.

The most important question for this study is how to link this pattern of ties with the industry's economic context. Alternatively put, to what extent are the form of relations in steel affected by the industry's economic factors, and how do these relations affect companies' relative influence? To some degree, this pattern of relations owes something to China's general political institutions. Even though the government initiated the launching of associations in the 1980s, it has since adopted specific regulations that are not supportive of associations, even for ones it ostensibly controls. In addition, because it is not formally accountable to society, the Chinese government in general has not promoted the transparency of the policy process.

Beyond these general political conditions, it also appears that several economic factors have still been quite significant. Most broadly, the shift away from planning has made firms, even SOEs, see themselves as distinct from the government and interested in policy matters. Moreover, the particular weakness of associations and stress on direct ties have been encouraged by two economic factors. The first of these economic factors is the dominance of SOEs, which have historically had direct ties to the bureaucracy, reducing the incentives for associations. While some private enterprises entering the industry have been somewhat more interested in associations, in general they have followed the lead of their SOE counterparts in focusing on direct ties (most of their interest in associations has been directed at those outside the industry). This suggests not only that an individual company's ownership affects its preference for how to interact with the government but that the relative ownership share of an industry matters as well. The second economic factor is low firm-concentration, which, by making it difficult to collectively respond to price fluctuations, has also limited associations' development. The failure of price cartels reinforced the impression among companies that associations were not a useful tool for public action. And finally, size, while not having a clear bearing on firms' interests in associations, has had an effect on their relative degree of direct access to the government. While large SOEs lead in every dimension of direct contact, even large foreign corporations have had more access on policy matters with the central government than small SOEs.

These economic circumstances have had consequences for firms' relative influence. Larger firms, SOEs in particular, have been best able to operate in an environment of weak associations. They have utilized their relative access to government to influence various policies of concern to them, the most important involving pricing and international competition. Large SOEs have not had to pay much attention to environmental policy because of their metallurgy bureaucracy's activism on their behalf, something that could change with the government's restructuring. If so, we will likely see greater efforts by steel companies to water down environmental regulations before they are adopted rather than violate them once announced.

Those interested in democratization and greater accountability have generally welcomed the opening of the policy process to nongovernmental influences. Societal influence is not an either-or proposition. Some elements of society can have greater access and hence more influence than others in certain circumstances. In the case of steel, large SOEs' relative political influence has permitted them to push for economic policies that challenge the economic liberalization advocated by more efficient domestic and foreign companies. Even if sometimes rebuffed by the counter lobbying of others, their efforts suggest that steel companies will continue to have some success lobbying for policies that shield them from domestic and foreign competition, even after China enters the WTO. Steel companies also appear poised to fight against greater environmental controls as the bureaucracy that has shielded it is dismantled. In steel, industry has entered the playing field, but it is far from an even playing field.

# ～ 4

## The Consumer Electronics
## Industry: Sending Mixed Signals

$S$TEEL HAS always been a priority sector to the PRC government and software may be the industry of the future, but in the post-
Mao era, light industry, and consumer products in particular, are more
closely associated with the country's economic and social transformation. In the first decades following the revolution, most Chinese farmers and urbanites made do with the bare necessities, spending little on
entertainment and goods that could ease their personal lives. By contrast, the grand promise of the Reform era and a redefined socialism
has been to materially improve the everyday lot of ordinary Chinese.
The PRC has also become one of the largest markets for consumer
electronics on the globe.[1] In the 1980s, it was the dream of urban
households to own a refrigerator, color television, and washing machine; to that list has been added an air conditioner, cell phone, and
personal computer.[2] In 2001, for every 100 urban households in China
there were over 120 color TVs and 40 video compact disc (VCD) players on which they could watch movies made from Xi'an to Hollywood
and London.[3] In the past few years, a growing proportion have up-
graded to digital versatile disc (DVD) players. Right alongside this consumer market have grown industries employing over a million workers,
in cities large and small, on the coast and in the interior. In 2000, the
electronics and telecommunications industries, of which consumer

96

electronics is a large component, employed about 70 percent as many workers as in steel, but produced almost 60 percent more goods.[4]

Because the consumer electronics industry includes such a wide spectrum of products, this chapter focuses only on companies that manufacture color televisions and VCD players, two of the sector's most prominent products. Besides being complementary goods, the economic characteristics of companies that produce them have similarities that distinguish them from steel and software, but they also have some differences that allow for comparison within the industry. As with the other two sectors, the move toward the market has politically energized consumer electronics companies; their attention and attempts to influence public policies that affect their interests are unmistakable. However, the economics of steel and software more clearly point toward likely patterns of how business and government would interact. In consumer electronics, by contrast, the industry's economic characteristics are more muddled and, as a consequence, so too are the industry's pattern of politics. Associations are somewhat more developed and active than in the steel industry, but they are on the whole less mature than those in the software industry. Hence, direct contact between companies and the state has still outweighed the use of associations. The growth of influence of large nonstate companies has been accompanied by an increase in the tensions over the old norms of government-business relations, particularly industry deference to government. When considering how to characterize this overall pattern, it is apparent that the corporatist framework does not apply, but the uneven development of associations is likewise inconsistent with pluralism.

Large state-owned consumer electronics makers have a great degree of influence, but so do large domestic and foreign private companies. It is critical to understand that, in contrast to the steel industry, consumer electronics firms' interests cut across ownership and nationality boundaries, making for new and shifting alliances based on economic complementarities. As a result, which firms are part of the coalition that achieve policy victories depends on the issue.

This chapter begins by introducing the industry's economic characteristics to show that they contain elements that both promote and hinder associations. The following section then discusses how TV and video player associations are on average somewhat more autonomous and active than those in steel but subject to more criticism than those in software. The next section shows how important direct ties still are, but how consumer electronics companies of all types have become increasingly uncomfortable with government intervention in the industry. Finally, these points are reinforced by a discussion of three recent policy issues critical to the industry's development: pricing and competition, taxes, and technical standards.

## The Economics of TVs and VCD Players

China's color TV industry was born in 1980 when some Chinese state-owned factories launched joint ventures with Japanese makers, who provided the designs, components, and manufacturing equipment. Production and sales quickly grew, and over the next decade the government approved hundreds of companies around the country to make parts and finished TVs. By 2001, China annually produced over 40 million color TV sets.[5] By contrast, the VCD player industry emerged suddenly in the mid-1990s. In the late 1980s and early 1990s, a similarly large number of enterprises produced VHS video cassette recorders (VCRs), but in 1992 two Chinese engineers from a small private company in Anhui and an American video compression company, C-Cube Microsystems, combined their skills to give audio compact disc players the ability to handle pictures.[6] Their product, which they named video compact disc (VCD) player, first made it to Chinese stores in 1994. Fueled by the existence of cheap pirated discs manufactured in Hong Kong and Guangdong and a relatively low installed user base of VCRs, sales of VCD players skyrocketed, while VCR sales plummeted.[7] Not surprisingly, the number of companies producing VCD players grew dramatically. By the late 1990s, companies participated in an integrated national market, producing and marketing their TVs and VCD players across the country.

The color television and VCD player sectors share four characteristics that collectively set them apart from steel and software. First, as in steel, consumer electronics producers face high economies of scale, with average costs dropping with each additional unit of output. As of the mid-1990s, China's 146 TV enterprises had 173,000 employees producing TVs, yielding an average size of almost 1,200 workers per company.[8] The largest, Sichuan Changhong, has twenty-seven thousand employees, with most working on their TV assembly lines. There is no comparable reliable data on the VCD industry, but anecdotal evidence suggests that VCD makers on average employ somewhat fewer workers than in TV, perhaps five hundred to seven hundred, but still more than the typical software company.[9] Right after the players hit the market, there were hundreds of small, unlicensed shops in southern China assembling VCD players from parts smuggled from abroad, but most of these shops have since gone out of business.[10]

Second, as a result of companies closing or switching to other products, over time the TV and VCD player markets have grown more concentrated. By 1997, the top four TV producers had a collective market share of 50 percent, and the top ten producers 74 percent. The VCD player industry had already become even more concentrated, with four- and ten-firm concentration levels of 66 percent and 87 percent, respectively.[11] These figures are double those in steel and triple those in software.[12]

The industry's third economic characteristic is the tendency by firms to use extremely competitive pricing strategies. Like luxury consumer goods everywhere, TVs and VCD players have high elasticities of demand, so that a small change in price is more than offset by a change in sales. This situation, which creates a natural incentive to lower prices, was accentuated in China in the TV industry by an expansion in the number of factories supported by cheap credit from Chinese banks answerable to local officials interested in increasing output if not profits. Until the late 1980s, overinvestment had little effect on prices because prices were administratively set. But in 1988, when radical price reforms were first introduced, TV prices were freed. At the time, demand far outstripped supply, sending prices higher. But since 1992, the expansion in investment has led to a growing disparity between supply and demand. As expected in an era of free prices with so many competitors and oversupply, the consequence has been a consistent fall in prices.[13] The TV industry saw six to eight rounds of price wars between 1992 and 2000. Each time prices stabilized for a while before one company—usually Changhong—attempted to capture a greater market share by lowering prices, forcing competitors to follow suit. In 1997 alone, prices fell 20–30 percent.[14] Similarly, the price of VCD players (which were never subject to government price controls) fell from over RMB 4,000 in 1995 to RMB 1,200 in 1997.[15] While price wars have been a boon to consumers, they have been the main reason for the departure of firms and decline in profits in both sectors. The Ministry of Information Industry (MII) estimated that in 1998 price wars cost the industries a combined RMB 10 billion in profits.[16]

And fourth, there is a large foreign presence in China's color TV and VCD player sectors. Besides there being several joint ventures in both industries, Chinese companies are integrated into global supply chains, purchasing parts from more advanced foreign makers and exporting a portion of their final output. There are dozens of TV components producers, but a significant portion of the most important part, the picture tube, are either imported (legally and otherwise) or produced in joint ventures. Makers of Chinese VCD players are even more dependent on foreign suppliers for video decompression chips and other critical technology. Most consumer electronics exports go to Asia, but the United States has emerged as a new market for Chinese companies.[17]

While China's color TV and VCD player industries are similar in many respects, they differ in two ways. The first is the much larger role of domestic private companies in the VCD player market. In contrast to the television industry, VCD players emerged off the government's radar screen. Private companies were quicker to exploit this opportunity than their state-owned counterparts and, as a result, have long had a larger share of the market.[18] Though not to the extent in software, private producers of VCD players are even more highly represented in terms of the sheer number of companies. By contrast, the specific market leaders for TVs in China have changed since the 1980s, but they are still predominantly state-owned enterprises (SOE).[19]

The other distinction between the two industries concerns technical standards. Typically, the existence of standards are helpful to producers and consumers by ensuring that their products are compatible with supporting infrastructure (for example, telecommunications signals) or with peripheral products used in conjunction with them (for example, video compact disks). Some standards (for example, what side of the road people drive on) are market neutral. They have no impact on companies' success; rather, they simply make life more convenient. Other standards, including those in electronics, can have a dramatic effect on market shares. Companies can develop products that they hope will capture a large market share and become the de facto industry standard, with the result that other companies are either locked out altogether or required to pay royalties to use the standard in their own products. Given the potential economic benefits, governments have also taken a strong interest in standards as a way to promote (or protect) domestic industry. As a result, "standards wars" have become a common feature in the electronics industry.[20] Standards can have market-shaping effects in both the TV and VCD player industries. However, the standards wars over color television were fought between the 1950s to 1970s, and Chinese TV makers are just beginning to show interest in digital television, at least for the domestic market.[21] In the video recording industry, which includes VCD and DVD players, standards are still evolving, giving firms and the Chinese government a stronger incentive to shape them.

These economic characteristics have mixed consequences for how business and government interact. Some foster and some inhibit the development of associations. If we first consider those characteristics the two product makers share, high concentration levels should help foster interfirm cooperation and associations. But the tendency to use aggressive pricing strategies promotes price competition, and high economies of scale give firms the sense they can individually influence public policy, making interfirm cooperation more difficult. These factors work against associations. If we then consider those factors where TVs and VCD player producers diverge, the situation is also somewhat muddled. The predominance of SOEs in the TV industry further weakens incentives for associations. While the existence of more private firms in the VCD player market should spur associations, conflicts over standards could divide the industry and make cooperation harder. In sum, there are some economic incentives promoting associations—high concentration levels and the growth of private VCD player companies—but there are other economic factors pushing in the other direction—high economies of scale, competitive pricing tactics, the predominance of state-owned TV companies, and evolving VCD standards.

These economic factors have also determined the issues around which relations have revolved. By far the most important issue affecting China's TV industry, and one that has been almost as important in the VCD player market, has been deflation. Just as in steel and other industries, the crux of the debate has been how to characterize the deflation: is it dumping intended to eliminate competition, or is it common-sense competition that will eliminate inefficient companies and the monopoly rents they previously had? The answer leads in two very different policy directions, either to permit intervention by government or others to stop the price falls or to allow prices to continue falling until inefficient producers exit the market and prices stabilize naturally. Besides deflation, the most prominent issue in the VCD industry has been a fight over the setting of technical standards. Eager to grab or increase their market shares, firms became deeply engaged in the policy process. Ironically, disagreements about the norms of the decision-making process became just as contentious as those over the technical standards themselves.

How these and other issues have been resolved will be taken up once we address the problem of how the industries' economic circumstances affect the general pattern of government-business interaction.

## The Uneven Growth of Consumer Electronics Associations

Reflecting the mixed economic characteristics of the consumer electronics industry, associations in the sector vary in their autonomy and activism. While not corporatist, their mixed utility and their tendency to avoid confrontation with the government mean the sector's associations do not meet the definition of pluralism either.[22] Significantly, the variation between associations within consumer electronics also seems related to economic differences between the TV and VCD player industries.

There are three national-level associations whose mandates encompass the television and VCD player industries (see Table 4.1). Outwardly, they all appear to have similarly mixed levels of autonomy from the government. As in the other industries, the initial impetus for them came from the central government. The Number Four Machinery Industry Ministry, which became the Ministry of Electronics Industry (MEI) in 1982 and which merged with two other ministries in 1998 to become the Ministry of Information Industry, established the National TV International Competition Committee in 1979 to help it regulate TV makers. In 1986, MEI turned the committee into the China Electronic Video Industry Association (CVA, *zhongguo dianzi shixiang hangye xiehui*). Similarly, the China Electronic Audio Industry Associa-

**Table 4.1** Autonomy of selected consumer electronics associations in China (Y=yes; N=no; darker shading signifies greater autonomy)

| Business association | Chinese govt initiative? | Affiliation | Staffed with (former) govt officials? | Financially dependent on govt? |
|---|---|---|---|---|
| China Electronic Video Industry Association (CVA) (1979) | Y | MII | N | N |
| China Electronic Audio Industry Association (CAA) (1981) | Y | MII | N | N |
| China Electronics Chamber of Commerce (CECC) (1988) | Y | MII | Limited | N |

tion (CAA, *zhongguo dianzi yinxiang gongye xiehui*) began in 1981 as the National Recorder Inter-Factory Competition Committee (*quanguo luyinji changji jingsai weiyuanhui*). In 1983 it became the China Recorder Industry Association (*zhongguo luyinji gongye xiehui*) and in 1986 took on its current name, expanding its scope to cover all audio products, including radios, stereo equipment, and compact disc players. The China Electronics Chamber of Commerce (CECC, *zhongguo dianzi shanghui*) was formed two years later to replace MEI's sales bureau, which had been eliminated as part of a broader government restructuring effort.[23]

Despite these official origins and continued affiliation with MII, the associations do have elements of autonomy. None of the three are run on a daily basis by present or former government officials, and none receive government financing.[24] To accentuate their autonomy, the audio and video associations, at their own suggestion and with MII's approval, have been headquartered in Shanghai and Nanjing, respectively. CAA wanted to be close to the center of the recording industry, which in the 1980s was in Shanghai and Zhejiang but has since spread south to Fujian and Guangdong. Since its inception, CVA has been run by Nanjing-based Panda Electronics.[25]

Neither do the associations reflect other elements related to corporatism. Membership in each is not mandatory, and all three have some foreign companies or joint ventures as members. There is no hierarchical relationship among the three associations, between them and trans-sectoral associations like the China Industrial Economy Federation, or between them and regional industry associations. They also have no strict jurisdictional monopolies. Although VCD players project video, the CAA became the primary association for the sector because many VCD player producers originally made CD players and stereos. The video association later set up its own Video Disc Sub-Association, but it failed to attract VCD player makers to join.[26] In addition, the electronics chamber has both TV and VCD player manufacturers as members and has become involved in the same policy issues as the China Audio Association and the China Video Association. Moreover, there are also some local, separately founded electronics associations, particularly in Shanghai and Guangdong, that have overlapping memberships and interests with the national associations. Finally, companies' participation in multiple associations also has further reduced any possibility for representational monopolies.

The organization of consumer electronics associations differs distinctly from corporatism. Yet despite the associations' similar levels of autonomy, they have different levels of activism. This is best seen through a comparison of the two primary associations, CVA and CAA. The video association has not been controlled by MII, but it still has not been able to attract much industry support. Although it receives no government funding, it also has never charged membership dues, likely because companies would not pay. Without support, its activities have been minimal. It has no publications and has not hosted many exhibitions. On policy matters, CVA was involved in several attempts to establish price cartels up until 1998, but since then it has not participated. Not surprisingly, it has difficulty attracting some of the more recent market leaders in the industry (TCL, Kangjia and Chuangwei are not members), and existing members ridicule the association. Every CVA member interviewed for this study said the association had absolutely no utility to them.[27] Some credit for CVA's weakness must go to the fact that China's TV industry is dominated by large SOEs, which have never seen much value in associations. They have neglected the video association, and as a result, it has largely sat dormant for much of its existence.[28]

By contrast, the audio association has been far more active with regard to market promotion, influencing government policy, and self-regulation, drawing praise from some of its members and the government. On its own initiative and that of its members, CAA has established six sub-associations, five specialized committees, and four regional representative offices.[29] CAA regularly sponsors product exhibitions and produces publications dealing with audio technology and market trends. Through conferences and meetings, CAA and its sub-associations have been involved in a variety of policy issues, including pricing, taxes, technical standards, and international trade. CAA's authority was strengthened in late 1998 when MII authorized it to represent Chinese firms in negotiations with the DVD Forum and other international business groups over how much in royalties Chinese companies would pay foreign patent-holders for the right to use their standards and components to manufacture DVD players.[30]

CAA's activism has been supported by many of its members and the government. Its 360 members, which include several foreign companies such as Sony, collectively hold a very high percent of the VCD player market; only Jinzheng, a private producer from Guangdong province, has not joined. Unlike CVA, CAA collects annual dues. More significantly, officials and top industry executives make a point to attend its meetings and events. In addition to their active participation, several of its members and government officials interviewed for this study praised the association. None questioned CAA's independence from the government, saying that it was "popular" (*minjiande*) and represented its members. And they contrasted CAA's activism with that of the video association.[31]

CAA's higher productivity is likely related to the much higher proportion of private companies in the VCD player industry. The product emerged without government financial or technical support. In addition, private producers did not have established avenues to policy makers in Beijing; conversely, MII found it easier to directly regulate SOEs under its jurisdiction than private companies. These factors created the opportunity for CAA to play an active role in the industry.[32]

What is somewhat surprising—and needs an explanation—are those members, state-owned and private, who have a low regard for the audio association. In interviews they maintained, some quite vociferously, that CAA was of no utility to them. Their criticisms are due to several factors, which when understood allow the distinction between the audio and video associations and the reason for their differences—variation in composition of members' ownership—to still hold. First, some members grouped CAA with Chinese associations in general. One company executive said that in China "associations are too distant from the market." Along similar lines, another questioned even the possibility of having strong associations in China. Since Chinese SOEs have close relationships with the government, they "aren't standardized; so how could associations be? A building can't stand if the earth under it is soft."[33] Second, the impression among some that CAA is weak is reinforced by its typically nonconfrontational posture toward the government. CAA promotes its members' interests in as conciliatory a manner as possible. In its brochures and in discussion, it stresses that it "does not fight for power with the government" but rather "takes a supporting role in industry regulation."[34] These firms would like the association to be more outwardly aggressive, a characteristic these firms display in their own behavior. Third, several believe that CAA is partial to Xinke, its largest member, located two hours west of Shanghai. Because of Xinke's financial support, CAA has been accused of siding with it on several issues, the most important being the fight over technical standards in 1998. And fourth, the association was blamed for its perceived inability to solve some of the industry's economic woes (such as deflation) and was not credited for its efforts on policy matters that did bear results (such as tax policy).[35] This combination of factors is responsible for the gap between these companies' impressions of CAA and its actual activism and achievements.

The above discussion shows that the autonomy and activism of consumer electronics associations on the whole sit in between that of the steel and software sectors, a finding attributable to the sector's economic characteristics. This point is reinforced by the effect that differing ownership compositions of the TV and VCD player industries have on the vitality of the video and audio associations. Yet despite the objective differences in the two associations, many CAA members are not satisfied with its performance. Even if their appraisals are not entirely accurate, they still shape these firms' political behavior. While TV companies obviously rely little on the video association on policy issues, most VCD player makers do not heavily rely on the audio association either. Consequently, direct interaction is still extremely important for all consumer electronics firms that seek to influence national government policy.

## Direct Contact: Taking Offense

As with the other sectors, direct business-government contact on policy is quite common, which is another factor that distinguishes China from the corporatist framework. The various aspects of direct ties—the depth of firms' involvement on policy matters, the degree to which companies show deference to the government, and the significance of patron-client ties—show some similarities to both the steel and software industries but are closer to that of the latter. In addition, increased media coverage of the industry's policy issues has enhanced the policy process's transparency. As a result, direct government-business interaction in the consumer electronics industry is more consistent with pluralism than any other model.

As in the other two sectors, size is a critical factor enabling firms to interact with the national government directly. And as in the steel industry, the threshold for what counts as a large firm that has the wherewithal to seek and deserve regular access is high, over one thousand employees. But in contrast to steel, consumer electronics firms' form of ownership is far less important in gaining access to the government on policy matters.

Large SOEs clearly have more regular contact with the government organ to which they are attached on administrative matters. Often their most senior executives are still appointed by the government. They have to obtain approval for certain investments, and they have been forced into actions they otherwise would not have taken. For example, Mudan, which used to be one of the most successful TV companies in the country, has been buried under a mountain of debt because it was compelled to take over four other Beijing government-owned factories.

But on issues of public policy, the distinction between large firms of different ownership forms has been reduced. The prerequisite for the growing similarity of policy-centered relations has been the greater clarity of firms' profits and losses and the long tenure of most executives, factors which have sharpened the boundary between SOEs and the government, particularly relations beyond their immediate supervisory organ. Changhong's president, Ni Runfeng, took up his post in 1985. Although an alternate member of the Chinese Communist Party Central Committee, he has been fiercely loyal to his company, something that could be said about the heads of all China's large consumer electronics makers.[36] Because of the importance of policy, and not just administrative fiat, the old monist framework has been eclipsed. Large SOEs in consumer electronics are keenly aware of and interested in influencing the direction of policy. Said one executive, "When the interests of enterprises and the government are not the same, enterprises will proactively provide opinions."[37]

Large domestic and foreign private consumer electronics companies are as equally interested in industrial policy. All large consumer electronics companies meet with national-level officials on a regular basis. Whether a company is based in Beijing matters little, since those based outside the capital have representative offices in the city, and their executives frequently travel to Beijing and meet officials elsewhere. Large TV and VCD player companies of all ownership types have interacted with officials across the national bureaucracy, including MII, the State Economic and Trade Commission (SETC), the Ministry of Foreign Trade and Economic Cooperation (now the Ministry of Commerce), the General Administration of Customs, and the Ministry of Finance. Government officials admit to the change in relations over the past two decades. During the planning era (which extended into the 1980s), only large SOEs would seek out officials to obtain special benefits for their individual enterprises. By contrast, officials now regularly meet with what they describe as "representative, relatively large companies" in the industry regardless of ownership type, often at the firms' initiative, to discuss policy, which gives firms a "certain influence" on policy debates.[38] Many meetings take place in government offices, but on several occasions consumer electronics companies have hosted conferences with other companies and officials from a variety of agencies in attendance.[39]

The depth of direct ties has been the most important factor in increasing transparency of the policy process, but increased media coverage has also helped. Besides the official *China Electronics News*, several other far more market-oriented publications cover the consumer electronics industry, among them the All-China Federation of Industry and Commerce's daily *China Business Times* (*zhonghua gongshang shibao*) and *China Business* (*zhongguo jingying bao*), a weekly newspaper run by the Chinese Academy of Social Science's Institute of Industrial Economics. Both regularly carry stories about the industry's economic trends and policy announcements and occasionally run stories providing insights into how businesses and government interact during the policy-making process. While not as detailed and regular as similar coverage in democracies, the reporting supplements the information needs of policy participants and opens a window into the process for outsiders who lack direct access.

The next notable feature of direct relations in the industry is the increasingly critical posture of companies toward government intervention in the market and their willingness to act on that belief by openly challenging the government's authority. Producers and associations in the other two industries analyzed in this study generally take a deferential posture toward officials. Even in software, which is dominated by the private sector, companies and associations usually do their best not to offend bureaucrats. While such an attitude exists in consumer electronics associations and many companies, a growing number of companies have acted on their dissatisfaction with government authority. In interviews, both state-owned and private companies were critical of government intervention in the market in general and on specific policy issues, in particular with regard to pricing and competition policy and the setting of technical standards.[40] In these instances, as will be discussed below, firms have brazenly acted on their sentiments, knowing full well they were violating the official norms of deference and cooperation. The sense of tension between old and new norms of government-business interaction has been greater in consumer electronics as compared to software, likely because in the former firms are larger in absolute size, giving them confidence to act this way, and because the specific policy issues they have encountered have gone precisely to the issue of what role the government should have in a market economy.

The final aspect of direct government-business ties that deserves mention concerns the low salience of personal connections (*guanxi*) and patron-client ties on national policy problems. Firms consistently held that *guanxi*'s relevance has declined substantially, particularly for larger firms. An electronics maker in Guangdong said that a patron could help a smaller firm avoid paying some taxes, which if fully collected would eliminate any chance of profitability, but that once the firm became large, finding and nurturing a patron would be a waste of time.[41] One large East Asian firm interviewed for this project hired a Chinese national to interface with the national government. He said that with growing rule of law, his Chinese assistant could use his relationships with officials to better understand or comment on existing laws, but those connections would not allow his company to avoid abiding by the law. He concluded, "Good products are much more important than good *guanxi*."[42]

Even companies that clearly had good connections credibly downplayed their importance. Ye Minghua, the president of Shenzhen-based Xianke, is the fourth son of Ye Ting, a civil war general who fought with Deng Xiaoping before being killed by the Kuomintang (KMT). Ye Minghua was then adopted and raised by Zhou Enlai, something Zhou did for other orphans, the most prominent being former National People's Congress Chairman Li Peng. In early 1992, when Deng Xiaoping made his famous "southern tour" to reignite economic reforms, he purposely visited one company—Xianke. On the walls of Xianke's headquarters hang pictures from Deng's trip and subsequent visits of other senior Politburo members, including Jiang Zemin, Li Peng, Zhu Rongji, Liu Huaqing, and Zou Jiahua. (Hu Jintao and Li Tieying have also visited.) Despite Xianke's platinum connections, which the firm has used for public relations purposes, it is unclear if these ties have affected the company's bottom-line or given it a dominant position in policy debates. Xianke did not reach profitability until 1996, four years after Deng visited; it is difficult to trace their success to ties to him or other leaders. Xianke has also been active in policy debates, but its influence seems proportionate to its economic stature. Having patrons may help on an issue specific to a consumer electronics company, such as obtaining credit, but it seems less useful on public-policy problems where the range of actors and interests is much wider.[43]

⁓ EACH OF THESE ASPECTS of direct government-business ties—in-depth access to the policy process by large firms of all ownership types (supplemented by greater media coverage), companies' increasingly willingness to be challenge government authority, and the declining significance of patronage—all point toward a policy process consistent with pluralism. However, the mixed development of associations is the primary deficiency that has kept the consumer electronics industry's politics from more fully fitting within that framework. To demonstrate the uneven development of associations and growing assertiveness of large businesses on policy issues, the remainder of the chapter considers three policy issues that were hotly fought over in the latter half of the 1990s: pricing and competition, taxes, and technical standards. The first two concern both TVs and VCD players, the last only the VCD player market.

## The Price of Competition

As in steel, one of the most important issues facing consumer electronics companies since the mid-1990s has been the falling prices of their products. The story of how the industry has dealt with deflation provides insight into firms' growing influence on public policy, their willingness to challenge the government when policies go against them, and associations' frustrating attempts to gain greater respect and authority.

To appreciate how the sector has grappled with the problem of deflation, we need to recall the broader national debate, which climaxed in 1998, and the role that consumer electronics companies had in it.[44] Price declines across the economy split companies into opposing camps. Many large, inefficient producers and those that may have been more efficient but wanted to protect or increase their market shares called the widespread low prices "dumping" (*qingxiao*), a consequence of "vicious competition" (*exing jingzheng*) that had to be checked, either through government intervention or through cartels organized by associations or companies themselves. More efficient companies and even some inefficient ones who viewed such actions as counter to free market principles opposed any efforts to restrain competition. In some instances, as occurred in consumer electronics, those calling for price controls, in fact, initiated the price wars themselves; they changed their policy position depending on the circumstances of the moment.

Chinese law provided mixed signals on which position had the law on its side. The 1993 Anti–Unfair Competition Law forbade selling goods at below cost, but only if one could demonstrate that sellers were motivated by trying to "squeeze out competing opponents." Products that were overstocked were exempted from these constraints. The May 1998 Price Law banned the sale of goods below cost and at unreasonably high prices, and collusion or manipulation of prices. But as with the 1993 law, exceptions were allowed on both sides. The requirements to prove dumping were extremely onerous. On the other hand, when prices wildly fluctuate, the Price Law permits the government to temporarily set them, and allows industry associations to help their members "strengthen price self-discipline" (*jiaqiang jiage zilu*), that is, to set price floors or ceilings.[45]

Although firms did not have much direct influence on these two laws, they strongly affected how the laws were interpreted when policies were considered in the face of falling prices.[46] Proponents of intervention at first obtained the upper hand. In July 1998, thirteen large companies from a variety of industries issued two joint written appeals to the SETC, calling on it to help "standardize market order" by allowing associations to form price cartels. In large part due to their lobbying and that of others, the next month the SETC issued such a notice, "Idea on Instituting Industry Self-Discipline Prices for Some Industrial Products," which encouraged associations to set price floors for twenty-one products.[47] Some associations had already sprung into action, but the SETC's notice energized more to get involved. One subsidiary goal of proponents was to strengthen China's weak associations by giving them more responsibility.[48]

Just as some firms helped launch the policy, others worked to curtail it. Economists and companies hurt or offended by price controls successfully persuaded the State Development and Planning Commission (SDPC) to join them in attacking the self-discipline price policy as antithetical to China's market reforms. The SDPC, long a bastion of central planning, ironically was sympathetic to these companies' free-market overtures because the cartels reduced its own administrative authority over prices. With firms and others weighing in on both sides, the SETC and SDPC jointly issued a notice in late November 1998 that scaled back the right of associations to organize cartels, restored pricing authority to the SDPC, and set a higher threshold for proving dumping.[49]

Companies from a host of sectors, including those in consumer electronics, were involved in this debate. (The role of steel companies is discussed in Chapter 3.) Changhong and Idall (*Aiduo*), which held large market shares in the color TV and VCD player markets, respectively, signed the July 1998 appeal to the SETC. And at an extremely contentious conference involving all parties in the debate, held right after the November regulation was issued, Changhong made a forceful but futile plea to give associations more authority in organizing cartels.[50]

These firms' participation in the transsectoral national debate was typical of government-business relations in the consumer electronics industries in so far as both state-owned and private companies have been actively involved in policy circles. However, their participation was atypical in that their specific position on this policy did not reflect the diversity of opinion in their industry. Changhong and Idall's views were not borne out of pride from successful price controls in consumer electronics but out of frustration with their failure.

Other industries tried forming local cartels in the early 1990s, but color TV makers were the first to attempt one on a nationwide basis when they met in April 1996, following deep price cuts by Changhong.[51] The China Video Association, in response to complaints from most of the other large manufacturers, helped to arrange a truce. But in a pattern to be repeated, firms soon forgot their pledges and cut prices again, leading to the cartel's demise. Ironically, this was the association's only area of policy activism (see Table 4.2). In early 1998, following the initiation of another round of price cuts, CVA helped its ten largest members form a "market working committee" to stabilize prices. The cartel again soon gave way to cheating. Despite its failure, the CVA and some members responded to the SETC's August 1998 "Idea on Self-Discipline Prices" with another attempt, thinking the imprimatur of the SETC and MII's support might make a difference. It did not, and prices quickly resumed their downward trajectory.[52]

Soon after, the CVA found itself pushed aside, both by its members and by the government. CVA was in the middle of a battle for market

Table 4.2 Price floor attempts in the color TV and VCD player industries

| Date initiated | Firms involved | Association involved | Government agency involved | Result |
|---|---|---|---|---|
| *Color TV* | | | | |
| Apr. 1998 | CVA members | CVA | MEI | Failed |
| Jan. 1998 | Top 10 producers | CVA | MEI | Failed |
| Oct. 1998 | Top 10 producers | CVA | MII | Failed |
| Apr. 1999 | All firms in industry | — | MII, SDPC | Failed |
| June 2000 | 9 large TV makers | — | — | Failed |
| *VCD player* | | | | |
| May 1997 | 22 producers | CECC | MII | Failed |
| May 1998 | 7 large producers | — | MII | Failed |
| May 2000 | 4 large DVD makers | — | — | Failed |

dominance it could not officiate. Although another company, Gaoluhua, started the price cuts that led to the early 1998 attempt at price floors, Changhong was more often the instigator. It was doing everything in its power to obtain a monopoly, even if that meant dropping prices one day and criticizing price wars the next. Its most audacious move occurred in November 1998 when it announced that it had bought up most of the country's available color picture tubes.[53] Coming on the heels of a well-publicized crackdown on smuggling by customs that summer, Changhong's move put its competitors at an extreme disadvantage. Changhong was gambling that with all the tubes its market share would grow dramatically during the upcoming Spring Festival, when TV sales were at their peak. Ignoring CVA, several large makers formed, in the words of one executive, a "lobbying group" (*youshui jituan*) to pressure MII and customs to side with them. They even appealed to Wu Bangguo, a Politburo member responsible for industrial policy. In a dramatic New Year's Eve showdown of the major TV and picture tube producers hosted by MII—no one from CVA was invited—the aggrieved TV makers demanded that the government increase the quota for tube imports and that Changhong be forced to give up some of its tubes. Though the demands were denied that night, eventually tube import quotas were lifted and Changhong "voluntarily" redirected some of its tubes to other companies.[54]

Locked in a battle for market share, companies became even bolder, more directly challenging the government's authority. Convinced the battle for the color TV market had gotten out of hand and with associations no longer allowed to organize price cartels because of the November 1998 regulation, the SDPC and MII in early April 1999, without informing the CVA, issued mandatory price floors for both color TVs and picture tubes. But this reassertion of government power was quickly undermined. Within weeks, companies were advertising TVs at prices below the price floors. One consumer electronics executive, a critic of price controls, noted that "the government's issuing of this document left them without face."[55] And in May 1999, eight of the country's eleven picture tube makers announced the formation of a production cartel. The eight, who were members of the China Vacuum Parts Association's Color Picture Tube Sub-Association (*zhongguo dianzi zhenkong qijian hangye xiehui caise shixiangguan fenhui*), included several joint venture producers, including Japan's Matsushita and South

Korea's LG. Knowing they could not stop the cartel, MII and SDPC officials condoned their action. Despite their brazen behavior, cartel members soon cheated and production resumed ahead of schedule. Taking a page from their book, the following summer nine large TV producers (which did not include Changhong) announced their own privately organized price cartel, the China Color TV Enterprise Summit. This time, the SDPC called their move illegal, but no action was taken against them. However, as usual, their cartel collapsed within a few weeks.[56]

Although all of the cartels failed, they demonstrate TV companies' extremely aggressive attempts to dominate the market, turn public policy in their favor, and if not successful ignore government sentiment by taking matters into their own hands. The China Video Association, which was involved in the early efforts, was discarded by the government and large SOEs, who thought the association was simply getting in the way.

Makers of VCD players also attempted to set price floors with an association's help, but unlike their color TV counterparts, failure quickly led most companies to lose enthusiasm for such arrangements. Their initial attempt in mid-1997 was extremely ambitious. Following drastic price reductions by Idall, the China Electronic Chamber of Commerce's periodical, *World Electronics Express* (*shijie dianzi kuaixun*), organized an industry "roundtable" (*yuanzhuo huiyi*) in Guangdong. The twenty-two participants drafted and signed the "China VCD Enterprise Competition Self-Discipline United Manifesto" (*zhongguo VCD qiye jingzheng zilu lianhe xuanyan*), which called not only for price floors but also for ethical advertising and other elements of fair competition. It gave the *World Electronics Express* and a board of signatories the right to monitor and report on firms' behavior and "castigate" (*bianda*) violators.[57]

While an ambitious effort that was a large step toward self-regulation (MII officials attended the roundtable and approved of the manifesto), price floors did not hold for very long. In a classic case of prisoner's dilemma, participants quickly defected from the deal with the hope of expanding their market shares. As a result, most firms lost hope of ever being able to manipulate prices. In May 1998, when seven of the industry's key firms met with MII officials, some argued for another attempt. While the participants orally accepted the restraints and specific floor prices were identified, some avoided signing the written pledge. (The pledge was a five-point agreement that dealt with multiple issues, including floor prices.) Since the signatures were never obtained, no real effort was made to implement the deal.[58] Signaling the waning enthusiasm for price cartels, none were ever tried again for the market's primary products, VCD and Super VCD players. Two years later only four companies that sold DVD players could be persuaded to join a cartel, which again did not survive long.[59]

VCD player producers' flagging interest in cartels was also reflected in the lack of activism of the China Audio Association on this issue. Although it had been involved in arranging price floors for radios and VCRs in 1989, it increasingly agreed with the vast majority of its members that price floors were unenforceable and should not be tried.[60] Thus, on this issue, it was CAA's inaction that demonstrated its links to its members.

To summarize, first, consumer electronics companies have had a major influence on the industry's pricing and competition policies. They persuaded the government to support price cartels and to allow associations to have a significant role in their adoption. Second, the policy to encourage associations to organize price cartels as a way of strengthening them had the opposite effect. CVA's reputation was weakened even further by its impotence on the issue. And third, large TV companies, state-owned and private alike, displayed a lack of deference to the government on several occasions, showing that this norm was no longer widely accepted. (Many VCD player companies would show the same attitude in the standards conflict discussed below.)

Perhaps the most puzzling aspect of this saga is why cartels consistently failed in a sector with relatively high concentration levels, the primary reason being offered in Chapter 3 as to why most steel cartels met a similar fate. One explanation is that the data overstates concentration in the TV and VCD player markets. Another is that the concentration levels were still not high enough in a country China's size, along with the attendant difficulties for monitoring cheaters. More likely is that high concentration levels did, in fact, facilitate the meeting of key firms and their initial cooperation but that high concentration alone could not guarantee firms would abide by their commitments. Other economic conditions which have been found to supplement high concentration, such as having a high-tech hook or significant import protection, did not exist. The integration of Chinese consumer electronics companies into global supply chains has manifested itself in low barriers to trade and investment, distinguishing China from Japan, where cartels have been more successful.[61] But in addition, it makes sense that cartels work best when participants enter them in good faith. It is clear that in these cases, some firms, such as Changhong and Idall, promoted cartels knowing they would violate them as soon as they had the chance. Several rounds of cheating reduced trust, making the possibility of success even more remote. Firms had the ability to influence the government but not to control one another.

## Fighting Off the Tax Man

In contrast to the frustration that consumer electronics associations and companies encountered in their attempts to set floor prices, the industry has had more success on tax policy. The chance to have taxes reduced (as occurred in the software industry) or the threat of having additional taxes levied (as in the case to be discussed here) promoted industry unity, encouraging firms to act jointly through associations.

In January 1998, the Ministry of Finance (MOF) was preparing to institute a special consumption tax on VCD and DVD players, stereo equipment, and large-screen televisions. Zhu Rongji, then still vice premier but the central leader most responsible for economic affairs, encouraged the ministry to take this step. Reportedly, in the fall of 1997 Zhu became convinced that the industry was "overheating." Not only were prices falling because of expanding production and firms' attempts to increase their market shares, but consumer electronics makers, especially VCD player companies, were also spending huge sums on TV advertising. Idall, then one of the industry's most dominant companies, was crowned "Label King" (*biaowang*) in 1997 for leading the country in spending on TV commercials.[62] Zhu thought the industry needed to be tamed and so approved the consumption tax (whether the initial suggestion was his or the ministry's is unclear).

Within a few weeks, word of the proposed tax reached the China Audio Association and some of its members, none of whom were initially consulted on the proposal. Before long they responded to this threat on their profits. In March 1998, the association organized a meeting with its ten largest members and officials from the SETC, the State Taxation

Administration (STA), and MII. They also invited reporters from the major media outlets, including Xinhua News Agency, *Economics Daily*, and *China Electronics News*. The association and companies argued that in contrast to the general perception of a booming industry, profits were meager because of the price wars. Moreover, if a special consumption tax was instituted, large, law-abiding companies would comply, but smaller firms would avoid paying. By giving, however unintentionally, a competitive advantage to small companies, the tax would inhibit the industry consolidation that Zhu Ronji and other government officials wanted for the economy in general. Finally, those present argued that the tax would hurt an industry that was doing its most to relieve growing unemployment caused by slowdowns in other sectors, such as steel. In addition to this meeting, individual companies also sought out officials in these and other ministries to press their case. MII inherently supported their views, but the voices of companies and the association energized MII to also defend their interests in other meetings. To top it off, several large companies persuaded deputies to the National People's Congress, which at the time was holding its annual plenum, to speak up on the industry's behalf against the consumption tax.

Their lobbying paid off. Besides whatever newspaper articles he may have written, the journalist from *Economics Daily* attending the CAA meeting wrote an internal report about the meeting for the State Council, which found its way to Zhu Rongji's desk. Based on these reports and perhaps the statements of the NPC deputies, in April 1998 Zhu reversed his position and ordered the Ministry of Finance to cancel its plans for the tax.[63]

Most participants gave primary credit to the VCD player companies and MII for successfully fighting off the special consumption tax. At a couple of points in the 1980s when the consumer electronics market "overheated," the industry had mixed results in staving off similar consumption tax plans: in 1985 they were successful; in 1989 they were not.[64] But the first major difference between the policy conflicts over taxes in the 1980s and 1998 was the far stronger reaction companies had toward the plan in 1998. Greater sensitivity to sales and profits made even SOEs staunchly oppose the plan. But the second difference between the two periods was the audio association's greater activism, something for which it did not receive much credit from some of its members. (By contrast, the video association, less attuned to the policy process and its members, never became involved. TV makers, regardless of whether they also made VCD players, benefited from the audio association's activism.) The association's influence may have been subsidiary to that of its members, but it played a significant role in organizing its members and providing a fora for the airing of views that then filtered back to the key decision-maker in the government.

## The Standard of Influence

One reason some members may not have been inclined to give the audio association its due credit was that the industry was in the middle of a battle that left members of the association sharply divided—a standards war. The conflict, which took over a year and a half to resolve, reveals how economic factors have reshaped government-business relations in China. The combination of large economies of scale, a growing market share for domestic and foreign private companies, and the importance of standards in digital technology pushed China's VCD player makers into a policy process for which China's political institutions and norms were not prepared. These economic factors shaped how the problem of standards was turned into a policy issue; affected how the VCD player companies interacted with one another, their association, and the government; and largely determined the outcome of the policy debate.

China's formal standard-setting system is geared not for standards wars but for cooperation. As in France, the government is expected to take the initiative in establishing and monitoring standards.[65] China's 1988 Standardization Law and its 1990 implementing regulations specify that technical committees that draft standards should be composed of "customers, production establishments, trade associations, scientific and technological research institutes, academic organizations, and experts from relevant [government] departments." However, these parties are expected to work collectively for the greater good and be subordinate to the government. The law allows companies to set "enterprise standards" (that is, de facto standards), but only in the absence of any government-approved national, industry or regional standards.[66] In short, China's system is inclusive but it frowns upon companies acting on their own.[67]

This system operated without much difficulty in the 1980s. In 1987, even prior to the Standardization Law's adoption, China's State Quality and Technical Supervision Bureau (SQTSB) established the Recording Standards Committee (*quanguo luzhi shebei biaozhunhua jishu weiyuanhui*). Its eighty members consisted of technical specialists from plodding SOEs, research institutes and universities, and government officials. Its responsibility was to draft standards and forward them to the Ministry of Electronics Industry, which could reject them, issue an industry standard, or forward them to the SQTSB, which would then issue a national standard. For the first decade of its existence, everything went smoothly. In the course of adopting more than eighty standards related to VCRs, audio recorders, and karaoke machines, the committee's members rarely quarreled. The sharpest disagreement centered over whether the minimum operating temperature for VCRs should be 0 or -5 degrees Celsius; unable to resolve their differences, the committee decided to recognize both temperatures as legitimate standards. And consistent with the norm of cooperation, no member ever expected or demanded they be given intellectual property rights over any of the standards they helped set.[68]

By the mid-1990s, more domestic and foreign private companies sensitive to profits had entered the market, and they recognized the value of leveraging the intellectual property rights of a proprietary standard in information technology. These changes set the conditions for the launching of a standards war that also put the industry on a collision course with the formal standard-setting system.[69] In 1996, the VCD player market was growing extremely quickly. Sensing more profits and taking a cue from the global VCR industry, VCD player manufacturers wanted to issue a more advanced machine with resolution higher than that of existing VCD players but not as high as the resolution of DVD players. Foreign companies owned the intellectual property rights to DVD player components, which would require Chinese companies to pay royalties, reducing their profits. Because compatibility between players and discs is so important (companies wanted existing VCDs to be able to play in the new generation of players), a standard would have to be created. So, in late 1996 and early 1997, VCD player manufacturers pressed the Ministry of Electronics Industry over the need for a new standard.[70] MEI, which had little knowledge of the VCD player market, was receptive to their advances. As a poor, developing country, China had never set an international technical standard in information technology. This was China's chance to move from the status of rule taker to that of rule maker and promote domestic industry by China having control over the standard. In keeping with past practice, MEI charged the Recording Standards Committee with drafting a standard that it hoped would first be set as a national standard and then be submitted to the International Electrotechnical Commission (IEC) as an international standard.

After several months of discussion and meetings, the process hit a roadblock. Support emerged for two different standards, SVCD (super video compact disc) and CVD (China video disc). Though differing in a number of respects, the key distinction was their different resolutions, with the SVCD standard having higher clarity.[71] Supporters for the alternative standards split into two opposing camps, what could be called the CVD Team and the SVCD Team. Table 4.3 lists the members of the teams that either participated in the committee or were otherwise involved in the policy discussion. What stands out are the similar characteristics of both sides. In keeping with the tendency for only large companies to have a political voice, large companies alone became involved in this process. Both teams consisted of foreign private, state-owned, and domestic private companies, and both teams had companies from different parts of China. As occurred in the software

**Table 4.3** The two teams in the standards conflict

| CVD Team | | | SVCD Team | | |
|---|---|---|---|---|---|
| Company | Ownership* | Location | Company | Ownership* | Location |
| C-Cube | FP | United States | ESS | FP | United States |
| Philips | FP | Netherlands | Xinke (Shinco) | SOE | Jiangsu |
| Xianke | SOE | Guangdong | Xiongmao (Panda) | SOE | Jiangsu |
| Changhong | SOE | Sichuan | Jindian | SOE | Sichuan |
| Wanlida | SOE | Fujian | Shanghai Broad. | SOE | Shanghai |
| Xiaxin | SOE | Fujian | Wanyan | PE | Anhui |
| Mudan (Peony) | SOE | Beijing | Chuangwei | PE | Guangdong |
| Jinzheng | PE | Guangdong | | | |
| Bubugao (BBK) | PE | Guangdong | | | |
| Aiduo (Idall) | PE | Guangdong | | | |

* Ownership: SOE—state-owned enterprise; PE—domestic private enterprise; FP—foreign private enterprise.

industry, companies crossed ownership and regional boundaries to ally with other companies based on technological compatibility, market position, and other economic factors.[72]

The VCD standards conflict not only upset old rivalries but also challenged the old norms of policy making. As one reporter put it, the SVCD Team followed the "official route" (*guanfang luxian*), while the CVD Team took the "popular route" (*minjian luxian*).[73] Cognizant of the expectation of cooperation, the SVCD Team at every step explicitly recognized the government's authority to manage the process. By contrast, the CVD Team took a much more competitive posture. At key moments, they departed from the position of the Recording Standards Committee and challenged the government's very right to have a say over the standard.

In May 1998, at the same meeting hosted by the Ministry of Information Industry in which price floors were discussed, key VCD player companies also agreed in principle to jointly develop a common technical standard. But a few weeks after the meeting, five of the companies in attendance (Xianke, Idall, Wanlida, Xiaxin, and Bubugao) broke their promise. They and several others secretly collaborated with C-Cube in developing an alternative standard, CVD, which they unveiled on June 9, 1998. They intentionally did not invite any officials to their press conference or notify them ahead of time of their plan.[74] The CVD Team's strategy was a textbook case of companies trying to set a de facto standard by being first to market.

While such a tactic would have been perfectly acceptable in many industrialized countries, where standards wars are commonplace, it startled the Chinese policy community for its brashness. The CVD Team was criticized for challenging the government's authority. Most criticism was directed at C-Cube, which was portrayed as not understanding that in China foreign companies "had to adjust to the norm" of working with the government.[75] Said one observer, the press conference was like a protest against the government: "It was not illegal, but it violated basic common knowledge" of what was expected. Another concurred, charging that C-Cube "broke our country's rules of the game."[76] By contrast, observers praised ESS, the foreign company on the SVCD Team that was seen as sensitive to the traditional norms of government-business relations.

The distinction between C-Cube and ESS may be valid, but it overlooks the fact that the CVD Team was also composed of domestic state-owned and private companies that knew they were trampling on the old norms. But they did so anyway, maintaining that in a market economy, companies have the right to sell what they want. Said one CVD Team member, "As long as you have a product that consumers like, that's enough. Firms can set standards by themselves; they don't need government intervention." Another concurred, stating unequivocally, "The standard is the market. If consumers buy it, then that's the standard."[77] What began as a fight over technical standards evolved into a fight over the proper standards of behavior for business and government.

The conflict also set the CVD Team against the China Audio Association. Because the Recording Standards Committee served as the forum for government-business dialogue and because it knew its firms were divided over the issue, CAA had little role in the process. However, after the CVD Team released their product, CAA issued a statement siding with the SVCD Team and the government's position. They stressed that the government had the right to lead the process and that the forthcoming standard issued by the committee and then MII would be mandatory.[78] CAA's position was interpreted by many observers as the work of Xinke, which they believed had disproportionate influence over the association.[79] Even if CAA acted on its own accord, the conflict led some of its members to question if the association represented all its members equally.

The climax and outcome of the war also reflected the industry's economic characteristics. After the CVD Team announced their product, the SVCD Team quickly raced to issue their own and move the formal standard-setting process forward. In August 1998, the Recording Standards Committee met, and its members overwhelmingly voted to approve the SVCD standard.[80] Since the committee's vote was just a recommendation to MII, both teams continued their fight by aggressively pressing their cases with MII officials. The CVD Team found sympathetic ears in officials from MII's Science and Technology Division and from a vice minister. They argued that since consumers had already bought so many CVD players, approving the committee's decision would be akin to saying consumers had bought an illegal product. They suggested that MII issue a dual standard that included both CVD and SVCD players. Persuaded by their arguments and knowing that it would be extremely difficult to actually take CVD players off the market, MII revised the standard accordingly. Besides allowing variable resolution quality and creating an alternate location for storing information, it required that all companies' players be compatible with all other machines and discs on the market. The revised standard was issued a few weeks later.[81] To hide the fact that it was a compromise, MII also changed its English name from SVCD to Chaoji VCD, *chaoji* being the romanized Chinese word for "super." The CVD Team, on the strength of its market power, challenged the old rules of the game and still managed to obtain a partial policy victory.

A couple of observers suggested that the CVD Team obtained enough support from MII to have the standards modified because the firms tried to bribe MII officials or because their coalition included Changhong and Xianke, the first led by an alternate member of the Communist Party's Central Committee, the latter having a history of ties to Deng Xiaoping.[82] If accurate, they would show the importance of patronage in the policy process. While such charges cannot be fully disproved, the weight of the evidence does not fit such an interpretation. The great majority of principals to the contest believe that MII's decision was based on the arguments of the CVD Team about the VCD player market. This conclusion is reinforced by the fact that even members of the SVCD Team acknowledged that the compromise was probably the best possible outcome, even if it hurt their chances to corner the market.[83] In addition, both sides were stocked with large companies, state-owned and private, with a history of policy engagement with the national government. Throughout the entire episode, neither side had any difficulty accessing MII.

That clientelism was not the deciding factor in the outcome did not mean that participants were satisfied with the process by which the standards were set. Many complained that the Recording Standards Committee was a poor vehicle for the process. It had too many members who were not in the VCD player industry and only three who were on the CVD Team (Changhong, Xianke, and Idall). The process was, thus, too democratic in that too many voices were involved, and not democratic enough in that both sides were not evenly represented. In addition, some felt that the standards war would have been resolved far more quickly had the government's role been less important.[84]

The VCD standards conflict proved to be a watershed event. In response to these complaints, MII revised its standard-setting process. It still maintained its right to authorize standards, but it admitted that the most important producers in an industry should have a much stronger voice in the process. To this end, in late 1998, MII abandoned the Recording Standards Committee and formed a committee directly under the ministry's control composed of key Chinese and foreign VCD makers in an attempt to revise the standard so that it could be submitted to the IEC, which occurred in September 2000.[85] And the China Audio Association, not the government, then successfully represented the industry in negotiations to reduce royalty payments to patent holders of DVD-related technology, earning it the respect of former critics.[86]

There also has been a torrent of subsequent efforts to establish standards for other consumer electronics goods, among them a more advanced video player, the EVD (enhanced versatile disc), a third generation (3G) mobile phone, and a new audio-visual coding standard (AVS) that could be applied to a range of electronics devices.[87] Although in no case have companies followed the CVD Team's example of unveiling a new standard without first consulting the government, industry consistently has been proactive in suggesting the need for standards, has played a central role in the formal decision-making process on committees, and has informally lobbied the government to accept their plans. And in several cases, firms have split into competing alliances, all of which often have both Chinese and foreign companies. Most standards proposals, thus, combine domestic and foreign technology, thwarting government hopes to create a purely Chinese standard that privileges domestic industry at the expense of foreign producers.[88] These cases collectively demonstrate that the dynamics of the consumer electronics market have shaped the agenda and outcome of standards efforts in ways one would not anticipate by focusing only on China's formal standards institutions.

## Conclusion

The pattern of politics in consumer electronics is more muddled than in the steel and software sectors. Its associations are unevenly developed, yet large companies of all ownership forms have become more willing to vigorously defend their interests through direct contact with officialdom, even at the risk of offending the government. While its associations are not fully mature, the direct aspect of ties seems most consistent with pluralism. This mixed state of affairs can be explained by reference to the industry's economic characteristics.

High concentration levels and the emergence of domestic and foreign private producers have encouraged associations. High concentration facilitates cooperation, and associations create a link to government that private firms did not originally have. On the other hand, some economic characteristics have hindered associations by making cooperation more difficult (competitive pricing tactics and the importance of standards for market share) and reducing the need for associations (SOEs have natural links and large companies can develop them). Consequently, companies have no confidence in the China Video Association. The China Audio Association is much more developed, but even it does not have the full support of its members. Similarly, associations have had more success in policies where industry cooperation was relatively easy to generate (fighting the special consumption tax), as opposed to those that generated conflict (engaging in price and standards wars). One irony of the price floors fiasco is that this failure was a blow to the development of associations and consequently political liberalization but a boost to economic reform, since collusion was defeated.

While the picture concerning the avenues by which government-business relations occurs is mixed, the growing assertiveness of the industry is crystal clear, a trend also related to the industry's economic characteristics. Consumer electronics is dominated by large companies involved in an extremely competitive market, making any economic or policy advantage a company can gain extremely valuable. The importance of pricing, technical standards, and other aspects of competition have made consumer electronics companies much more attentive to policy debates. Companies' generally large size has given them the confidence to be more aggressive in seeing that these policy debates turn in their favor and, when they do not, in following their own preferences anyway. As time wore on, Changhong and the other large color TV makers dropped prices or tried to fix them regardless of the government's position, and the CVD Team was bold enough to issue its own standard and then convince the government to legitimize it. And a united industry, with the help of some NPC deputies, turned back the Ministry of Finance's tax plan.

So even with less than fully developed associations, industry influence has grown tremendously, changing the fundamental nature of sector's policy making. A Chinese journalist's observation that the standards war signaled that the "top-down" process of the planning era was giving way to the "bottom-up" process consistent with the market could apply to the industry's politics as a whole. Since firms are now free to follow government instructions on a voluntary basis, he wrote, the government increasingly has to listen to them when they disagree.[89]

The final question is which firms benefit from this pattern. On the one hand, the obvious answer appears to be large firms. Their direct access has given them disproportionate influence over policy compared to smaller companies. Even the defeat of the consumption tax, which should benefit big and small companies alike, may have been a relative loss for smaller firms if larger firms' arguments about smaller ones' ability to avoid paying the tax are correct. On the other hand, while large firms are the primary winners, since coalitions vary by issue depending on firms' perceived economic interests, which large companies actually win policy debates also changes. Consequently, companies that lose in one arena may win in another. In the VCD player industry, the alliances for and against price cartels differed from those created to develop technical standards. Idall had little luck in enforcing price cartels, but as part of the CVD Team, it succeeded in having its standards preference find its way into the final policy. And foreign companies regularly find themselves in alliances with Chinese companies against other coalitions that combine both Chinese and foreign members. As a result, Chinese firms' integration into global supply chains means that the interests of foreign firms are rarely entirely rejected. Thus, knowing a large company's form of ownership or nationality will not tell an observer which side of an issue the company is on or whether it has any influence. That judgement must be made on a case-by-case basis.

# ~ 5

# *The Software Industry: Approaching Pluralism*

$I$N A COUNTRY where agriculture occupies the lives of over 320 million people and one one-thousandth of that number work in the software industry, it might seem strange for a study trying to get to the heart of China's political economy to focus on software. Having emerged as a global industry in the early 1980s, software does not have nearly the same legacy as farming or steel do in China. Although China apparently had 20,000 software engineers in 1984, the first genuine software firms did not open until a few years later, and the vast majority that currently exist registered in the 1990s.[1] In addition, the steel and consumer electronics industries dwarf software. The sector's 400,000 employees and RMB 74 billion in sales in 2001 accounted for just 0.05 percent of employed workers and 1 percent of sales of all goods and services that year.[2]

However, while still dwarfed by steel and consumer electronics, the software industry has been growing annually at over 30 percent since the mid-1990s. More important than the absolute size of the industry proper is its significance to China more generally. Information technology is becoming a part of the everyday vocabulary and lives of more and more urbanites, and it has also become a tool of business and the government. In 2001, more than 8 million PCs were sold in China, bringing the installed user base to 34 million units. Most PCs are in offices, but urban home ownership has risen quickly. By 2003 China had

68 million "netizens," or Internet users, while the media, companies, and government agencies—not to mention every variety of social organization—had all gone online, setting up hundreds of thousands of Internet sites to inform readers, attract customers, and explain policies to citizens.[3] All of these computers and Internet sites are dependent on software. Finally, the rampant nature of software piracy and the extensive efforts to avoid the Y2K problem in China likewise speak to sector's underlying significance.[4] In short, software has woven itself into the fabric of Chinese society.

The surprising degree to which information technology's reach has expanded in China makes the software industry worth understanding in and of itself, but its distinct economic characteristics make it valuable for our purposes. This chapter tracks the extent to which these factors— among them the prominence of private firms, domestic and foreign— have affected the avenues and outcomes of government-business interaction. To some degree, relations between software companies and the government mirror those found in the steel and consumer electronics industries. Direct ties are still important to software companies. And in comparison to Western democracies, China's software associations' autonomy is circumscribed, and their activities are unsophisticated. However, what stands out are the ways in which government-business relations in the software industry are distinctive. In comparison to associations in consumer electronics and, even more clearly, steel, software associations are more numerous, independent, and active on behalf of their members. In addition, the importance of company size in determining the depth of direct contact with government is still detectable, but the threshold for what constitutes a large company is far lower and more flexible than in the other industries.

This chapter argues that the industry's economic characteristics have pushed government-business ties further in the direction of pluralism than either of the other two sectors. The organization and functions of associations and the existence of alternative paths of contact with the government on public policy issues differ fundamentally from corporatism. As in the other sectors, nurturing personal relations with officialdom can occasionally be helpful, but the clearer trend is the attenuation of *guanxi*'s utility, suggesting the limited applicability of the clientelism framework. Although companies and associations do not openly confront the government, and the policy process is not completely transparent, companies still try to promote their interests, often with success, in a manner approaching pluralism.

To demonstrate how these findings were reached, the chapter begins by outlining the software industry's economic characteristics and the main problems that have become issues for policy debates. It then shows how the association system has grown in ways politically beneficial to companies. The focus then turns to other signs of pluralism—direct ties on policy matters and increased transparency. These points are finally reinforced by an in-depth discussion of three recent policy issues at the center of the industry's development: the value-added tax (VAT), the protection of intellectual property rights, and the creation of technical standards.

## The Economics of Software

No matter where one looks in the world, the software industry has several characteristics that distinguish it from the steel and consumer electronics sectors. First, while technology is important to all three industries in this study, software is the most knowledge-intensive. Employees' expertise is far and away a firm's most important asset. A software firm typically has an extremely young, but a very highly educated workforce whose skills are not as easily substitutable as those of employees in steel or consumer electronics companies. Creativity is particularly valued in the software industry, because firms succeed to the extent that they can differentiate their products from that of their competitors. Second, since software development is predominantly a knowledge-intensive activity that requires relatively limited financial investment per unit, there are very low economies of scale, and hence software firms globally tend to be small.[5] Anyone with a bright idea, access to a PC, and a limited amount of financing can potentially produce and market software on a wide scale. And third, although the industry is extremely competitive, there is an unprecedented level of interfirm cooperation, even between companies that otherwise fight for customers. Some alliances form around a base product that all firms share (for example, software developers who use Sun Microsystems' Java code or firms that write applications for Microsoft's Windows operating system). And firms with different yet complementary talents forge alliances when expanding into new technology or market niches.[6]

When translated into the Chinese context, the differences between steel, consumer electronics, and software are further sharpened. But it is important to first mention a common feature that these sectors share in China. Like the other two industries, China's software industry is national in scope. Although firms' headquarters are concentrated in Beijing, Shanghai, and Guangdong's Pearl River Delta, most large firms have subsidiaries spread around the country. And even where firms lack a permanent presence, they utilize their own roving sales force, a bevy of distributors, or retail outlets, not to mention pirates, to ply their wares. Several domestic software retail chains have opened. The most prominent, Federal, has over two hundred stores throughout China.

But there the similarities end and the differences begin. First, as a knowledge-intensive industry, China's software firms have a far better educated staff on average than their steel and consumer electronics counterparts. Most employees have college degrees, often in computer science, and a plurality have advanced degrees. It is, thus, no surprise that much of China's software industry is located in the northwest quadrant of Beijing in close proximity to over thirty universities and the Chinese Academy of Sciences. Relatedly, software employees are typically quite young. The average age of employees at UFSoft (*Yongyou*), a leading provider of financial management software, is just twenty-eight.[7] When founding the company with a friend in 1988, Wang Wenjing was just twenty-three. Ninety percent of Peking University's Founder Group's (*Beida fangzheng jituan*) directors and vice presidents are under thirty-five.[8]

Second, software firms in China tend to be extremely small. In 2001, 60 percent of firms had less than fifty employees, while just 15 percent had more than a hundred. Only a few have more than a thousand, and even that statistic can be deceiving. For example, China Software and Technical Services Corporation (CS&S, *Zhongruan*) has its two thousand employees scattered among forty-three subsidiaries.[9] As elsewhere, low economies of scale encourage small firms. But in addition, the high rate of software piracy in China keeps firms from making the returns on their investments needed to expand.

Third, the industry's overall market concentration is low, likely well under 20 percent.[10] China's software industry consists of thousands of small firms, most trying to find a niche market in which they can survive and grow. Although some product categories—such as operating systems, periodical publishing, and financial management—are dominated by a small number of firms, no one firm sells the full range of software products. By cutting into legal sales of operating systems and some applications, piracy has also led to a lower market concentration.[11]

Fourth, a majority of software companies in China are privately run domestic and foreign firms.[12] There are no definitive, detailed data on ownership structure, but an unsystematic scanning of the media and of store shelves yields far more references to private firms than to state-owned enterprises (SOEs). In almost every segment category, domestic private firms are prominent: UFSoft and Kingdee (*Jindie*) in financial management, Kingsoft (*Jinshan*) in word processing, and Kelihua in education and training.

Although domestic private firms likely outnumber others, foreign firms, mostly American, are the industry's leaders. This should not come as a surprise since seven of the world's top ten software firms are from the United States.[13] Foreign companies control two-thirds of the Chinese software market.[14] The importance of foreign industry goes far beyond market share. The sector's hub is not in China but the United States. The concepts and programming languages used to develop software are imported into China and are often used in English.

Foreign involvement is also critical because of the high degree of cooperation between foreign and domestic software producers. Just as with the industry in general, firms in China regularly cooperate on everything from basic research to product development, marketing, sales, and service. Horizontal links are a natural part of the business and in China regularly cross the domestic-foreign divide that hobbles such cooperation in other sectors, such as in steel.[15] The transfer of knowledge and resources is not one way but is bidirectional. Foreign firms rely heavily on local talent to adapt their products to Chinese users (what is called "Sinification," or *hanhua*) and to manage their business operations. Thus, notions of "Chinese-made software" and "foreign-made software" are artificial constructs that mask a more complex reality.

The majority of the software industry's economic characteristics—high knowledge intensity, low economies of scale, predominance of domestic and foreign private companies, and the importance of interfirm technical cooperation—clearly foster interfirm cooperation on matters of public policy. The high-tech nature of software means that firms have expertise that government cadres generally lack and need in making decisions that affect the industry. Small size and the predominance of private firms mean that most software companies do not have voices loud enough to be heard on their own and do not have natural allies in government to support them. The emphasis on cooperation in business creates an incentive for joint activism in trying to promote common public-policy objectives. And the extent of domestic-foreign interaction on the business side of software reduces conflicts of interest between them on policy issues, facilitating truly industry-wide concerted efforts on relevant policies. Low overall concentration could make industry-wide cooperation more difficult, but this problem would apply mainly to issues on which firms have an incentive to violate agreements (such as pricing guidelines).

These factors only affect *how* firms interact with the government. It is the existence of a series of problems that has generated industry activism in the first place. The largest threat to the industry has been piracy. Just as in China's entertainment industry, which depends on the sales of compact discs and tapes, the number of illegal copies (*daoban*) of software installed in computers or in use far outnumbers those legally purchased (*zhengban*). Piracy has severely limited the industry's ability to make profits and grow, and hence has been one of the most important issues firms have raised with the government. But the depth of piracy and the limited ability to deter it has also raised companies' sensitivity to tax policies that take away further from their income or make it difficult to raise funds from capital markets, both privately from venture capitalists and publicly by listing on stock markets. Other issues that have affected the industry include incompatibility between software in the same market niches and obstacles keeping firms from entering certain markets, particularly government procurement. Some of these issues have arisen simply because the industry is relatively new to China, while others seem chronic to all creativity-based industries, especially in developing countries. In addition, as an executive from a foreign company noted, despite not having the legacy of central planning and despite continued attempts to micromanage outcomes as in the steel industry, software is a "highly regulated industry" that requires firms to be attentive to the policy process.[16]

To see how these issues have been addressed, we must first understand how business and government generally interact on public policy, both through associations and other intermediaries, and through direct communication.

## The Growth of Software Associations

The clearest sign of the influence of economic factors on the pattern of government-business relations is the industry's well-developed system of associations. Compared to their counterparts in steel and consumer electronics, they appear much more pluralist than corporatist.[17] First, except for the industry's initial association, by most measures software associations have a relatively high degree of autonomy (see Table 5.1).

The original impetus to set up a national software association derived from the same source as in steel and consumer electronics: government fiat. Since its establishment in September 1984, the China Software Industry Association (CSIA, *Zhongguo ruanjian hangye xiehui*) has resembled other national associations formed around the same

Table 5.1 Autonomy of selected software associations (Y=yes; N=no; darker shading signifies greater autonomy)

| Business association | Chinese govt initiative? | Affiliation | Staffed with (former) govt officials? | Financially dependent on govt? |
|---|---|---|---|---|
| China Software Industry Association (CSIA) (1984) | Y | MII | Y | Limited |
| **Regional Associations** | | | | |
| Beijing Software Industry Association (BSIA) (1986) | Y | None | Limited | N |
| Shanghai Software Industry Association (SSIA) (1986) | Y | Shanghai Sci-Tech Comm. | Limited | Limited |
| **CSIA Sub-Associations** | | | | |
| Accounting and Business Mgt Sub-Assn (ABM) (1995) | N | CSIA | Limited | N |
| Touch Systems Sub-Assn (1998) | N | CSIA | N | N |
| **Foreign Associations in China** | | | | |
| Business Software Alliance (BSA) (Early 1990s) | N | None | N | N |
| U.S. Information Technology Office (USITO) (1995) | N | None | N | N |

time. Its staff and financing were fully provided for by the Ministry of Electronics Industry (MEI), then headed by Jiang Zemin.[18] Not surprisingly, its offices were in the ministry. In the 1990s, its official color only marginally faded. CSIA chairman Yang Tianxing headed the computer and software division at MEI until he retired. Only three of CSIA's twenty vice chairs are from a ministry proper (six are from ministry-controlled research institutes), but they have no genuine decision-making authority. One of its vice chairs, who is also a co-secretary-general, Chen Chong, has concurrently served as a deputy division head within MII, violating the usual ban against officials at and above the rank of deputy section chief from serving as an association official.[19] Although CSIA has begun to obtain a greater proportion of its income by sponsoring exhibitions, it still depends on the government to cover most of its costs, including the salaries of its leaders.[20] CSIA did move its offices out of the ministry but into space given to it by a ministry-owned software company (CS&S).

Beyond CSIA, though, there has gradually emerged over the next decade and a half an array of associations that are substantially more independent. CSIA's founding was followed by the creation of regional software associations across the country.[21] Although local government initiative was important in their establishment, their ties to officialdom have been attenuated. For example, when the Beijing Software Industry Association (BSIA) was founded in 1986, it did not have a government sponsor (*guakao danwei*). Its "responsible business unit" (*zhuguan bumen*), the Beijing Electronics Information Industry Office, was corporatized in the late 1990s, giving up its regulatory functions. BSIA's secretary-general came from the local bureaucracy, but the rest of the staff were hired from a talent exchange center and had no government experience. And since its founding, BSIA has depended on membership dues and other outside sources to cover its operating expenses.[22] The Shanghai Software Industry Association (SSIA) has had a similar semi-official background. Its secretary-general has been an engineer, not a government official, and part of SSIA's income has consistently come from dues and consulting.[23] And the offices of both BSIA and SSIA are not on government premises.

The most significant development in software has been the proliferation since the late 1980s of issue-specific associations, established at the initiative of firms, not the government. The range of these associations is broad, dealing with issues that span the industry (such as intellectual property rights, artificial intelligence, and open software) or that revolve around discrete market niches (such as financial management, multimedia, and games).[24] To maintain the pretense of officialdom, these issue-specific associations often have a current or former bureaucrat in a nominal leadership position, and since 1992 all issue-specific software associations have been subsumed under the umbrella of the CSIA as sub-associations (*fenhui*). But most of their genuine leadership comes from firms, as well as their financing and office space. Rather than block or co-opt their functions, MII and CSIA have permitted the sub-associations to expand significantly.

Added to the domestic associations are several foreign software-related associations that have been operating in China since the 1990s. They include the Business Software Alliance (BSA), a U.S.-based group of a dozen software makers that focuses on countering piracy, and the U.S. Information Technology Office (USITO), a coalition of six U.S. trade associations (including those in software, computers, telecommunications and electronics) which collectively have six thousand corporate members.[25]

Second, in addition to the associations' relative autonomy, participation in software associations has never been mandatory. CSIA's one thousand members account for 15 percent of all software firms.[26] All the large domestic software firms are members of CSIA, but they describe their membership as voluntary. The same rule of noncompulsory participation applies to the other software associations as well.

Third, there are no hierarchical relationships among associations. CSIA and the regional software associations are regular members of, respectively, the national and regional branches of the China Industrial Economy Federation (CIEF), but just as with the steel and consumer electronics associations, they are not subject to its oversight. The software associations attend CIEF meetings but do not take instruction from the latter and are not conduits of policy information between the CIEF and their own members. And none of the software associations are members of the All-China Federation of Industry and Commerce (ACFIC). There is also no hierarchy among national associations within information technology; instead, each is directly accountable to a national ministry, either the Ministry of Information Industry (MII), the Ministry of Science and Technology (MOST), or the Ministry of Finance (MOF). And within the software industry, although the China

Software Industry Association provides formal oversight of its various sub-associations, in practice CSIA does not supervise them. Still further, CSIA has no regulatory authority over the regional software associations, which are registered with their local governments.[27]

Fourth and finally, software associations lack jurisdictional monopolies. The sub-associations individually are supposed to deal with a narrow range of issues, but in practice their concerns are broad and overlap with one another as well as those of the regional associations and CSIA. In addition, the regional associations occasionally cooperate on activities with CSIA, but more often than not the regional and national associations compete with each other for firms' support and influence on the government.[28] The regional associations also have sub-associations and specialized committees that overlap with those of the national association. Even within a region there are multiple local associations that deal with similar issues.[29] And lastly, associations that span information technology deal with many of the issues with which software-specific associations grapple. For example, the China Digitization (3C) Industry Alliance (*zhongguo shuzihua* (*3C chanpin*) *chanye lianmeng*), founded in June 1999, has a software working committee.[30]

The absence of jurisdictional monopolies is reinforced by the fact that Chinese and foreign software firms regularly belong to multiple associations and transsectoral chambers of commerce. Many of the firms in the China Software Industry Association are also in one of the regional associations and one or more of the sub-associations. Because of the growing diversity of its business interests, Founder tops the list with membership in twenty associations, but even smaller firms belong to more than one. For example, Sina (previously SRS) joined CSIA, BSIA, the China Software Alliance (*zhongguo ruanjian lianmeng*), and China Internet Content Providers United Development High-Level Conference (*zhongguo ICP lianhe fazhan gaoceng huiyi*).[31] Most recently, foreign firms with offices in China have begun to join domestic associations. In addition to being a member of the BSA, USITO, and the American Chamber of Commerce, Microsoft has also joined the domestically initiated China Software Industry Association, the Beijing Software Industry Association, the China Software Alliance, and the China Digitzation (3C) Industry Alliance. In sum, if firms so choose, they have multiple formal routes to learn about policies or to air their positions.

Reflecting their relatively pluralist bent, software associations are active on behalf of their members. Their activities fall into three categories: market promotion, the government policy process, and market self-regulation. The software associations regularly host exhibitions, hold press conferences, and conduct and report on product-quality tests to publicize the industry's firms and their products, activities which may lead to future business opportunities. More importantly, the software associations participate in the policy-making process at their own initiative or that of their members. Most of the associations, domestic and foreign, host seminars and meetings on the myriad issues that affect the industry, including intellectual property rights, difficulties raising capital, the need for tax relief, and government procurement. Before and after the meetings, associations write reports to relevant government agencies, not just to the agency with which they are affiliated, that analyze existing policies and suggest changes. Unlike in the steel industry, most of this activity is initiated by the software associations and their members, not the government.

The exception is CSIA, which has had the mandate familiar to other government-controlled associations of being the "bridge and belt" (*qiaoliang he niudai*) between the ministry and software companies. However, it has not proactively fulfilled its mission. By and large, CSIA is rudderless and takes no initiatives without prior approval from MII. It has hosted meetings at which firms have aired their opinions about various problems, but these chances have been few and far in between. And while CSIA has adopted positions against that of some government agencies, such as the State Taxation Administration, it has never been at loggerheads with MII.[32] CSIA's passivity pales in comparison to the other associations' activism.

Last, some software associations have begun to gain some authority in actually regulating the industry themselves. CSIA's Accounting and Business Management Software Sub-Association (ABM, *caiwu ji qiye guanli ruanjian fenhui*), founded in 1995 by companies that produce accounting and financial management software, issued its own "industry agreement" (*hangyue*) in August 1996.[33] The pact details legitimate business practices for its members (fifty-five in 1998) regarding competition, employee responsibilities, intellectual property rights, and the sharing of technology and ideas. Because of a history of price cutting, which was perceived as unfair competition, members are required to publish the prices of their software and charge for post-sales service. Significantly, the agreement gives the association the right to arbitrate disputes among members or sanction a member if violations of this code of conduct are found. ABM has occasionally held meetings to criticize members' behavior, such as producing overly misleading advertising or selling below cost, but it has yet to fine a member or dismiss one from the association. Reportedly, behavior among ABM's members has improved since the pact was instituted.[34] Another sign of the pact's success is that it is being imitated by others. In late 1998, CSIA issued its own "basic convention" (*jiben gongyue*), which was strikingly similar to ABM's. CSIA has since encouraged its other sub-associations and the regional associations to follow suit.[35]

These software associations have been active despite having less than absolute autonomy. Being founded at their members' initiative and not being dependent on the government for finances has ensured their orientation toward their members. Their autonomy has been attenuated by having to register with a government agencies (directly or via CSIA) and having some former officials on their staffs, but these requirements have not had a crippling effect. On the one hand, the associations tend to adhere to the norm of quiet consultation rather than open confrontation. These associations are occasionally more critical of MII and government policy than CSIA, but they operate quietly and try not to intentionally antagonize any party to a policy debate. On the other hand, associations genuinely oriented toward members have also been able to use these official links to gain access to the government. To them, the modest sacrifice in absolute autonomy has been offset by a chance to influence policy, even if it is done in a cooperative and incremental fashion.[36] For example, the BSIA's original secretary-general was a relatively effective voice for his members, but his success was partly due to his previous position in the municipal government. During the 1999 round of elections, the membership kept him from retiring because of his utility. When he stepped aside, his replacement also had worked in the municipal government.[37] In sum, the inverted-U-shaped relationship found between autonomy and influence in steel associations applies to software associations as well. A high degree of autonomy for domestic software associations is a prerequisite to being advocates for their members, but absolute autonomy is an impediment to effective representation because the government will not accept them.[38]

The political environment also affects the style in which foreign associations promote their members' interests. While independent of government control, foreign associations have to be careful not to antagonize the government, and thus they also tend to stress cooperation and quiet diplomacy just as domestic associations do. In addition to hosting their own meetings, where they invite government officials to meet with their members, they also work with Chinese associations and research institutes when possible. And they frame their positions as "win-win" for foreign and domestic concerns, a stance which is plausible since foreign software makers have an identifiable ally in the domestic software industry.[39]

The proliferation in the number and level of activity of software associations is clearly tied to the industry's economic characteristics. The need for cooperation on business activities helps facilitate joint behavior in associations among all software companies. It is the prevalence of domestic and foreign private companies in the industry, though, that helps bridge that link. Interviews demonstrate that domestic and foreign private companies are relatively more interested and active in software associations than state-owned companies.

Though far from unanimous, private firms tend to be more active in associations, even initiating some, and see associations as useful in forwarding both their interests and those of the industry as a whole. Private firms are more disposed than their state-owned counterparts to use software associations to obtain information or criticize or propose ideas on policy. This relationship seems to hold regardless of the size of private firms. The large financial management software leader UFSoft, which is active in policy debates, was one of the chief forces behind the creation of the ABM Sub-Association. Federal and SunTendy were the chief industry advocates behind the creation in 1995 of the China Software Alliance, a CSIA sub-association that focuses on intellectual property rights.[40] Even private firms that interact considerably less with the government than UFSoft tend to see associations as a source of information, albeit not the only source. Despite having only ten employees, multimedia software designer Haojie joined CSIA and has attended meetings of another association in the hopes of learning more about government policies.[41]

Perhaps most intriguing is a Beijing-based maker of document digitization software (akin to Adobe's Acrobat but geared specifically for Chinese-language documents). Despite its small size and limited resources, in 1997 this private company began organizing a "software salon," an informal gathering among software makers. The monthly meetings typically have brought together mid-level employees to discuss a range of topics, including venture capital, electronic commerce, and case studies of successful and failed software companies. Although government officials rarely attend, the salons regularly discuss policy issues.[42]

Private enterprises are not completely satisfied with software associations. Not surprisingly, their strongest criticism is directed at the CSIA. Because of its bureaucratic dominance, most software firms would agree with two company executives who said that CSIA "cannot represent its members" and that "it is better to call it the government than an association." The CSIA "does not understand the industry" and thus "is not of any real utility to us." Several admitted that if the CSIA disappeared it would have no affect on their business or the industry.[43] By contrast, to the extent some were disaffected with other software associations, they claimed the associations were not appendages of the state but of *other* members. As the discussion of setting standards below shows, such a charge was made with regard to the Accounting and Business Management Sub-Association.[44]

Private software firms were also critical of transsectoral associations such as the All-China Federation of Industry and Commerce and the Private Entreprises Association (PEA). The smaller private entrepreneurs did no more than pay their annual dues, which they perceived as a tax, to the PEA. One challenged the ACFIC's image as a chamber of commerce representing small and private businesses. He correctly noted that many of its leaders are descendants of former capitalists from the pre-1949 days. He interprets this fact to mean that these leaders' interests differ from his company's. He concluded, "there's no real association for small businesses."[45]

Most of the foreign software firms see participation in international associations that have offices in China as useful. Adobe, a global giant in graphics software, has had a very small contingent in China and thus has been reliant on the Business Software Alliance to fight for anti-piracy measures.[46] And Kalsoft actively participates in the Shanghai-based American Chamber of Commerce. Foreign firms have less praise for domestic associations. Those that join local associations do so largely for public relations purposes. None of those interviewed for this study actively participate in the China Association of Enterprises with Foreign Investment (CAEFI), and some executives who are responsible for government affairs did not even know if they were members. Praise, or at least grudging respect, was given strictly to some of CSIA's sub-associations, in particular the ABM and the China Software Alliance.

In comparison to their private cousins, as we have seen in other sectors, state-owned software firms are consistently unenthusiastic participants in associations. Although they are often in multiple associations and even hold positions as vice chairmen in many of them, their participation is by and large formalistic. These firms' senior executives rarely attend association meetings, preferring to send lieutenants in their place. "They do not have any utility at all," summed up one senior executive.[47] Many admitted that they participated in associations strictly for public relations purposes.

The one exception among state-owned software firms interviewed for this study was Tiko, a maker of public information terminals, or kiosks, that are placed in office lobbies, airports, and train stations. Following ABM's lead, in late 1998 Tiko organized fourteen other kiosk makers to set up the CSIA Touch Systems Sub-Association (*chumo xitong fenhui*). Their goal was to bring order to what they saw as a chaotic yet burgeoning market. But hiding behind Tiko's state-owned veneer was a private firm that "wore a red hat." Tiko was founded in 1997 as a joint venture between the state-owned Beijing Number 1 Computer Factory and the private company Taigu. Beijing Number 1 was the majority shareholder, but Taigu really ran Tiko and was the source of Tiko's interest in an association.[48] But in late 1998, Tiko was bought out by two state-owned enterprises, including Capital Iron and Steel (*Shougang*). Taigu ceded control to managers sent from Shougang, a large SOE with extensive government contacts. Although the new management expressed interest in the association, their commitment proved temporary, as the Touch Systems Sub-Association appears to have stopped operations in 2002.[49] Tiko's change of behavior is another sign that ownership affects interest in associational activity.

## Other Signs of Pluralism

Although most software associations are vigorous advocates for their members, direct interaction with the government is still a critical way by which companies learn about and try to influence policies. Software associations on the whole are more useful than those in steel or consumer electronics, but they primarily supplement one-on-one contact on policy issues. This depth of interaction, modestly supplemented by a large number of semi-independent trade journals, has made the policy process more transparent.[50] The prevalence of direct interaction on public-policy issues geared to promote firms' interests, like the association system, is also more consistent with pluralism than corporatism or clientelism.

As in the other sectors, there is variation in the depth of firms' involvement with the government, but the pattern is closer to consumer electronics than to steel. Just as in consumer electronics, firms of all ownership forms and nationalities interact intensively with the government; and larger firms tend to have greater contact with the government on policy. (In steel, large SOEs have the most contact with government on policy.) Software, though, is distinguished in that the benchmark for what constitutes a "large" firm is far lower and somewhat more elastic than in steel or consumer electronics.

In contrast to the steel industry (where there are no large domestic private companies), state-owned, domestic private, and foreign private firms all deeply interact with the government on policy. This is surprising given the legacy of central planning and the state's continued role in personnel decisions of state-owned enterprises. In fact, CS&S president Tang Min is married to Chen Chong, the mid-level MII official who also is vice chairman of the China Software Industry Association. Despite this history and such links, the majority of interaction of large state-owned software firms like CS&S and Founder with the government increasingly resembles that of large private firms, domestic or foreign, than it does small state-owned enterprises.

Large private firms contact the national government as often as Founder and CS&S. UFSoft and Microsoft are in touch with some part of the local or national government several times a day, not just to sell their software, but to discuss policy problems.[51] Microsoft's former general manager for China, Duh Jiabin, emphasized the importance of having the Chinese government understand Microsoft and vice versa, something that requires constant attention.[52] For state-owned and private firms alike, regular interaction with the government is an integral component of their broader business strategy.[53]

Large firms of all types regularly interface with a broad swath of ministries and departments, which have included MII, the Ministry of Science and Technology, the National Copyright Administration (NCA), the State Economic and Trade Commission (SETC), and the State Taxation Administration. (As was the case in steel and consumer electronics, software firms pay only limited attention to people's congresses at the national or local levels, since the legislature less regularly passes laws that clearly affect the firms' interests.) And because of their prominence, these firms have access to senior officials in these ministries as well as the occasional opportunity to meet more senior political leaders.[54] A look at the pictures that adorn their offices and their brochures shows that many Politburo members have visited Founder and UFSoft. Large foreign firms use the visits to China of their own high-level executives as occasions to meet with China's elite.[55] In each of his visits China, Microsoft co-founder Bill Gates has been hosted by at least one member of the Politburo Standing Committee.[56]

Software firms regularly interact with officialdom in both face-to-face encounters and through reports and other correspondence. Not surprisingly, officials sometimes meet with just one or two larger software firms in private encounters or public events. Besides meetings strictly focused on policy, the larger software firms all invite officials to their press conferences and product announcements. Even though officials usually can have only a very limited effect on a product's development or sales, their presence and occasional remarks lend an air of official endorsement. For example, medium-sized Kingsoft used just this tactic when it released its word processing software, WPS2000, in early 1999. It invited officials from various ministries to its press conferences; the officials then openly praised Kingsoft's product and obliquely criticized its main competitor, Microsoft. The announcements were followed by private banquets in which the product and broader policy issues were discussed.[57] Kingsoft's intent was to gain sympathy and support by portraying its software as the Chinese challenger to Microsoft Word. Since then, specialists and domestic companies who do not cooperate in business with Microsoft have drawn on nationalist sentiment in meetings with officials to promote the Linux operating system as a viable substitute for Windows.[58]

Whether in person or via written documents, larger software companies and the government discuss the entire spectrum of issues that affect the industry. Firms update officials about their products and give their views on industry trends, and they also try to learn about the state of policy deliberations, offering their own criticisms and suggestions. Founder, UFSoft, and Microsoft all take a very proactive posture in trying to advance their agendas on a regular basis with many parts of the local and national governments simultaneously.

The smaller the firm, the more circumscribed their involvement with government. Medium-sized firms typically meet mid-level ministry and senior municipal officials. Whereas Founder displays photos of Jiang Zemin's visits, the medium-sized Tiko trumpets visits by the Beijing vice mayor and other local officials to their production facilities, while Kalsoft can be proud of its participation in meetings with Shanghai's leaders. A smaller firm said even if it wanted to influence the government, there were no established channels for small firms to do so, directly or via associations.[59] The smallest firms' only contact with the government at any level was the moment they first registered and each month when they pay taxes. Executives from most smaller firms never considered the possibility that they—or any firm—could influence government policy. One summed up government-business relations as those of "the decider and the decidee" (*juedingzhe he beijuedingzhe*). He saw meetings not as honest exchanges but as window dressing to cloak pre-made government decisions with the veil of corporate support.[60]

As in other industries, on policy matters firms typically interact with government agencies, not Chinese Communist Party (CCP) organizations. (Senior leaders' meetings with the visiting heads of multinational corporations and their tours of companies are usually public relations events.) This practice applies to state-owned, private, and foreign firms alike. The head of a large state-owned software company, who is also a party member, and a foreign company executive both said the CCP is important to China politically, but they seek out officials based on their government posts, not their party positions.[61] One private company executive said that a party official might be helpful in a firm gaining a business contract, but not in dealing with broader policy issues.[62] Another private company salesman was more adamant. Although a party member himself, he would never inquire whether a potential client, in or out of government, was a party member, and he likewise would not mention his own party affiliation. "That would be like telling someone whether or not I was wearing underwear," he said. "No one cares, and I certainly would not tell them."[63]

The development of associations and in-depth direct contact on policy matters are the most significant markers that have made government-business relations in software more closely approach pluralism than they do in other sectors. These aspects have been modestly supplemented by the wide coverage of the industry in the print media. In addition to the standard ministry-run trade newspaper, *China Electronics News*, and staid technology journals, there are a host of newsletters, tabloids, and magazines. Many of these trade publications owe their existence to International Data Group (IDG), a global publishing and consulting company based in Massachusetts. Since launching its first joint venture publication in 1980, IDG has partnered with MII in setting up at least twelve information industry periodicals that have national circulation and are estimated to have almost 20 million readers.[64] Most of these publications have launched Internet editions. They carry up-to-date news about the Chinese and global markets and have a relatively open and broad discussion of domestic and international policy issues. Though the coverage of process is dwarfed by reports on substance, this media can be a useful supplement to large companies with extensive ties to the government or at least provide basic news on industry policy trends to smaller companies with far less official access. While not as focused on policy as trade publications in the United States, the information industry media in China has modestly increased the transparency of the policy process, moving the software industry slightly further in the direction of pluralism.

## The "Normalization" of Relationships

In addition to making associations more relevant and lowering the size threshold by which firms have significant communication with the government over policy, the economics of the industry have also affected the role of personal relations and the importance of displaying closeness with the government. Clientelism strictly defined (a sustained pattern of symbiotic ties between a state patron and nonstate client based on personal ties) does not characterize any of the sectors studied for this project. Yet many firms see fostering a good rapport with the government as significant in helping them resolve firm-specific problems. In the software industry, though, there are signs that some firms have de-emphasized maintaining harmonious ties with the government in general or with particular potential patrons.

Software firms of various ownership forms have used many of the same tactics as their fellow businessmen in steel and consumer electronics to nurture ties with the government. They typically invite officials to press conferences and banquets. Some private companies have accepted investment from state-owned companies, believing they could use the investors' links to government to their benefit. Executives from larger state-owned and private firms have accepted positions in people's congresses or the Chinese People's Political Consultative Conference, a government advisory body made up of people from different social groups. To reduce the cultural distance in their relationship with government, almost all of the foreign software firms interviewed for this study have had ethnic Chinese as their local general managers.[65]

Perhaps the epitome of using connections and emphasizing one's closeness to the government is reflected in the financial software maker UFSoft. Prior to founding the company, Wang Wenjing worked for five years in the finance division of the State Council's Regulatory Bureau for Organizational Affairs (*jiguan shiwu guanliju*). There he helped draft the central government's administrative accounting system and establish computerization standards for that system. The experience gave Wang an understanding of the accounting business, but, even more, it was invaluable in helping him develop important relationships with the Ministry of Finance and other national government offices. These ties were critical when he started his company in 1988 and sought government agencies as customers. Wang has been candid about the importance of what he calls "relationship cultivation and management" (*guanxi yingxiao*) in making UFSoft successful.[66] In addition to developing ties with various bureaucracies, he himself has accepted government appointments, in 1993 becoming a member of the Beijing People's Political Consultative Conference and in 1998 a deputy to the Ninth National People's Congress (a post that he kept in the Tenth National People's Congress, which commenced in 2003). His powers as a deputy are extremely limited; and while he has been able to be an advocate for the industry as a whole, he has not been able to use the positions to directly benefit his company. Yet the prestige afforded him by holding these seats certainly cannot hurt UFSoft's business opportunities.

But UFSoft's behavior is not the rule. A counter-example is that of an equally large private financial software firm based outside Beijing. Like Wang, its president worked in the government for several years before founding his company in the early 1990s. As the firm grew, the municipal government began to court him and invited him to meet with vice mayors and people's congress members. And in 1998 he became a member of a district-level people's political consultative conference. Despite attempts to gain his allegiance, he has maintained an arms-length relationship with government. Except when there is a clear need to discuss his firm's situation or a policy matter, he refrains from interacting with officialdom. He has refused meetings with local politicians, and in meetings he has attended, he has been outwardly critical of government policies. And he rarely attends sessions of the local consultative body to which he was appointed, finding it a waste of time.[67]

This company is symbolic of the decline in the currency of personal relationships for promoting a company's interests. Good relations with the government are significant if one wants to influence policy, and all the larger software companies are familiar with officials in the various bureaucracies that regulate their industry. But many software firms believe that the utility of close relations with the government is declining and, in fact, may be harmful to a company.[68] One executive stressed that companies often invite regulators to press conferences and act deferentially toward officials because this is expected behavior, but that it does not imply hidden favoritism on either side's part.[69]

The "normalization" of personal relations in the software industry owes much to the influx of private and foreign firms, the high degree of competition, and the high-tech nature of the product. Inferior software immediately has a negative effect on customers' operations, and with so many alternatives (except for operating systems) switching software is quite feasible. These factors have led to a more inclusive discussion of software-related policies that are not as easily manipulated by a single firm or official.

To BETTER APPRECIATE how the software industry and the state interact on public policy, the remainder of the chapter examines three policy issues: the excessive burden of the value-added tax on software companies, weak copyright protection, and the use of standards as a market barrier in the financial management software business. The three case studies highlight, respectively, the potential influence of associations and company lobbying on specific industrial policies, industry's subsidiary yet expanding role in shaping broader legislation, and the difficulty companies have manipulating associations at the expense of other members.

## The VAT: Revaluing the Industry

Over the first decade and a half of the Reform era the Chinese government's tax receipts dwindled substantially, from 31.2 percent of GDP in 1978 to 12.6 percent in 1993.[70] To stem this tide and shift a greater proportion of tax receipts to the central government, in 1994 China introduced a major overhaul of the tax system. One important component was the implementation of a 17 percent value-added tax (VAT, *zengzhishui*) on the sale of all goods.[71] While perhaps an important innovation from a national perspective, the tax placed a unique burden on software developers because of how it is calculated. The seller of a good is charged 17 percent of the difference between their sale price and the costs incurred in purchasing the inputs. Though not specified in the regulation, in practice only material inputs are counted as part of production costs. Given that the cost of producing software is primarily creativity, an intangible asset, the effective VAT that software developers have paid is far greater than that for ordinary manufacturers.[72]

China's software industry in the early 1990s was young and certainly could not derail such a wide sweeping change of the tax code. Aside from particular relief given to foreign-invested firms, the government initially made a point not to provide preferential treatment to any industries. Despite the government's declaration, the software industry was unsatisfied and began to mobilize in opposition. This was an issue that united all software firms, state-owned and private, domestic and foreign. Over the following years, medium- and large-sized software firms of all ownership stripes complained vociferously to various parts of the national government, principally MII, the Ministry of Science and Technology (known as the Science and Technology Commission until March 1998), the Ministry of Finance, and the State Taxation Administration. CSIA, the regional associations, and even at least one issue-specific association (ABM) organized meetings with these government agencies, met with officials on their own, and wrote numerous reports. They collectively argued that the tax was unfair to an industry that was supposedly critical to China's modernization and that because of the industry's small size, an exemption or reduction would not have a significant impact on the government's revenue stream.[73]

As the years passed, the industry believed that the State Taxation Administration would never relent. By late 1998, firms and associations saw tax relief as a distant and fading hope, leaving some to complain that the dialogue with the government was superficial.[74] Some also grumbled about the lack of association initiative. But to almost everyone's surprise, in June 1999 the tax agency notified associations that it had decided that software firms in Beijing would have their VAT slashed from 17 percent to 6 percent.[75] Six months later the tax break was enacted nationally.[76]

The larger software firms deserve a great deal of the credit for finally persuading the government to enact the tax reduction. Without their regular criticism, there would have been no incentive on the part of government to make the changes. Officials at MII and the Ministry of Science and Technology, which also represented the industry in discussions within the government, emphasized that firms protested regularly, spurring their own activism.[77] In addition to the regular interaction with ministries, Wang Wenjing and Wang Xuan, the leader of Founder, used their positions in the National People's Congress to call for greater government support of high technology, including software. Even though they lacked the authority to enact changes themselves, they raised the visibility of the issue.[78]

As significant as larger firms' activism was in raising the stakes of the issue, the software associations shaped the outcome as well. In late 1997, CSIA and BSIA met with the Science and Technology Commission and others and persuaded them of the need for the tax break. In the following months, the associations offered alternative plans, including counting 70 percent of a software product's retail price as the input cost or reducing the VAT to 5 percent. Once the State Taxation Administration accepted the 6 percent rate, BSIA came up with the plan of how to determine which firms and which products could be eligible to receive the tax break. After the policy change was announced, firms praised the associations for their efforts.[79] Just as the failures to enforce price floors in steel and consumer electronics hurt the reputation of associations in those sectors, successes such as the reduction in the VAT imbue the software associations with new legitimacy in the eyes of their members, suggesting associations' role in future policy debates will likely rise.[80]

Tax relief on its own would not change the fortunes of the industry as a whole, but it likely has helped most firms to a moderate degree. Not all firms were satisfied with the reduction, arguing that they should be exempted entirely from the VAT.[81] However, in the late summer of 1999 the number of newly founded software firms in Beijing jumped dramatically, and many existing companies moved to Beijing from other regions.[82] By dint of their actions, firms showed how much they welcomed the change.[83]

The VAT reduction episode suggests that business-government relations in the software sector are structured in a pluralist fashion. Firms of varying ownership forms and associations working in concert and individually all repeatedly argued for a revision of the tax code, and they did so by focusing on the merits of their position. Although larger firms were the ones with access, large and small companies benefited from the policy change. And so in this instance, the industry as a whole gained from the actions of a few.

## Copyright Protection: Joining the Fight

As quickly as China's software industry has grown over the last decade, the consensus is that the industry is smaller and less profitable than it should be.[84] The best indicator that the sector is stunted is that in China hardware sales outnumber software sales by a ten-to-one margin, whereas globally software sales are 22 percent greater than hardware sales.[85] By far the greatest impediment to the expansion of the industry is the rampant violation of software developers' copyrights. Throughout the 1990s and into the 2000s, pirated software accounted for over 90 percent of the software installed in computers in China.[86] The lost income from piracy to individual software companies has been staggering. The vast majority of Internet browsing software produced by SRS, the multimedia software developed by Haojie, and the word processing software developed by Kingsoft that is installed in computers are pirated copies for which these companies have received no payment.[87] Many foreign software makers fare no better, and piracy has kept some from making a greater commitment to sell and produce in the Chinese market.[88]

The primary impetus to counter piracy and establish a regime for intellectual property rights has come from abroad, mainly from the U.S. government and the World Trade Organization (WTO), both of whom have been heavily pressured by large multinationals.[89] In the 1990s, China signed three memoranda of understanding (MOU) with the United States that stipulated steps the Chinese government should take to improve protection of intellectual property rights. U.S. pressure was instrumental in having China accede to the Berne Universal Copyright Convention and to commit to revising its domestic copyright laws to be consistent with the WTO's Agreement on Trade-Related Aspects of Intellectual Property Rights (TRIPS).[90] Tellingly, China issued updated versions of the Copyright Law and the Computer Software Protection Regulations in late 2001, just prior to its WTO accession.

While international political pressure has been critical, the software industry in China has also played a visible role in promoting change. Domestic firms have acted as a group and individually, and they have also cooperated with foreign software makers and associations. In 1995, twelve domestic companies, mostly private, formed the China Software Alliance, partly modeled on the antipiracy association based in the United States, the Business Software Alliance.[91] Although CSA has had an extremely limited budget and only two regular employees, it has been involved in a variety of activities to promote popular awareness of copyright issues, enforcement of existing laws, and changes to existing laws and policies. CSA has written newspapers articles as well as encouraged its members to do so.[92] On the enforcement side, since 1995 CSA and BSA have jointly run a national hotline for people to report piracy (it has annually received one thousand leads).[93] And CSA has cooperated with the software retailer Federal to make the latter's stores double as "observation posts" (*guanchazhan*) that are supposed to give regular reports on piracy.[94] On the policy side, CSA and its member firms have regularly hosted or attended meetings with the various government agencies responsible for enforcement and policy making, including the State Administration for Industry and Commerce (SAIC), MII, the National Copyright Administration, the State Council, and the

National People's Congress. Through these meetings and CSA's reports, the association and member firms have pushed for revisions to the Copyright Law and other relevant regulations.

Larger domestic firms individually have taken some steps to promote software protection. Many have established internal controls to ensure that programs are kept secret, and some have hired lawyers that specialize in intellectual property rights law to help them register their software and represent them in legal disputes.[95] And they have regularly complained to the local and national offices of the National Copyright Administration and others about the laxity of enforcement and weaknesses of existing laws. UFSoft's Wang Wenjing, Founder's Wang Xuan, and Legend's Liu Chuanzhi jointly issued a resolution at the second plenum of the Ninth National People's Congress in March 1999, calling for increased protection against piracy.[96] Kingsoft's founder, Qiu Bojun, has been the most consistent public voice among domestic software producers for enforcing copyrights and has repeatedly admonished authorities, saying, "The greatest support the government can give us is to stop copyright piracy, so that we have room to survive and grow."[97]

As active as domestic firms have been, by far the most active firm on copyright issues has been Microsoft.[98] Working through its own staff and via associations, Microsoft has engineered a three-pronged strategy to "educate" Chinese society and government to accept its interpretation of intellectual property rights norms, to make the government enforce existing laws, and to lobby for passage of stricter laws. In addition to supporting BSA and CSA, the company has: (1) set up training programs in universities and certification programs for software firms that distribute Microsoft products or develop Windows-compatible applications;[99] (2) signed memoranda of understanding and cooperation with various regional governments in which the latter pledge to use legal software and cooperate with Microsoft in developing their information networks;[100] (3) sued several domestic firms for copyright violations;[101] (4) provided evidence of piracy to the government in the hope it would take administrative measures against pirates; and (5) offered specific suggestions regarding changes in the Copyright Law and the Computer Software Protection Regulations to drafters in several national agencies.[102]

According to industry and government sources directly involved in the drafting process, industry lobbying certainly affected the substance of the revised Computer Software Protection Regulations and the Copyright Law.[103] The China Software Alliance persuaded the government to revise the separate regulation protecting computer software rather than eliminate it by absorbing certain elements into the Copyright Law, as the National Copyright Administration had originally preferred.[104] The CSA also convinced drafters to add clauses to the Copyright Law that prohibit purchasers from trying to decipher software that makers had encrypted to prevent piracy, as well as to add language requiring that written works placed on the Internet include information on the author, publisher, and date of a publication.[105] Domestic and foreign industry persuaded drafters of the Copyright Law to improve administrative enforcement by easing seizure of suspected pirated items. And because of lobbying, the new laws make private end-users legally liable for unauthorized use of software, not just commercial users as is required by TRIPS.[106]

Such influence represents a significant change from the early 1990s, when the original Copyright Law and Computer Software Protection Regulations were enacted. On the other hand, one should not overstate the power of the industry, particularly on the domestic side. Like most associations, CSA took a very conciliatory approach and refrained from openly criticizing the various government agencies responsible for cracking down on piracy and drafting the new copyright law. Some of its meetings were held at the request of the government, not its members. And because the National People's Congress's deliberations were secret, the CSA, other associations, and software firms were unaware that the draft was running into major difficulties because of an unrelated dispute and was actually withdrawn from the NPC and sent back to the NCA for further revisions in the summer of 1999.[107] Without the pressure of the U.S. government and China's impending accession into the WTO, the laws may never have been revised, or at least not so fully.[108] It was the external pressure that created the opening for industry to have a voice in the first place. The domestic software industry has been a subsidiary, albeit growing, force for change.

Just as important, revising the laws was just one step of the process. Because of the many interests in society and government that benefit from pirated software, enforcement has proven much more difficult. Industry is just beginning to learn how to use the administrative enforcement procedures to their benefit. As such, the sweeping legal changes may wind up being smaller victories than they first appear.

## Standards: Erecting and Dismantling Barriers to Entry

The story of video compact discs (VCD) showed that standards can be the critical issue that shapes an industry and thus directly affects firms' interests. The same is no less true in software, where firms struggle to make their products the de facto standard in some niche. And because Chinese is a character-based language, in China (and other East Asian countries) there are also standards for character input methods and for their graphic representation. A less mentioned area is that software designs are supposed to conform to standards originally devised for noncomputer processes, such as in manufacturing or business management. Regardless of the actual issue, standards can bring order to a market by keeping out poor products, but they can also be used as unfair market barriers.

As mentioned, CSIA's Accounting and Business Management Subassociation has drawn praise from various circles as one of the most active associations in the industry. But like the other software associations, ABM is not fully autonomous. While the initiative for its founding and financing both came from its member firms, ABM's secretary-general has been Xu Jiangang, up until 1998 an official with the Computerization Section in the Accounting Division of the Ministry of Finance. As the person that ran ABM's day-to-day operations, Xu simultaneously wore two hats, one as the industry's primary regulator, the other as the industry's chief representative.

What made the potential for a conflict of interest particularly high was the sector's efforts to apply rigorous standards to accounting software. Starting in the late 1980s, the Ministry of Finance tried to institute new standards for the accounting system used by government departments and firms through the country as well as to promote the move away from pen and paper to the use of software. In 1989 the ministry began to formally regulate accounting software. Following discussions with existing firms, it instituted a formal "appraisal system" (*pingshen zhidu*) to ensure that domestically sold accounting software conformed to the Ministry of Finance's general accounting guidelines. In response to the growth in the number of software firms and changes to the Accounting Law, the regulations were substantially revised in 1994. The new regulations stated that software approved by the national Ministry of Finance's Accounting Division could be sold throughout the country, whereas software approved by a provincial accounting bureau could only be sold within that jurisdiction. Not only were the regulations directed at producers, but they also encouraged governments and firms to purchase only software that had been approved for their local market.[109]

When ABM was founded the following year, it took great interest in the appraisal system, ostensibly believing that it was a systematic way to weed out small firms that develop mediocre products sold at cut-rate prices. Although the ministry maintained its authority to approve or reject software, Xu's dual position made ABM integral to this process. By early 1998 at least three dozen firms' software products were approved by the ministry to be sold nationally. However, some companies with software of equal or better quality had not been approved, raising the possibility that the ministry and ABM had shown favoritism. In particular, some firms charged that the ABM was "the puppet of UFSoft" and Xu its chief assistant.[110]

As noted, UFSoft's Wang Wenjing has openly stressed developing personal relations to promote his business interests. Wang himself had participated in the work on accounting standards while in government, and he continued his discussions with the Ministry of Finance after he started UFSoft. Some other firms insist that the ministry, led by Xu, intentionally rejected their applications year after year to help UFSoft protect its market share, in 1998 estimated at 40 percent. They and others cite evidence that Xu has been materially rewarded for his efforts.[111] Stonewalled in Beijing, these firms had to obtain approval province by province, a time-consuming and not always successful process.

ABM's history suggests that an association borne out of industry initiative can become manipulated by individual members at the expense of others. The irony is that the association's greater autonomy and activism made it more susceptible to clientelism than the more official and staid CSIA. However, clientelist relations are only as stable as their patrons. In mid-1998, following the national government's restructuring that spring, the office that Xu Jiangang led was merged into another, and half of its staff, including Xu, were dismissed. And in April

1999, the Ministry of Finance decided to eliminate the appraisal system altogether. It appears that much of the impetus for Xu's firing and the system's cancellation lays with domestic firms, who complained about Xu and the approval system to the new head of the Ministry of Finance's Accounting Division (Xu's boss). This final twist indicates that vigorous market competition makes clientelist relationships more difficult to sustain.[112]

## Conclusion

Business-government relations in the software industry are distinctive. True, China's software associations are not as independent and aggressive as those in the United States, and the process behind the consideration of policies related to software is still not entirely transparent. But within the context of China—in comparison to other sectors, particularly steel—the recent politics of the software industry represents a significant contrast. Its associations are relatively independent, voluntary, and decidedly flat in their organization, and they have no jurisdictional monopolies. Although some people in associations view some form of ties to the government as helpful—such as a secretary-general with former government experience—software associations that seek to influence policy also value the independence they can reasonably garner. Besides these associations, companies have extensive direct contact with officialdom, which, when supplemented by a coterie of young, semi-independent trade publications, have increased transparency and created opportunities for influence. Software comes closer to the pluralist framework than any of the other sectors in this study.

The ways in which software companies have interacted with the Chinese government have been heavily affected by the industry's distinctive economic characteristics. High knowledge requirements, low economies of scale, strong economic incentives for interfirm cooperation, and the predominance of domestic and foreign private companies have fueled the growth of more robust software associations. The importance of ownership is reflected in the fact that private companies, irrespective of size, are relatively more disposed toward taking an active interest and role in associations than their SOE counterparts. Size is a much more important factor in determining the depth of direct interaction companies have with the government on policy issues, but size is relative. A large software firm like UFSoft with significant access to the national bureaucracy would be considered a small steel or television maker and be left out of policy circles. In addition, as was demonstrated in the case of accounting software standards, the very competitive nature of China's software industry has made it more difficult for patron-client ties to determine economic or policy outcomes.

The industry's economics have led to business alliances between foreign and domestic companies that in turn have created the foundation for common policy positions, which was visible in the case of intellectual property rights protection. These ties give weight to foreign firms' stated position that their policy preferences also benefit the domestic software industry. As a consequence, shared interests have made it more difficult to adopt and implement policies that discriminate against foreign software. In the past few years, the government has issued several documents ordering government agencies to purchase only domestically made software, which is part of the broader effort to promote Linux and wean from dependence on Microsoft. However, the likelihood of genuine implementation is low because most domestic software applications are written for the Windows platform. Not only would Microsoft, Oracle, and other foreign firms be shut out from the potentially lucrative procurement market, so would much of domestic industry, unless it switched platforms, something it does not seem interested in doing. If the government does forge ahead with such a policy, one should expect that much of domestic industry will oppose the step just as strongly as Microsoft would.[113]

The industry's business structure and the resulting pattern of interaction likewise have had clear implications for influence. As in the steel and consumer electronics sectors, larger software companies have had the most influence on policy matters. The imbalance in direct access has ensured large firms' disproportionate role in policy. What is distinctive about software is that a foreign company, by dint of its mass and critical place in the industry, has had the most policy influence of any single software firm. This turn of events has occurred despite officials' regular carping about Microsoft and efforts to direct business to domestic competitors.

The growth of associations has also given the industry more influence than it otherwise would yield, helping it to achieve some policy victories that have benefited all software firms, large and small. That said, even with relatively more vibrant associations, the software industry's influence should not be overstated. CSA and others in the industry helped shape the copyright legislation, but most of the laws' content and its path to passage were the result of far larger economic and political forces. China's domestic software industry would benefit from the proposed changes, but its diminutive stature limited its lobbying powers. However, despite continued high rates of piracy, China's software industry has grown at a fast pace. Continued expansion combined with active associations should eventually make the industry more powerful in national policy debates.

# ~ 6

## Conclusion:
## China's Political Economies

Open up an American newspaper and find a story about China, and it will not take long to be reminded that the Chinese government is authoritarian. Stories about leadership changes made behind closed doors, human rights abuses, and controls on the media all feed the image of a strong, undemocratic state that is not consistently or systematically responsive to societal pressures. As accurate as these individual stories of China are, this book's exploration into the politics of business in China demonstrates that they present far from the full picture. Spurred by marketization, companies—domestic and foreign, private and state-owned—are involved in a tug of war with the government and one another to gain policy advantages that help their bottom lines. Their efforts have yielded victories on scores of issues, including trade, taxes, intellectual property rights protection, technical standards, and competition. Although individual fingerprints are sometimes hard to find, there are fewer and fewer industry policies that have not been touched by industry's hands. Surely, the notions that a strong leader dominates Chinese politics or that the bureaucracy controls the scene no longer capture critical elements of the political process.

At the same time, the politics of China is not of a piece. The market economy and its attendant regulatory foundation have spurred lobbying across industries, but the shape and consequences of business activism vary widely. The comparison conducted in earlier chapters of

160

firms' interaction with the government in the steel, consumer electronics, and software industries also shows that companies' economic circumstances affect whether they lobby at all and, if so, how and to what effect. So, while it is important to recognize the basic fact that the Chinese government is now subject to greater nonstate pressures than ever before, it is equally critical to notice that such pressure is not exerted evenly or similarly across the economy.

This chapter begins by drawing together the strands of analysis developed in the case studies of the steel, consumer electronics, and software sectors to demonstrate exactly how the political behavior of companies are affected by their respective economic circumstances. This comparison suggests the need to revise generally accepted conceptions of Chinese politics, and it also adds weight to the perspective seen in the broader political economy debate about the critical effects that economic factors have on political action. Thus, this study offers a corrective to the recent trend in political economy scholarship to focus primarily on the importance of national political institutions. Countries do not just have one political economy, but multiple political *economies*.

The discussion then shifts to considering the implications of these findings for how we view state-society relations and the policy-making process in China. This book both confirms and challenges earlier findings on China and, more significantly, offers a new approach toward unifying these two issue areas, which to date have been analyzed separately. This new strategy could be applied to other countries as well. After next looking at the implications of this study for China's democratization, the discussion concludes with a consideration of the implications of two alternative reform packages for associations, one akin to corporatism, the other consistent with pluralism. The central point of the analysis is that both reform options are problematic.

## Linking Economics, Interaction, and Influence

This book's central focus concerns the degree to which economic factors shape the ways in which business and government interact and the effect that such interaction in turn has on businesses' relative influence on policy. While the research debate that inspired this study's design focuses on the first of these two questions because of the consequences for countries' quality of governance and economic performance, the implications for relative political influence are equally visible. Drawing on the evidence presented in earlier chapters, we will first clarify the link between economic contexts and patterns of interaction and then explain the consequences for political influence.

Previous scholarship that compares capitalist states is divided over the relative effect of economic and political factors on patterns of government-business relations. One of the primary criteria used to measure the relative effect of economic and political factors is sectoral convergence: are business-government relations in the same sector across countries more or less similar than government-business relations across economically diverse sectors within the same country? While some have pointed to evidence of sectoral convergence (such as the chemical industry in Western Europe and the dairy industry globally), others have found that government-business relations in the same sectors in different countries are not as similar as different sectors in their own respective countries.[1]

If sectoral convergence was the only yardstick by which to judge the influence of economic factors, then much of the evidence in this study, when compared to research on the same sectors in other countries, would likely point toward the relative weight of political institutions and official norms. China's steel industry has not been organized like the steel industry in Japan, where a strong association (the Japan Iron and Steel Import-Export Association) has helped organize price and production cartels since at least the 1960s. Nor are China's steel associations as politically active as the American Iron and Steel Institute, the primary association for U.S. manufacturers. Similarly, the electronics associations in Japan and Western Europe have been more instrumental in mediating relations between their companies and governments and in facilitating self-regulation than either the China Video Association (CVA) or the China Audio Association (CAA).[2] China's software industry is the only one whose political organization may approach that of industries in other countries. The autonomy and activism of its associations and the relative proactiveness of its firms bare some similarities to the American and Indian experiences. But this comparison is based only on anecdotal data.[3] There has yet to be a systematic study of the organization of software associations and other methods of lobbying in the United States or elsewhere.

Although potentially telling, the existence or lack of cross-national convergence may be highly misleading. Besides differences in political institutions, countries' economic conditions also vary, more broadly and at the sectoral level. Sectors across countries do share some economic characteristics, but they also have traits that are specific to a country, creating the likelihood that it is political institutions *and* these economic differences that are creating the divergent patterns of government-business relations in the same sectors. For example, the steel industry has high economies of scale and is vulnerable to price fluctuations everywhere, but China's steel industry is distinct from Japan's in that it is dominated by state-owned enterprises (SOEs) and has a much lower concentration level. These economic circumstances can affect steel companies' interest in and ability to maintain associations. Moreover, politics can also be a source for the convergence of political economies, as is demonstrated in the example of East Asian countries being forced to make concessions regarding domestic institutions and industry governance to the International Monetary Fund and other lenders in the late 1990s to receive economic aid. In short, since convergence (or divergence) can be caused by both economic and political factors, one should not conflate lack of convergence with the irrelevance of economic factors (or divergence with the strength of political ones). To minimize the problems that can be introduced by comparing across different political institutions, this study has examined government-business relations in multiple sectors within one country. By holding political institutions constant, one can more safely attribute variation found across different types of companies and sectors to economic factors.

In some regards, China's political institutions and official norms do shape government-business relations on public policy with respect to association autonomy, the significance of direct interaction, the level of firm deference toward government, and the degree of transparency. First, few trade associations are completely independent. China's political environment provides incentives for maintaining some ties, however limited, with the state, yielding an inverted-U-shaped relationship between autonomy and influence. As was seen in the case of a steel association founded by a private company, the Stainless Steel Department, too great a degree of independence may actually impede an association's ability to exist and interact with the state.[4]

Second, the political system also promotes direct interaction between industry and the national government. The history of the state's administrative and regulatory control of SOEs has encouraged direct interaction on policy issues for state, private, and foreign firms alike. Moreover, while firms regularly lobby different parts of the government bureaucracy, they far less frequently interface with Chinese Communist Party organizations on public-policy issues. The state has developed myriad complex institutions that are responsible for regulating the economy, particularly at the level of industrial policy, and business executives lobby these institutions as if they have genuine decision-making authority. The party rank of government officials that staff these organization is usually not apparent or perceived as significant to industry. Party officials are more often sought after on firm-specific issues, which most often arise at the local level.[5]

Third, associations in all sectors and companies in most sectors tend to avoid challenging the government's authority; instead, deference to the state and finding win-win outcomes is the most common strategy to persuade the government to adopt policies consistent with one's own interests. And fourth, China's political system promotes an opaque policy process, which is consistent with the historical practice of compartmentalizing information and not sharing it with the public.

While political factors have had a major effect on government-business relations in China, there is also strong evidence that the influence of economic factors has been equally, if not more, significant. If political factors predominated, then one would expect to see a consistent pattern of relations across industries, since they are all subject to the same political environment.[6] Such consistency does not fully exist.

Government-business relations on public policy matters vary across industries, though these differences do not conform to the frameworks typically used to describe how government and society interact (pluralism, societal corporatism, state corporatism, clientelism, and monism).[7] Monism is only a memory in any of the sectors since SOEs' sense of identity has been strengthened and relations between them and the state have expanded far beyond their administrative unit and issues of internal governance. No sectors' government-business relations fully fits within the corporatist model either, societal or state. Few associations have compulsory membership; few are hierarchically ordered or have genuine jurisdictional monopolies; and in no sector do associations dominate business-government interaction. Limited autonomy of an association may make it appropriate to describe that individual organization as corporatist, but that adjective is less apt when applied to how associations are organized or how government and business interact more broadly in any of the sectors.[8] Nor is clientelism a fitting descriptor for the politics of any of the sectors. Although there were signs of patronage involving a large steel factory in Jiangsu province, the Accounting and Business Management Sub-Association (ABM), and (possibly) the setting of the VCD player technical standards, patron-client relations were not found to be significant to companies' interaction with the national government on public-policy issues. The limited evidence for corporatism and clientelism in all of the sectors in China is partly related to the move to a market economy that has brought with it an expansion of competition, domestic and international.[9]

Rather than neatly varying according to those models, government-business interaction across the sectors were found to differ along four dimensions: the relative development of autonomous associations useful to their members, the depth of firms' direct contact with officialdom on policy matters, firms' willingness to vigorously defend their interests even when they conflict with that of the government and other companies, and the transparency of the policy process.

These differences are directly tied to firms' and sectors' economic characteristics (see Table 6.1). First, although China's business association system is formally standard across the economy, its actual development and operation vary widely. The preponderance of large SOEs with a low level of market concentration have made associations an extremely low priority for steelmakers. Instead, most companies in the sector "walk on one leg" and interact with the government almost entirely through direct interaction alone. The only area where associations have developed to any degree has been in the stainless steel segment of the market, where there are a large number of small domestic private producers. But even the stainless steel associations lead a borderline existence. Consumer electronics associations are overall more developed than those in steel. That portion of the consumer electronics industry in which there is a higher proportion of private companies (VCD players) has stronger associations than that part still controlled by SOEs (color TVs). The China Video Association is relatively independent of government control, but its members have ig-

**Table 6.1** Linking economics, interaction, and influence

| Industry | Economic characteristics | Pattern of interaction | Relative influence |
|---|---|---|---|
| **Steel** | 1. High percent of SOEs<br>2. High economies of scale (large firms)<br>3. Low concentration<br>4. Vulnerability to price fluctuations<br>5. Inefficient | 1. Weak associations<br>2. Hierarchy of direct contact (large SOEs, large FIEs, all small)<br>3. Nonconfrontational approach<br>4. Limited transparency | Large SOEs |
| **Consumer electronics** | 1. High percent of SOEs in TV, lower in VCD players<br>2. High foreign presence large companies<br>3. High economies of scale (large firms)<br>4. High concentration<br>5. Competitive pricing strategies<br>6. Standards critical to VCD players | 1. Varied associations<br>2. Direct contact for all<br>3. Nonconfrontational associations, more aggressive direct contact<br>4. Greater transparency | Large companies of all ownership types; coalitions vary by issue |
| **Software** | 1. High percent of domestic and foreign private companies<br>2. Low economies of scale (small firms)<br>3. Low overall concentration<br>4. Knowledge-intensive product<br>5. Habit of interfirm technical and business cooperation | 1. More developed associations<br>2. Direct contact for all large companies<br>3. Nonconfrontational approach<br>4. Greatest transparency | Large companies of all ownership types, with some indirect influence by smaller firms |

nored it in favor of informal alliances and direct contact with the government. Competitive pricing strategies, central to all consumer electronics products, have been a drag on the sector's associations, while competition over technical standards have weakened some VCD player makers' confidence in the China Audio Association. In even further contrast to steel, in the software industry, with the plethora of small domestic and foreign private companies that have a habit of cooperation on business and technical matters, associations are much more numerous, independent (though not fully), and active on behalf of their members. Low market concentration matters less in software than in steel or consumer electronics because of the habit of cooperation and the fact that many of the policy issues facing the industry have not induced companies to defect and undermine one another. Direct interaction still is critical for software companies, but it has been significantly supplemented by associations.

Second, direct interaction is important in every sector, but there is variance in the depth of interaction across sectors. In the SOE-dominated steel industry, large SOEs have the most regular interaction with officialdom in the widest variety of settings and over the broadest range of issues. Large foreign steel companies interact with national officials less regularly and on a narrower range of issues. At the bottom of this hierarchy sit small steel firms of all ownership types, who have no access whatsoever to national policy circles. In software and consumer electronics, where domestic and foreign private firms are more numerous and have greater market shares, size is the key distinguishing feature between firms' degree of involvement on policy issues. The only difference between the two industries is that size is relative: a large software maker with significant access would be a small consumer electronics (or steel) maker with much less access. While perhaps not surprising in capitalist countries where SOEs are a small share of the economy, except in China's steel industry, size has become more significant than ownership form in determining companies' relative involvement on policy. Size was regularly mentioned in interviews by large and small companies alike (and government officials) as reasons why firms could or could not influence the policy process.

Finally, although deference and limited transparency have not been fully displaced, there are signs of change that are related to economic factors. The greater willingness of consumer electronics companies to be more confrontational with the government (for example, on pricing and technical standards policies) is associated with the fact that these are relatively large companies in extremely competitive markets, where the ability to turn prices and standards in their favor are critical to the success. The software industry's smaller firms, though predominantly private, are less confident they can violate the official norms of behavior and not eventually be penalized in some fashion. However, even though software companies (and their associations) maintain an external face of cooperation, they still have been able to achieve significant policy victories (for example, reduction of the value-added tax). The higher proportion of domestic and foreign private companies has also spawned the greater media coverage of policy debates in the software and consumer electronics industries. This is most clear in the software industry, where a foreign information technology publisher has invested heavily in local trade periodicals. By contrast, with its less diverse media, the steel industry policy process is less publicized.

The software industry's economic characteristics help explain why that industry's pattern of government-business relations approach pluralism. Although government-business relations in the steel industry are not organized in a corporatist fashion, the differences with the software industry are pronounced. Aside from the aggressive lobbying tactics used by consumer electronics makers, the consumer electronics industry's pattern of relations falls roughly in between that of steel and software.

The explanation for why the politics of business vary among the steel, consumer electronics, and software sectors is strengthened when the scope is expanded to other parts of the economy. Based on the evidence gathered from these three sectors, we should expect other sectors in China with similar economic characteristics to have similar patterns of relations along the dimensions just discussed. To take just the first dimension (association development), in sectors dominated by large, inefficient SOEs with low concentration levels, we should expect little associational activity. However, in those sectors with a predominance of relatively smaller private and foreign companies where technical cooperation is common, we should see greater industry desire for and more prominent associations.

Evidence from the automobile and market research industries— two sectors that are economically similar to steel and software, respectively—suggests that the patterns found in my cases apply more generally in China.[10] The auto industry has an extremely weak government-initiated association that has been largely unable to organize its firms to cooperate on economic or political issues. The auto association failed to institute price cartels as miserably as associations in other sectors with large SOEs and low concentration levels. In the absence of a strong association, large auto manufacturers interact with national senior officials and ministries directly.[11]

By contrast, the market research industry is composed predominantly of hundreds of small private companies that conduct technically sophisticated surveys. None dominate the sector (the top five firms have 30 percent of the market). Foreign firms do not have the market share of their software counterparts, but they interact extensively with domestic survey companies. Consciously following the practice of private entrepreneurs who held "industry dinner parties" in Shanghai in the 1950s, several market research firms began meeting informally in late 1997 to discuss business trends and policy issues. Over the next four years, they became increasingly organized and in 2001 registered the China Marketing Research Association (CMRA, *zhongguo xinxi xiehui shichang yanjiuye fenhui*) as a sub-association of the China Information Association. With its membership swelled to over three hundred companies in 2003, accounting for 95 percent of the industry's business, CMRA has become active in technical training, industry self-regulation, and policy advocacy. Unlike many other national associations, it has adamantly refused to accept any current or former government officials on its staff. A competing association set up by the National Bureau of Statistics is far less vibrant.[12]

The relationship between economic characteristics and associational development usually holds in other individual cases and also more generally, regardless of whether one looks by sector or region.[13] According to a government review of over three hundred national industry associations, the most active and successful associations are in sectors with a higher proportion of private firms where the government permitted them to form associations relatively early.[14] Industry associations have also been found to be more fully developed in regions with a high proportion of small private companies, such as Wenzhou, whereas they have floundered in regions dominated by state-owned enterprises, such as Shanghai.[15]

With the link between economic factors and patterns of interaction established, the next question is to what extent those differences actually matter. Comparative research has focused on the implications that patterns of interaction have on economic growth and the quality of governance, while scholarship on China has been most concerned with the consequences for political reform.[16] Although the latter issue will be addressed below, this study is more concerned with the consequences that economic factors and patterns of interaction have for firms' relative influence on policy making.

This study arrives at mixed conclusions about the consequences of associational activity. On the one hand, associations helped smaller private companies and sectors in which such firms are predominant to gain some access to the policy process that they otherwise would have lacked and that associations did help them to achieve some policy victories. The most significant example in this study involved the reduction of the value-added tax for software firms, but even a stainless steel association helped persuade the government to exempt firms with electric furnaces from being closed as part of the government's effort to eliminate furnaces below a certain capacity. Several associations also cited examples of helping smaller members with firm-specific problems.

On the other hand, associations did not always work to the advantage of their smaller members, state-owned or private. Individual large members have attempted to manipulate associations in China, as displayed by UFSoft's control over the ABM. In addition, associations have worked to the benefit of large members more generally, as when CAA helped to halt the specialty consumption tax on consumer electronics and when the China Electronics Chamber of Commerce tried to organize their largest members into cartels. Associations have made a difference in helping companies influence public policy, but they do not consistently redistribute the balance of influence in favor of smaller firms.

In addition, and of greater significance, the scales of influence tilt even further in the direction of larger firms when the effect of direct interaction is factored in. While smaller firms in the software industry have obtained some political voice, leading companies in each sector—larger SOEs in steel and larger companies of all ownership types in software and consumer electronics—have much more influence on public policy than their smaller counterparts due to their far deeper direct access to the political system. Even foreign companies, such as Microsoft in software, have turned their economic weight into political clout in China. (Foreign firms, though, are not always in conflict with their Chinese counterparts. As was shown, in industries with greater foreign involvement, political alliances commonly cross nationality, putting Chinese and foreign firms on the same side of issues.) In short, as one Chinese observer put it, "The greater an enterprise's contribution to society, the greater its input into policy."[17]

The evidence from the cases investigated here suggests that the relationship between companies' size and influence should predominate in other sectors as well. Although this conclusion appears unsurprising in some respects, it runs counter to the conventional wisdom that in China state-owned enterprises are more politically powerful than private and foreign companies, not to mention usually on the opposite side of policy fights. Increasingly in the People's Republic, size, not ownership or nationality, determines a company's ability to influence public policy.

While this study has highlighted the significance of economic factors, there are three possible alternative hypotheses that deserve consideration to possibly explain the patterns of interaction and influence with regard to the role of associations. The existence of different patterns of interaction has been associated with differing economic factors, partly based on the assumption that all industries in China face a common political environment. If, on the other hand, different industries face different political environments, then that fact might account for variation in patterns of interaction. The best evidence that this situation might be the case is that some Chinese officials and others have expressed a desire to reform the country's associations, while also asserting that the associations of sectors central to the country's national security or of critical importance to the economy need to be kept under official control indefinitely.[18] It would be reasonable to assume that steel is more important to the country than color TVs, VCD players, and software. If this is accurate, it would explain why the China Iron and Steel Association is still dominated by the old metallurgy bureaucracy and why there has been less official resistance to the development of associations in the other sectors.

However, while this theory is enticing, it lacks explanatory power. First, the view that there need to be different levels of government control of associations depending on their centrality is not universally held by all officials. As noted in Chapter 2, there is widespread disagreement within the government about its policy toward associations. Relatedly, those who share this general viewpoint have never specifically identified which industries' associations must be controlled. In fact, one official cites the need to control associations related to new high-technology sectors, which would reasonably include software and VCD players.[19] But even if such views were government policy, that would explain only the political space for more independent and active associations to exist. These views could not account for companies actually taking the initiative to start or support associations to fill this space. Associations for makers of stainless steel, VCD players, and software have depended heavily on their members. In addition, if politics were paramount, one would also expect that all noncritical sectors would have more autonomous and active associations, while all core sectors' associations would be more official and used primarily as vehicles for regulation. Although I do not have systematic data on a large number of associations in both conceptual categories (which are ill defined in any event), that situation does not appear to be the case, as variation across sectors does not fit this pattern (the weakness of the China Video Association is just one example).

Another alternative hypothesis rooted in politics concerns the age of companies. The idea would be that companies founded during or prior to the Mao era already have established patterns of interaction with the state that stress direct contact, whereas more recently founded firms have less institutionalized patterns of contact, and hence industry and the state have been more open to use associations as an avenue for influence or control. Evidence obtained for this project about the age of companies does not strongly support this hypothesis. If correct, one would expect newer SOEs, unencumbered by historic patterns, to be more sanguine about associations than their older counterparts. That is not the case. More recently formed large state-owned software companies have as low regard for most software associations as their older counterparts in the steel industries do for theirs.

A final theory expands on the second, moving from the age of firms to the age of industries. Like the second theory, it could be framed politically and stress how older industries that emerged in the Mao era are more likely to use direct ties and eschew associations. On the other hand, this third hypothesis could also be framed from an economic perspective that distinguishes between old conventional industries and new high-technology sectors, the argument being that technological innovation acts as a strong incentive to promote interfirm business cooperation that then overflows into political cooperation.[20] Regardless of how it is framed, an industry's age or technological sophistication on its own cannot explain the variation found in China. An illustrative example is the computer hardware industry, a high-tech sector that emerged in China in the late 1980s and early 1990s. The computer industry does not have nearly as active associations as those in the software sector, and those that do exist are not significant vehicles for self-regulation or policy influence. Rather than the founding date, the explanation may lay in the fact that the computer industry is dominated by a small number of large (and relatively young) state-owned enterprises, such as Lenovo (formerly Legend), and foreign companies that appear to have little interest in or need for associations.

To understand why business associations actually develop and gain industry support, one must consider their members' perspectives, which are heavily shaped by their economic circumstances and not just the political environment. It should not be surprising that businesses' political behavior is heavily affected by their business. Moreover, the alternative explanations rooted in the assumption of varying political constraints (or technology alone) do not even address variation found in other aspects of relations—depth of direct contact, willingness to challenge government authority, and transparency—that have also been shown to be linked to the economic conditions of companies and their industries.

Although prediction is not the only basis for determining the efficacy of theories, looking forward and then looking backward after a certain period complements other analytical tools. If the argument put forward in this book is correct, one should expect that government-business relations in China will only converge across sectors to the extent that economic circumstances of the sectors more closely approximate one another. The Chinese government may adopt policies that liberalize associations and direct interaction over policy. If so, there likely would be a spectrum shift toward greater political activism, both via associations and through direct links. However, there likely would still be distinct differences in the quality and utility of associations and the depth of direct interaction attributable to continuing differences in firms' and sectors' economic circumstances. Similarly, one should expect that as private and foreign firms gain a larger share of sectors historically dominated by SOEs, the new entrants' level of direct contact with national leaders on policy issues should deepen, the policy process should become more transparent, and, if firms are relatively large, they may adopt a more confrontational lobbying style.

To summarize, this study's chief theoretical findings are that economic factors have induced a variety of patterns of interaction between business and government in China and that, while small firms are occasionally aided by associations, one economic factor in particular, size, has decisively shaped companies' relative ability to influence public policy. As a result, it makes more sense to speak not of China's political economy, singular, but of its political *economies*, plural. Given that China has an authoritarian government that heavily intervenes in the economy, China is a critical case. Since economic factors displayed their effects and led to variation in political organization and outcomes in such an inhospitable context, one can be confident that such processes are at work more generally. The utility of referring to the political economy, singular, of any country is on the decline. The landscape of business-government relations often varies within states and in some ways shows signs of continuity across states. That there is a lack of convergence toward a common pattern in sectors across countries does not necessarily demonstrate the weakness of economic factors, since the local economic contexts of sectors across countries often diverges. Analysts would, thus, benefit from maintaining their attention on both political and economic factors in analyzing any particular country's or sector's political economy.

## Chinese Politics: Adapting Models and Integrating Sub-Fields

In addition to contributing to our understanding of political economy in general, this book's findings also have implications for debates over Chinese politics. The study provides new insights into the nature of state-society relations and the policy-making process in China.

Previous research that alternatively has highlighted corporatism, clientelism, and pluralism (the last often referred to as civil society) has made significant contributions to our understanding of how different elements of society interact with the Chinese state. The corporatist argument reminds us that we should not lose sight of the state's powers; clientelism, that officials are capable of using their authority to engage in illicit exchanges with nonstate clients; and pluralism, that economic liberalization can generate incentives for society to become interested in public affairs. However, these frameworks also fail to fully grasp important aspects of state-society relations. This is in part because China is a moving target, and as it changes, so too must the models used to describe it. But it also appears that these models have also been limited by their own assumptions.

The corporatist model fits, and only partially so, when the focus is on association autonomy, but this is only one of the four aspects of corporatism.[21] But even here, there is significant variation in associations' autonomy across industries and over time, as more government-initiated and staffed associations have come to depend on their members and clients for their financial solvency. Just as important, in corporatist systems elsewhere, associations dominate state-society relations as either a control mechanism for the state, in the case of state corporatism, or as the key channel for negotiations, in the case of societal corporatism. In China, associations at most complement the more prevalent direct interaction of business executives and government officials. If one can conceive of an association system as a pipe that channels the water of control and influence, China's association system is, to say the least, extremely leaky.

The clientelism framework also seems unable to account for the totality of government-business relations in China over the last decade.[22] This conclusion must to some extent be tentative because of the difficulty of discerning patron-clients ties.[23] However, the evidence collected suggests that competitive markets have made patronage less useful than in the past.[24] To the extent clientelist relations exist, they most likely revolve around companies' interaction with government officials on issues specific to that company (such as obtaining a license or loan). Studies that have uncovered patron-client networks in China may have been driven to their conclusions by focusing on certain types of companies that interact with local officials on company-specific issues.[25] More broadly, the clientelism model privileges viewing direct one-to-one contact between officials and businesspeople as inherently involving illicit exchanges that benefit the official and the company at the expense of the general public good. The cases of direct lobbying described in previous chapters are consistent with trends in the United States, Western Europe, and Taiwan, showing that companies increasingly rely on themselves to lobby the government directly on public-policy issues and that such contact is not necessarily part of a patron-client relationship.[26]

The present study shares some affinities with the pluralist (aka civil society) framework, which captures a fundamental change in state-society relations: economic reform has made society far more interested in public policy than during the days of a planned economy.[27]

Companies, particularly large ones, are interested in politics when the issues under discussion relate to their interests. To many Chinese companies, public policy *is* business.

On the other hand, the present study diverts from the pluralism model on two scores. First, the pluralist framework, as outlined in Chapter 1, expects associations to develop evenly across all industries in the wake of economic reforms. This expectation is based on the framework's assumption that all markets are alike and that the only distinction that matters is between plan and market.[28] Instead, associations have developed irregularly across the Chinese landscape due to variation in the economic conditions of different industries. Different markets in China provide a greater or weaker incentive for associations to develop, depending on a variety of economic factors, including the prevalence of state-owned enterprises, market concentration, and price volatility. Second, the pluralism model as applied to China would lead one to expect associations to develop in tandem with societal interest in public policy. Where associations have been found to be wanting, it is assumed that society's influence on policy has been equally limited. Studies of this kind were driven to their conclusions by making associations the central protagonists in the greater drama of whether China was developing a civil society: if associations are weak, members of society ipso facto must also be weak.[29] In fact, companies' political influence has run far ahead of the development of associations, even in the software industry. As a consequence, this study finds that signs of civil society exist only in those parts of the economy where companies, in addition to interacting directly with the state, are also involved in relatively autonomous and active associations (such as those in the software industry and parts of the consumer electronics industry)—but that despite the uneven presence of signs of civil society, society's influence on the state has increased across all sectors.

The findings in this book also suggest that existing models of policy making in China need to be updated to take into account the growing *direct* role that societal actors have in the policy process. There is already a wealth of research showing that society has exhibited an ability to influence the Chinese state. Protests by farmers, factory workers, religious groups, and students, among others, have contributed to changes in government policy during the post-Mao era.[30] Most of such activity occurs well outside formal structures, though as individuals' sense of rights have grown, some protesters have used legal tactics, such as lawsuits and petitions.[31] Most observers have seen the Chinese state and society as influencing each other, though acting in parallel yet separate universes: society's protests engender a state policy response or vice versa.[32] The finding of some steps toward attempting to influence the state through formal procedures represents a departure from what could be called an action-response model of state-society relations. The great majority of such developments have been documented at the local level, at the very edges of the political system, with very few recorded cases of society's direct encroachment into the national policy-making process.[33]

The growth of businesses' direct involvement in economic policy making undermines even more thoroughly the action-response model of state-society relations, insofar as some members of society have become inside participants in the policy process itself. Business involvement in the policy process is not fully welcomed by all in government, and institutionalized paths such as hearings are only just emerging.[34] Nor is participation close to equal; "big business" has much more access than smaller companies, not to mention farmers, laborers, or noneconomic groups. Yet industry's entrance into the policy room means that policy-making models based solely on negotiations between different elements of the state no longer suffice.[35] Elites, bureaucrats, experts, and business are involved in an interactive process in which each side both sets agendas and responds to those of the others. As such, companies' greater political activism has made a process recently described as "organized anarchy" more chaotic, as the origins of policy ideas and the number of participants to the process have expanded and the norms which used to provide some sense of normalcy have in many instances been challenged.[36]

These remarks point to the need to update the frameworks used to explain Chinese politics. In addition, since scholars have to some extent been touching different parts of the elephant, they have been reaching different conclusions about what animal China is. The growing role of business in policy making offers an opportunity to join two sub-fields (state-society relations and policy making) that to date have carried on separate conversations, by stepping back to look at the entire elephant. This can be done by viewing any decision made by the state as a policy and recognizing that policies can differ in two respects—their range of

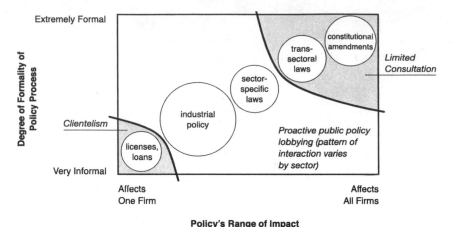

**Figure 6.1** Patterns of Policy Influence

impact and the degree of formality of the process by which they are adopted (see Figure 6.1). At the bottom-left corner of the figure are policies such as loans and licenses that affect only an individual firm and that can be decided in a very informal process. These policies are the most vulnerable to clientelism and likely account for the vast majority of corruption perpetrated by businesspeople (though one should also recognize that much of such interaction does not involve corruption). However, such policies encompass only a fraction of government-business relations. At the other extreme, the top-right corner, are policies that affect all firms and go through extremely formal deliberation procedures, such as constitutional amendments and transsectoral laws. In these instances it is likely that the influence of business is limited. These laws are more remote from businesses' interests, reducing firms' incentive to be involved. In these instances, lawmakers likely rely more on the bureaucracy, political elites, and experts, relegating business to providing limited consultation. Existing models of policy making likely have their most applicability in such cases.

It is in the wide expanse between these two extremes where the empirical evidence from this study falls. Businesses have been most interested in policies that affect their industry and have been most able to influence policies that go through moderately formal channels of deliberation. The methods by which firms actually exert their influence, though, varies to some extent depending on the sectors' economic circumstances. Given this overall pattern of government-business relations, the question then becomes one of identifying change over time. It seems most likely that over the past decade the area of the middle section (proactive public policy lobbying) has expanded and that the area of the two extremes (clientelism and limited consultation) has retracted toward the corners.

While the areas in Figure 6.1 signifying clientelism and limited consultation may continue to shrink, it is highly unlikely they will disappear quickly or entirely. Their disappearance would require the elimination of discretionary state authority on the one hand, thereby removing the basis for clientelism, and institutional political change on the other, thereby encouraging members of society to more fully participate in debates over even the broadest issues. Government officials will retain some powers even if economic reforms expand much further, while the chances of democratization are much more open to debate. It is to that latter question that we now turn.

## Incremental Democratization?

Whether predicting collapse or democratization, some observers have discerned a clear political future for China.[37] The evidence garnered from this study suggests that agnosticism is a more appropriate posture. The growth of business's policy influence has ambiguous implications for democratization.

On the one hand, business already affects how policy is made, and it may push for more sweeping changes. Economic reform has made companies much more attentive to public policy, both its substance and the manner by which it is adopted. Companies believe it is appropriate to lobby officials, and many officials expect them to do just that. But by virtue of their involvement in policy making, many companies have come to see the weaknesses in the process itself. Their dissatisfaction with some associations has led some associations to become empty shells, while others have reformed to be more productive tools of influence. As the proportion of private companies grows in more industries, it is possible that the number of representative associations will expand, particularly if the other economic aspects of these sectors provide incentives for associational activity. Further, it is possible that companies, having gained greater indirect and direct access to the government, will push

further to make such contact more institutionalized (by demanding regular and open hearings, for example, as well as comment-and-response
periods for draft regulations) and to make elite leaders and the bureaucracy more accountable for their actions. Incremental reforms that help
businesses may lead them to seek progressively greater changes. Although fundamental political change was not a consistent topic in my interviews, multiple sources from companies of various ownership forms
believe democratization is in the best interests of business and the country. This position is held even by those who benefit from connections.
Wang Wenjing, the young founder of the financial software firm UFSoft
who has extensive ties with officialdom, has used his position as a deputy
to the National People's Congress to urge authorities to make it easier
for private entrepreneurs to run for office in local elections.[38] Hence,
exploiting connections and advocating democracy are not necessarily
mutually exclusive strategies.

On the other hand, not all economic factors point toward democratization. While some sectors have seen the growth of more autonomous
associations, there is no uniform trend. Large companies in some sectors (such as software and parts of consumer electronics) have welcomed
associations, but the economic conditions of other sectors may not promote the development of associations even if the proportion of private
enterprises increases. To the extent that democratization is borne out of
a broad-based civil society, such a state of affairs is not on the immediate
horizon. Relatedly, even if support for democratization is growing
among China's millions of smaller entrepreneurs, it is likely that just as
with economic policies, large companies will have a greater say over
China's political trajectory. Many large firms, though dissatisfied with
existing associations, have still managed to have their opinions reach officialdom with some effect. Those with relatively significant influence
under current political circumstances may not see a need for much further modification. Once let in the door, the feeling may be, why allow
others in? While some interview sources from large companies support
democratization, others expressed skepticism about the benefits of radical change, particularly in the near term.[39]

That said, we should recognize that the mixed picture of the growth
of business influence provides only part of the story of China's political
future. Most importantly, the views and behavior of China's political
and military elites will have the largest and most direct effect on

whether the political system will ever intentionally be democratized through implementing competitive elections at the national level.[40] Even as industry displays greater influence, the Communist Party has not sat idly by and accepted the inevitability of its demise. It has been engaged in a multi-pronged strategy that involves coopting business elites into the party, promoting economic growth, fostering national pride, and undermining opposition movements. The Communist Party has surprised many by enduring so long. It may find ways to continue to prolong its tenure, regardless of the preferences of business.

Even if China does democratize, it is also important to consider the effect that economic factors have on the quality of democracy once initiated. Russia is a case in point. Because of high concentrations of wealth, large conglomerates have been able to wield the levers of political power in Russia to a greater extent than in the Soviet era.[41] Consequently, if democratization is not to promote only the interests of large corporations at the expense of small businesses, labor, and other noneconomic groups, it is important that concentrations of wealth and market power be limited.[42] Although market concentration in many sectors in China is still relatively low, the trend is pointing toward consolidation in many industries. Moreover, individual income inequality is also expanding quickly. In sum, trends at the sectoral and personal level may conflict with the goal of achieving a more equal distribution of political influence, regardless of the structure of China's formal political institutions.[43]

## Reform Alternatives: Beyond Liberalization

Given the myriad factors affecting whether China will democratize, it is more realistic to consider the implications of this study for more narrowly gauged reforms related to government-business relations. In particular, for the past several years, there has been a debate among officials, experts, and association representatives about how to modify regulations regarding China's associations. Participants in this debate almost universally agree that many of China's associations are dysfunctional and that changes need to be made. However, opinion is divided about what course of action to follow.

There have been two alternative competing reform packages that have received attention. The first would restructure China's association system along more corporatist lines by making the system hierarchical

and enforcing rules of monopoly of jurisdiction that have long been ig-
nored. At the same time, this side would leave in place requirements
that associations be affiliated with a government organization and that
they not be operated on a for-profit basis. Since late 1998, some initial
steps have been taken. As detailed in Chapter 2, several industrial ministries were first turned into bureaus of the State Economic and Trade
Commission (SETC), and then they were replaced with associations
when the SETC itself was eliminated in 2003. In addition, to promote
greater hierarchy, in December 1998, the China Industrial Economy
Association (CIEA) was formally made into a federation, and soon after
its counterpart in the trading and service sectors, the China General
Chamber of Commerce, followed suit. And beginning in 2001, the
ministries-turned-associations were given authority over more narrowly gauged trade associations. Based on these steps and on interviews
with officials and association leaders, the aim of these changes is to
make associations more authoritative channels for industry regulation
and to rectify what is currently viewed as a disorderly situation in which
associations lack regulatory authority and routinely overlap each others' jurisdiction and in which companies by default interact with the
government directly.

The findings of this study suggest that such modifications to China's
association system are likely to run into a great deal of opposition and
eventually to prove futile; they may even weaken industry regulation.
As noted above, corporatist systems are on the decline globally, as large
companies have become politically active and do not entrust associations to be their sole representative vis-à-vis the state. Corporatist systems have also been subverted by the growth of transnational business
ties. When companies' economic interests cross political boundaries,
their goals may not be consistent with those of either their home country or the countries in which they have subsidiaries. In the Chinese
case, political and economic factors do not favor successfully making
government-dominated associations the key avenue for state-business
ties writ large. Those sectors with a high percentage of SOEs will not
likely support such associations, and even private companies that are
more inclined toward associations in theory are not likely to have much
confidence in associations whose primary mission is regulation and not
interest representation. In addition, a corporatist system would also
conflict with the growing role of foreign firms in many sectors of the

Chinese economy. They would not likely countenance being corralled into sectoral associations that limit their flexibility without providing greater influence on policy. Furthermore, Chinese companies allied economically with foreign industry, as they are in the consumer electronics and software industries, would likely have the same hesitations. Finally, associations in China that are already relatively autonomous are unlikely to accept the regulatory authority of any other association. This group would include a range of national associations and sub-associations, local branches of the All-China Federation of Industry and Commerce, industry guilds, and foreign-based trade associations and chambers of commerce. In short, reforms along corporatist lines would likely face keen opposition, and associations would not fulfill their intended functions.[44] The recent elimination of industrial ministries and bureaus in the central and regional governments means that the failure of such reforms could potentially create a large regulatory vacuum, thereby hurting economic growth.

The alternative reform program advocated by some would be to liberalize the regulatory regime governing associations. Some officials, association leaders, and other observers have mentioned several changes that should be adopted: (1) Eliminate the requirement for associations to be affiliated with a government department (*zhuguan bumen*). Such ties ease access to that one government agency, but they may increase the difficulties of contacting other parts of the government. (2) Remove the formal requirement for jurisdictional monopolies. Overlap is already widespread, and encouraging competition between associations would make them work more diligently to serve their members. (3) Eliminate the government's authority to set employee quotas for associations, a practice that limits the chance of associations to attract new talent. (4) End the formal prohibition against making profits. This would allow associations to more easily finance their operations and provide more services for members. (5) Permit foreign companies to be full members in Chinese associations and their foreign managers to occupy leadership positions in these associations. Foreign companies are already in some Chinese associations, but their involvement should be legitimized in law. Given that foreign firms occupy an important part of many sectors, leaving them out of associations reduces the associations' utility. (6) Allow foreign trade associations to register and operate freely, as opposed to the current situation of operating on an ad hoc basis at the discretion of officials. Relatedly, a liberal reform package would allow Chinese companies to join foreign trade associations (a situation which current law does not address). Rather than two sets of laws apply to Chinese and foreign associations and chambers of commerce, have one set of laws that apply to all such organizations irrespective of their founders' or members' nationalities.[45]

The principal aim of liberal reforms would be to allow associations to more fully represent their members. And if associations are more financially self-sufficient, have higher quality staff, and have greater respect from their members, the associations would also be better equipped to take up the regulatory functions that the state could no longer manage on its own. Thus, from this perspective, more representative associations would also help China avoid the governance vacuum that would likely expand under the corporatist alternative.

The consequence of the liberal alternative would likely be to energize more associations. If one could imagine a spectrum with "direct contact" at one end and "associations" at the other, there would be a spectrum shift toward the "association" end of spectrum. Though there would likely still be variation in companies' interest in associations and in associations' effectiveness based on companies' and industries' economic circumstances, such a change might fulfill the conditions of pluralism and civil society, which would be well received by those primarily concerned about institutional political reform.

Some tentative steps in this direction have been or are being contemplated. At the local level, Wenzhou has had a relatively liberal association regime for several years, both for standard business associations and more informal financial associations. In 2002, the Shanghai municipal government adopted relatively reformist association regulations and created a new agency to promote association development.[46] There are also national-level officials advocating for the passage of a new law on business associations that would significantly break with the current regulatory regime.[47] However, they are locked in a stalemate with those worried about the political ramifications and "disorder" that could emerge.

As potentially beneficial as a more liberal regime for business could be for interest representation and industrial governance, this study's findings also suggest that such a state of affairs should not be expected to be unproblematic. As was seen in several instances, associations have not always been vehicles for a redistribution of political influence or liberal economic policies. Though small firms sometimes benefit from associations, larger firms have also been able to use associations to their advantage, occasionally pushing the association in a direction that conflicts with other members' interests. Associations have also been vehicles for anticompetitive practices, as occurred in the various attempts to institute cartels.

Since the latter half of the 1990s, China's deep economic problems have become more apparent. Reforms have provided two decades of growth but at the cost of growing debt by banks and state-owned enterprises.[48] Though almost all members of society have materially advanced, the gap in the standard of living between rural and urban residents and between Han Chinese and minority nationalities has grown. Various groups in society dissatisfied with their conditions are increasingly vocalizing their frustrations. China's admission into the World Trade Organization is supposed to propel economic reforms forward, thereby ensuring continued high growth rates that will allow the government to address the grievances of society. While WTO membership may result in long-term economic growth, in the short-to-medium term there are, to adopt the language of the debate in China, as many challenges as opportunities.

As this study has shown, companies and their representatives will not sit idly by while the government modifies its laws and regulations to conform to WTO standards. Beside the fact that many WTO norms are open to interpretation, businesses, Chinese and foreign, will in any case expend a great deal of effort to see that laws and regulations suit their interests. (In fact, industry pressure over regulatory changes has long since commenced.) Associations will no doubt be party to these debates. In some instances, they may be voices of liberalization, but in other cases, given the stakes, they may also be tools of anticompetitive measures geared to protect their members by seeking relief from intense competitive pressures. Even though many of these attempts likely will fail because of the low concentration of many sectors and China's preexisting openness to foreign trade and investment, this situation will not deter all associations (or companies in informal alliances) from pressing forward. Industry may also fight against greater environmental protection or more stringent public-health regulations, goals they have a greater chance of achieving if nongovernmental organizations continue to have difficulty organizing an even more disparate public. In short, greater industry influence is no panacea for China's many social and economic ills.

While the fear of business's political power run amok might lead some to suggest limiting such influence as much as possible or taking the reins off the rest of society, the choice is not only between clamping down and loosening up. As Steinfeld pointed out, successfully moving from plan to market is not achieved simply by liberalization of the economy. Instead it requires building complex institutions that promote efficient behavior.[49] Similarly, moving from a state-centered policy process to one in which the participation of social forces results in progress for the broader public involves more than dropping barriers to political organization, for business and nonbusiness interests alike. It means treating lobbying, whether by groups or individuals, as an industry unto itself. This requires designing and enforcing "rules of the game" that encourage those attempting to shape policy to act ethically. Thus, China needs regulations concerning nonstate policy participants' lobbying practices, income and expenditures, and conflicts of interest. Constructing such a system raises the chances of a better future for China in an era when business influence is sure to rise.

*Appendix*
*Notes*
*Index*

# *Appendix:*
# *Case Selection and Interviews*

The sectors analyzed in this study were chosen on the basis of their economic distinctness and their inherent importance to the economy. Potential industries were identified based on industries' characteristics as of 1997, and the final choices were made during the initial stages of fieldwork. As Table A.1 and the discussion in the main text suggest, the sectors varied along several economic lines, which offered the best way also to find differences in how government and business interact. The danger of a greatest-difference strategy is the difficulty of measuring the independent effect of individual variables. An alternative tactic would have been to select sectors that varied by only a single economic variable to more precisely isolate that variable's effect. Practically speaking, this would be extremely hard to do, given the enormous number of potential variables; Table 1.2, which is not exhaustive, lists almost twenty. Even if one could, focusing on just one or two variables also invites the danger of ignoring potentially important variables. And, quite frankly, it also would likely lead to a more boring story because of the numerous areas of overlap. The potential pitfalls that arise by choosing different sectors is ameliorated by having multiple firms from each sector and by focusing the research on uncovering which factors motivate the behavior of firms and associations.

Since China has such a large rural population and produces so much

**Table A.1** Economic characteristics of three sectors, 1997

| General Variable | Economies of scale (I) | Economies of scale (II) | Capital intensity | State-owned enterprise share | Foreign-invested enterprise share | Firm concentration |
|---|---|---|---|---|---|---|
| Specific Measure | Output/ enterprise (million RMB) | Employees/ enterprise | Capital/ employee (thousand RMB) | SOE output (% of total) | FIE output (% of total) | Top 4 firms' combined sales (% of total) |
| National Average | 15 | 133 | 44 | 41 | 21 | n/a |
| Steel | 63 | 525 | 61 | 70 | 4 | 32 |
| Consumer electronics | 92 | 584 | 40 | 34 | 46 | 58 |
| Software | 6 | 56 | n/a | <10 | 70 | 15 |

*Sources:*
National average: *China Statistical Yearbook 1998* (Beijing: China Statistical Publishing House, 1998).
Steel: *China Statistical Yearbook 1998; China Iron and Steel Industry Yearbook 1998*, pp. 81, 111, 112.
Consumer electronics: *China Electronics Industry Yearbook 1998* (Beijing: Publishing House of Electronics Industry, 1998); Sino-MR Corporation, "Zhongguo dianshiji shengchan qiye 1997 nian shengchang, xiaoshou, chukou qingkuang" (China television production enterprises' 1997 production, sales and export situation), April 1998; and Sino-MR Corporation, "Jiayong dianqi xiaoshou jiance: 1998 nian niandu baogao (yingdieji)" (Consumer electronics sales monitor: 1998 annual report, video disc players), March 1999. Comparable data was only available for the entire electronics industry; ad hoc data show consumer electronics is relatively similar to the entire electronics industry, except that concentration for individual products in much higher. The concentration figure here is the average for color televisions and VCD players.
Software: China Software Industry Association, *'98 zhongguo guoji ruanjian bolanhui ji jishu yantaohui (zhanhuikan)* ('98 China international software exhibition and technical discussion meeting, exhibition edition), Beijing, November 1998; Xinhua News Agency, "Overview of China's Software Market and Industry," September 19, 1998; and author's own estimates regarding SOE output and market share of Microsoft.

food, one might wonder why an agricultural sector, such as rice, was not chosen as a case. The first reason agriculture was avoided was practical: it would have been difficult to arrange extended fieldwork in both urban and rural communities in multiple parts of the country; fieldwork was easier to accomplish with three urban industrial sectors. But more importantly, despite its reputation, agriculture is a dwindling share of China's economy, having fallen from 50 percent of gross domestic product in 1952 to 28 percent in 1978, and to 16 percent in 2000. Industry and services are each larger and growing far more rapidly than agriculture, forcing farmers off the land and into rural and urban factories.[1] In this light, not including agriculture should not be seen as detrimental to understanding either China or the study's theoretical issues.

Specific firms were chosen as cases through several sources: industry directories, industry periodicals, and newspapers; and suggestions by independent industry analysts, journalists, other firms, and associations. No cases were based on recommendations by a government official.

Table A.2 summarizes the overall number of firms both by size and by form of ownership. Cumulatively, several firms fall into each category, and within each sector at least one firm fits within each segment. Categorizing firms was challenging. Determining a firm's ownership in the Chinese context is often a difficult task. In reality, ownership forms are arrayed along a continuum, but for the purposes of this study, firms were categorized as state owned, private domestic, or private foreign. Many state-owned firms have partially privatized or listed on a stock exchange, and some firms whose management is from the private sector have often registered as locally state-owned firms ("collectives"). These complexities make distinguishing between state-owned and private firms more difficult. This project has categorized firms' ownership based on which agents, specific individuals, or state bodies had identifiable claims over the firms' profits (for example, by their share of the company's stock). When claims over profits were impossible to determine or when investment came from both the state and private parties, the focus was shifted to determining which party had control over personnel, investment, and other management decisions. Ambiguous cases are discussed in the main text.

Firms were categorized by size based on the number of employees rather than total sales, market share, or other financial figures. A firm's

**Table A.2** Overall number of firm cases in each category, all three sectors combined

| Size | State-owned | Private-domestic | Private-foreign |
|------|-------------|------------------|-----------------|
| Large | 11 | 7 | 6 |
| Small | 6 | 9 | 4 |
| Total | 17 | 16 | 10 |

number of employees is a less sensitive piece of data, and it is less subject to manipulation than sales, since the latter is a basis for tax payments. Employee size is also significant in that it affects whether a firm
can devote human resources to interacting with the government.

It is also important to note two criteria that were *not* used to select
cases. First, there was no attempt to systematically compare firms from
different regions. Focusing on firms in just two regions was originally
considered as a way to isolate the significance of the regions' economic
characteristics, specifically the proportion of the economy in private
hands. However, during fieldwork, this strategy was deemed impracti-
cal and unrealistic for several reasons. First, there is a high degree of in-
terprovincial mobility of company employees (even of the most senior
executives), products, and government officials. Second, many firms
based in one province have production, marketing, and sales facilities in
other regions. Third, some provinces do not have firms in a sector that
covers each of the categories required for analysis. And fourth, many of
the most important issues facing firms are national in scope, and thus
they involve national-level associations that include firms from across
China as members and that are the jurisdiction of the national government in Beijing. Focusing on firms limited to only two locales and their
relations with local associations and governments regarding local problems would have been too restrictive and would have yielded less valuable results. Thus, the forty-three firms that constitute the central cases
are based in several regions: Beijing (twenty-one), Shanghai (eight),
Guangdong (six), Jiangsu (five), Zhejiang (two), and Sichuan (one). The
Beijing figure is inflated by the seven foreign firms that have their
China headquarters there, with only two in Shanghai and one in
Jiangsu.

Firms were also chosen without regard to which level of government
administration they were registered. Guthrie productively employs this
strategy in his study on enterprise behavior.[2] And others have noted the
differences between nationally and regionally owned enterprises in
how they varyingly interact with local governments. Within a sector,
firms in this study were chosen to maximize the ability to compare
companies of different size, ownership form, and nationality and not
administrative rank. The discussion only occasionally addresses this issue. If the focus was on comparing government-business relations at
different levels of government, this oversight would be a major detri-

ment. However, since this book's focus is on national policy making, the damage of not fully considering rank is less severe. It is also possible that while a firm's rank may affect its business size (by raising or lowering its access to capital, for instance), a firm's size can also affect its administrative rank, particularly for newer firms. Hence, rank may be more than a political indicator.

The bulk of interviews, approximately 250, were held with senior executives from firms, leaders of associations and other intermediaries, and junior and midlevel officials in the national and several local governments between August 1998 and August 1999 in China. Over seventy more interviews were conducted over the next four years, primarily in two subsequent visits to the field, in June and July 2002 and in August and September 2003. The great majority of meetings were arranged by me. The key exceptions are some interviews in Shanghai and Jiangsu that were scheduled by the Pudong Institute for the U.S. Economy. Only rarely did foreign affairs office officials arrange or attend interviews. In general, there was an overall low refusal rate for interviews, with the rate somewhat higher earlier in the research than later. Increased knowledge about a sector improved the "pitch" used to persuade people to agree to interviews and also led to more efficient and higher quality questioning. To the extent interview subjects saw me as a source, they were mostly interested in my analysis of an industry's economic conditions. I refrained as much as possible from making judgments about government-business relations, and I never revealed the views of other sources, a practice that would both be unethical and lead to biased results.

A compilation of the number of interviews is given in Table A.3. When multiple people were interviewed together (for example, two leaders of an association), I include them as one interview. But an interview source interviewed a second (or third) time is counted as multiple interviews. The table provides both the number of interviews and (in parentheses) the number of separate individuals interviewed in each category.

The initial interviews in 1998 and 1999 for each sector were done in sequential waves, beginning with software, then consumer electronics, and finally steel. Once progress was made on one sector, background research and interviews on the next would begin. This approach minimized the periods in which no interviewing was done and likewise minimized start-up times for each sector. It also permitted greater opportunities for follow-up interviews with subjects over time.

**Table A.3** Number of interviews by sector and occupation (separate individuals interviewed)

| Sector | Occupation total | | Firms | | Intermediaries | Government | Others* |
|---|---|---|---|---|---|---|---|
| General** | 107 | (92) | 6 | (5) | 32 (33) | 30 (22) | 39 (32) |
| Steel | 59 | (61) | 25 | (29) | 17 (14) | 13 (14) | 4 (4) |
| Consumer electronics | 55 | (52) | 28 | (29) | 10 (8) | 6 (6) | 11 (9) |
| Software | 102 | (88) | 56 | (50) | 19 (13) | 15 (15) | 12 (10) |
| Total Interviews | 323 (293) | | 115 (113) | | 78 (68) | 64 (57) | 66 (55) |

*Other interview sources included academics, researchers, industry consultants, and journalists.
**"General" includes interviews with people not in any of the three sectors, including representatives from transsectoral associations, national and local legislatures, transsectoral parts of the bureaucracy (for example, the State Economic and Trade Commission), and independent analysts who commented on the general nature of government-business relations.

Interview questions to firm executives were divided into several components: (1) a firm's economic circumstances; (2) an overview of its direct interaction with government and knowledge of the policy process; (3) an overview of its participation in associations and its use of other intermediaries, for example, public relations or law firms; and (4) a focused discussion of particular policy issues that affected its interests. An effort was made to determine the firm's knowledge of and position on issues, the ways it attempted to obtain information on and influence the outcome of policy deliberations, its level of satisfaction with the benefits it received from a policy outcome, a measure of the industry's importance in affecting the policy outcome, and the level of adherence to announced policies. Mirror interviews were held with associations and government officials to obtain their perspectives. Association representatives, most often the secretaries-general, were asked about their associations' organizational structures, membership, interaction with other associations, and the various types of activities in which the associations were involved (for example, market promotion, the policy process, and industry self-regulation). Government officials were asked about their interaction with firms, associations, and other government agencies in general and with regard to specific policies.

Most of the questioning was related to the recent past and current issues. When possible, subjects were also asked to compare the more recent context with that of the 1980s and early 1990s. However, some obstacles to retrospective interviewing did emerge: some firms were young (established in the mid-1990s), especially private ones; some interview subjects recently joined the firms or associations, or they had changed government departments; and some people naturally had faulty memories. As a result, discussions about earlier periods were less detailed.

Interviewing all three sides afforded a variety of perspectives on the general tenor of relations as well as on the process related to individual policy issues. It also allowed me to identify when a source appeared to be less than forthcoming and to probe further for more accurate answers. Supplemental interviews with other firms, industry experts, and academics and documentation from Chinese and Western sources also helped to make interviews more substantive and focused. When possible, I held multiple interviews with an individual to permit follow-up questions and probing of new issues.

Citations for interviews must balance the need to establish the authoritative nature of sources with the need to protect the interests of my sources and the institutions to which they belong. Reasons of politics, business, and unspecific personal beliefs motivated interview subjects to prefer to remain anonymous. Most of the information learned from interview sources was previously not public. Some information concerned individuals' sensitive judgments and information about other companies, associations, the government, and the Chinese Communist Party. It is clear that a promise of anonymity increased the positive response rate to interview requests and increased the amount and quality of information provided during interviews. And keeping to that promise with previous interview subjects raises the likelihood of future quality interviews.

As a result, this book errs on the side of caution by keeping all of my sources anonymous. Specific companies, government agencies, and associations are repeatedly referred to in the text, but no quotations or sources of information are directly attributed to a specific individual, and only on occasion are they connected to a specific organization. Instead, interview sources are coded.

To modestly help the reader (and to allow this researcher to track the sources used), interview codes contain a letter and number that is based on a consistent system. The letter indicates whether the interview primarily involved steel (#m_), consumer electronics (#c_), software (#s_), or government-business relations in general (#g_). The number indicates the order in which interviews were held. An important modification of this sequencing is that prior to numbering, interviews in each sectoral category were further subdivided into those involving representatives from companies, intermediaries, government agencies, and others; hence, a higher number within a sectoral category (for example, steel, #m_) does not always signify an interview preceded one with a lower number.

It is also important to recognize that the discussion of a company, association, or government agency was not entirely, or even primarily, based on sources from that organization but rather may have relied on other outside sources as well. Hence, the regular listing of an interview code during discussion of an organization in no way implies the source is from that organization, only that he or she is knowledgeable about it.

# Notes

## Chapter 1. Introduction: The Puzzle of Lobbying in China

1. The signatories, which met on several occasions before issuing their appeals, were Erdos Group, Sichuan Changhong Electronics Group, Chunlan Group, Guizhou Maotai Brewery, Tsingtao Beer Group, Idall Electronics, Tianjin Auto Industrial Group, Monkey King Group, Guangxi Yucai Machinery Co., Shanghai No. 1 Department Store, Beijing Wangfujing Department Store, Shenyang Zhongxing Commercial Building Co., and Dalian Department Store. Lu Zheng, ed., *Zhongguo gongye fazhan baogao 1999: gaobie duanque jingjide zhongguo gongye* (China industry development report 1999: Good-bye to Chinese industry's shortage economy) (Beijing: Economic Management Press, 1999), pp. 132–133; and Scott Kennedy, "The Price of Competition: Pricing Policies and the Struggle to Define China's Economic System," *China Journal*, no. 49 (January 2003), pp. 1–30.

2. It should be pointed out, though, that there is no single classical definition of pluralism that all scholars have cited. On the term's evolution, see Susan Gross Solomon, ed., *Pluralism in the Soviet Union* (New York: St. Martin's Press, 1983), pp. 4–36. On the growth in direct lobbying by firms, see Neil J. Mitchell, "The Decentralization of Business in Britain," *Journal of Politics*, vol. 52, no. 2 (May 1990), pp. 622–637; David Vogel, "Government-Industry Relations in the United States: An Overview," in Stephen Wilks and Maurice Wright, eds., *Comparative Government-Industry Relations* (Oxford: Clarendon Press, 1987), pp. 91–116; Wyn Grant and Jane Sargent, *Business and Politics in Britain* (London: Macmillan Education, 1987); and Amir Mahini and Louis T. Wells Jr., "Government Relations in the Global Firm," in Michael E. Porter, ed., *Competition in Global Industries* (Boston: Harvard Business School Press, 1986), pp. 291–312.

3. In the study of American politics, pluralism usually has been contrasted with elitism and class analysis. The debate has revolved around the extent to which political influence is limited to a privileged few or is more widely distributed among different interest groups. Robert Dahl, *Who Governs?* (New Haven, Conn.: Yale

University Press, 1961); C. Wright Mills, *The Power Elite* (New York: Oxford University Press, 1959). In the comparative politics sub-field, pluralism is usually compared with alternative forms of organization for business-government relations. The current study is consistent with the comparative politics sub-field's focus on varying patterns of interaction, but it also shares the American politics sub-field's more explicit concern with businesses' relative influence on politics.

4. Philippe C. Schmitter, "Still the Century of Corporatism?" *The Review of Politics*, vol. 36, no. 1 (January 1974), pp. 93–94.

5. Philippe C. Schmitter, *Interest Conflict and Political Change in Brazil* (Stanford: Stanford University Press, 1971); and Philippe C. Schmitter, *Corporatism and Public Policy in Authoritarian Portugal* (London: Sage, 1975). For a review of the ways in which corporatism has been defined and interpreted in the Chinese case, see Richard Baum and Alexei Shevchenko, "The 'State of the State,'" in Merle Goldman and Roderick MacFarquhar, eds., *The Paradox of China's Post-Mao Reforms* (Cambridge, Mass.: Harvard University Press, 1999), pp. 333–360.

6. Peter J. Katzenstein, *Small States in World Markets: Industrial Policy in Europe* (Ithaca, N.Y.: Cornell University Press, 1985), p. 32.

7. Alan Cawson, ed., *Organized Interests and the State: Studies in Meso-Corporatism* (London: Sage, 1985). For a criticism and defense of applying corporatism to the state's relationship with specific sectors or companies, see the exchange between Cox and Cawson. Andrew Cox, "The Old and New Testaments of Corporatism: Is it a Political Form or a Method of Policy-making?" *Political Studies*, vol. 36, no. 2 (June 1988), pp. 294–308; Alan Cawson, "In Defense of the New Testament: A Reply to Andrew Cox, 'The Old and New Testaments of Corporatism,'" *Political Studies*, vol. 36, no. 2 (June 1988), pp. 309–315.

8. Schmitter, "Still the Century of Corporatism?" p. 97.

9. Civil society refers to "a part of society comprising a complex of autonomous institutions—economic, religious, intellectual and political—distinguishable from the family, clan, the locality and the state." Edward Shils, "The Virtue of Civil Society," *Government and Opposition*, vol. 26, no. 1 (Winter 1991), p. 4.

10. Keane notes that the revival of the term *civil society* in the 1980s was directly connected to attempts to "revive the democratic imagination." John Keane, *Civil Society: Old Images, New Visions* (Stanford: Stanford University Press, 1998), p. 7. As examples, see Nelson Kasfir, ed., *Civil Society and Democracy and Africa: Critical Perspectives* (London: Frank Cass, 1998); Jeffrey Haynes, *Democracy and Civil Society in the Third World: Politics and New Political Movements* (Oxford: Polity Press, 1997); Victor M. Perez-Diaz, *The Return of Civil Society: The Emergence of Democratic Spain* (Cambridge, Mass.: Harvard University Press, 1993); and Peter J. Burnell and Peter Calvert, eds., *Civil Society in Democratization* (London: Frank Cass, 2004).

11. The broader comparative literature views societal corporatism as compatible with civil society. Schmitter, "Still the Century of Corporatism?"; Markus M. L. Crepaz and Arendd Lijphart, "Linking and Integrating Corporatism and Consensus Democracy: Theory, Concepts and Evidence," *British Journal of Political Science*, vol. 25, no. 2 (April 1995), pp. 281–288; Alan Siaroff, "Corporatism in 24 Industrial Democracies: Meaning and Measurement," *European Journal of Political Research*, vol. 36, no. 2 (October 1999), pp. 175–205. Some China specialists have taken a different tack. Pearson contrasts "civil society/democracy" with corpo-

ratism and clientelism. Unger and Chan show a similar perspective when they conclude, "To the extent China continues to loosen up politically, it is far more likely to involve such incremental shifts into societal corporatism rather than the introduction of any form of political democracy." Margaret M. Pearson, *China's New Business Elite: The Political Consequences of Economic Reform* (Berkeley: University of California Press, 1997); Jonathan Unger and Anita Chan, "Corporatism in China: A Developmental State in an East Asian Context," in Barrett L. McCormick and Jonathan Unger, eds., *China After Socialism: In the Footsteps of Eastern Europe or East Asia?* (Armonk, N.Y.: M. E. Sharpe, 1996), p. 129.

12. Civil society could be compared with other types of societies compatible with the other frameworks for state-society relations. "Controlled society" would be consistent with state corporatism, and "merged state-society" would exist in the context of clientelism or monism.

13. Solomon laments how the debate in Soviet studies over institutional pluralism, coined by Hough, sidetracked the entire field into focusing on whether the Soviet Union fit the pluralist model rather than attempting to gain a more direct understanding of Soviet reality. Solomon, *Pluralism in the Soviet Union*, pp. 4–36.

14. Pearson, *China's New Business Elite*, pp. 58–60.

15. Ole Bruun, *Business and Bureaucracy in a Chinese City: An Ethnography of Private Business Households in Contemporary China* (Berkeley: Institute of East Asian Studies, 1993); Gordon White, Jude Howell, and Shang Xiaoyuan, *In Search of Civil Society: Market Reform and Social Change in Contemporary China* (Oxford: Clarendon Press, 1996); and Pearson, *China's New Business Elite*.

16. Wank documents how the national-level Bureau of Industry and Commerce shut down a competing, locally-based civic association in the city of Xiamen when the latter began to draw away the former's members. David L. Wank, *Commodifying Communism: Business, Trust, and Politics in a Chinese City* (Cambridge: Cambridge University Press, 1999).

17. Kenneth W. Foster, "Associations in the Embrace of an Authoritarian State: State Domination of Society?" *Studies in Comparative International Development*, vol. 35, no. 4 (Winter 2001), pp. 84–109; and Kenneth W. Foster, "Embedded within State Agencies: Business Associations in Yantai," *China Journal*, no. 47 (January 2002), pp. 41–65.

18. Wang Ying, Zhe Xiaoye and Sun Bingyao, *Shehui zhongjianceng: gaige yu zhongguode shetuan zuzhi* (The intermediate level of society: reform and China's social organizations) (Beijing: China Development Publishing, 1993).

19. Thomas B. Gold, "Urban Private Business and Social Change," in Deborah Davis and Ezra Vogel, eds., *Chinese Society on the Eve of Tiananmen: The Impact of Reform* (Cambridge, Mass.: Council on East Asian Studies, 1990), pp. 157–178. R. M. Glassman, *China in Transition: Communism, Capitalism and Democracy* (New York: Praeger, 1991); and David Strand, "Protest in Beijing: Civil Society and Public Sphere in China," *Problems of Communism*, vol. 39, no. 3 (May–June 1990), pp. 1–19.

20. Benjamin L. Read, "Democratizing the Neighborhood? New Private Housing and Home-Owner Self-Organization in Urban China," *China Journal*, no. 49 (January 2003), pp. 31–60; Ian Johnson, "The Death and Life of China's Civil Society," *Perspectives*, vol. 1, no. 3 (September 2003), pp. 551–554.

21. White, Howell, and Shang, *In Search of Civil Society*, pp. 110, 153–183; Jonathan Unger, "'Bridges': Private Businesses, the Chinese Government and the

Rise of New Associations," *China Quarterly*, no. 147 (September 1996), pp. 795–819; Jude Howell, "Striking a New Balance: New Social Organization in Post-Mao China," *Capital and Class*, no. 54 (Autumn 1994), pp. 89–111; Vivienne Shue, "State Power and Social Organization in China," in Joel S. Migdal, Atul Kohli, and Vivienne Shue, eds., *State Power and Social Forces: Domination and Transformation in the Third World* (Cambridge: Cambridge University Press, 1994), pp. 65–88; Bruce J. Dickson, *Red Capitalists in China: The Party, Private Entrepreneurs, and Prospects for Political Change* (Cambridge: Cambridge University Press, 2003).

22.  Bruun, *Business and Bureaucracy in a Chinese City*; Wank, *Commodifying Communism*; and David L. Wank, "Civil Society in Communist China? Private Business and Political Alliance, 1989," in John Hall, ed., *Civil Society: Theory, History, Comparison* (Cambridge: Polity, 1995), pp. 56–79.

23.  David Zweig, "Undemocratic Capitalism: China and the Limits of Economism," *National Interest*, no. 56 (Summer 1999), p. 67.

24.  Wank, *Commodifying Communism*; He Qinglian, *Xiandaihuade xianjing: dangdai zhongguode jingji shehui wenti* (The pitfalls of modernization: The economic and social problems of contemporary China) (Beijing: China Today Press, 1998).

25.  Dorothy Solinger, "Urban Entrepreneurs and the State: The Merger of State and Society," in Arthur Lewis Rosenbaum, ed., *State and Society in China: The Consequences of Reform* (Boulder: Westview Press, 1992), p. 124.

26.  Maurice Meisner, *The Deng Xiaoping Era: An Inquiry Into the Fate of Chinese Socialism, 1978–1994* (New York: Hill and Wang, 1996), p. 514.

27.  Shue, "State Power and Social Organization in China"; Howell, "Striking a New Balance"; and White, Howell, and Shang, *In Search of Civil Society*.

28.  Victor Nee, "A Theory of Market Transition: From Redistribution to Markets in State Socialism," *American Sociological Review*, vol.54, no. 5 (October 1989), pp. 663–681.

29.  On the dichotomy between plan and market, see Charles E. Lindblom, *Politics and Markets: The World's Political Economic Systems* (New York: Basic Books, 1977); and Janos Kornai, *The Socialist System: The Political Economy of Communism* (Princeton, N.J.: Princeton University Press, 1992). On the focus on China's private economy and property rights, see Willy Kraus, *Private Business in China: Revival Between Ideology and Pragmatism* (Honolulu: University of Hawaii Press, 1991); Susan Young, *Private Business and Economic Reform in China* (Armonk, N.Y.: M. E. Sharpe, 1995); Jean C. Oi and Andrew G. Walder, eds., *Property Rights and Economic Reform in China* (Stanford: Stanford University Press, 1999); and William A. Kerr and Ed MacKay, "Is Mainland China Evolving into a Market Economy?" *Issues and Studies*, vol. 33, no. 9 (September 1997), pp. 31–45.

30.  On how states not only intervene in markets, but also how they, along with culture, can define markets' ownership rights, barriers to entry, access to credit, rules for pricing, and rules of exchange, see Andrew Walder, "Markets and Inequality in Transition Economies: Toward Testable Theories," *American Journal of Sociology*, vol. 101, no. 4 (January 1996), pp. 1060–1073; Neil Fligstein, "Markets as Politics: A Political-Cultural Approach to Market Institutions," *American Sociological Review*, vol. 61, no. 4 (August 1996), pp. 656–673; Edward Steinfeld, *Forging Reform in China: The Fate of State-Owned Industry* (Cambridge: Cambridge University Press, 1998); and Kellee S. Tsai, *Back-Alley Banking: Private Entrepreneurs in China* (Ithaca, N.Y.: Cornell University Press, 2002).

31. For example, my previous research that found the existence of greater firm activism on policy issues should be tempered since the study only examines a large nonstate firm in China's highly competitive and technology-intensive information industry. Kristen Parris discovered that private entrepreneurs' sense of rights varies widely, but the findings would have been more valuable had she systematically explored the extent to which their attitudes varied by their levels of education, industry, and location. Scott Kennedy, "The Stone Group: State Client or Market Pathbreaker?" *China Quarterly*, no. 152 (December 1997), pp. 746–777; Kristen Parris, "Entrepreneurs and Citizenship in China," *Problems of Post-Communism*, vol. 46, no. 1 (January/February 1999), pp. 43–61.

32. For example, Wank acknowledges that his findings of clientelism may be influenced by the fact that the coastal city of Xiamen is in a highly commercial region of China, but he leaves this line of inquiry unpursued. It may have also been significant that all of the merchants in his study were engaged in small-scale, standardized, labor-intensive activities that do not require much technical training, making them particularly vulnerable to bureaucratic pressure. David L. Wank, "Bureaucratic Patronage and Private Business: Changing Networks of Power in Urban China," in Andrew Walder, ed., *Waning of the Communist State: Economic Origins of Political Change in China and Hungary* (Berkeley: University of California Press), pp. 153–183.

33. Guthrie, though, stresses that the primary distinction in firms' actual use of connections is their administrative rank; those more highly placed need to draw on connections less often. Pei employs variation in his study of provincial associations by examining four industrial and four agricultural provinces, but whether the level of industrialization matters is left unanswered. Ole Odgaard, "Entrepreneurs and Elite Formation in Rural China," *Australian Journal of Chinese Affairs*, no. 28 (July 1992), pp. 89–108; Unger, "'Bridges'"; White, Howell and Shang, *In Search of Civil Society*; Doug Guthrie, *Dragon in a Three-Piece Suit: The Emergence of Capitalism in China* (Princeton, N.J.: Princeton University Press, 1999), pp. 175–197. Minxin Pei, "Chinese Civic Associations: An Empirical Analysis," *Modern China*, vol. 24, no. 3 (July 1998), pp. 285–318.

34. The explicit link between civil society and democratization made by White, Howell, and Shang is typical of how the research is framed: "This process of associational flowering and the shift in the balance of power between state and society which it reflects would undermine the existing authoritarian political order and provide the social impetus for a transition towards political liberalization and ultimately some form of democratic polity." *In Search of Civil Society*, p. 10. Also see Unger and Chan, "Corporatism in China": He Baogang, *The Democratic Implications of Civil Society in China* (New York: St. Martin's Press, 1997); and Xia Li Lollar, *China's Transition Toward a Market Economy, Civil Society and Democracy* (Bristol, Ind.: Wyndham Hill Press, 1997). Other China specialists who do not believe that China is moving in a democratic direction still orient their research around the theoretical relationship between civil society and democracy. Pearson, *China's New Business Elite*; Margaret M. Pearson, "Entrepreneurs and Democratization in China's Foreign Sector," in Victoria E. Bonnell and Thomas B. Gold, eds., *The New Entrepreneurs of Europe and Asia: Patterns of Business Development in Russia, Eastern Europe and China* (Armonk, N.Y.: M. E. Sharpe, 2002), pp. 130–155.

35. Some have even been satisfied with simply documenting the growth in the

number of associations without relating anything about how the associations actually operate. Kjeld Erik Brødsgaard, "State and Society in Hainan: Liao Xun's Ideas on 'Small Government, Big Society,'" in Kjeld Erik Brødsgaard and David Strand, eds., *Reconstructing Twentieth-Century China: State Control, Civil Society, and National Identity* (Oxford: Clarendon, 1998), pp. 189–215; and Pei, "Chinese Civic Associations."

36. This does not mean that the results presented here have nothing to contribute to the debates over democratization, economic growth, and the quality of governance. In fact, by not "looking directly into the sun," we may be able to say something about these issues after all. These questions are addressed in Chapter 6.

37. White, Howell, and Shang give anecdotal evidence of how the central government has consulted some associations, but they make no claim that the associations' members or the associations themselves proactively tried to influence public policy. *In Search of Civil Society*, pp. 115–117.

38. Kenneth Lieberthal and Michel Oksenberg, *Policy Making in China: Leaders, Structures, and Processes* (Princeton, N.J.: Princeton University Press, 1988); Kenneth Lieberthal and David M. Lampton, eds., *Bureaucracy, Politics and Decision-Making in Post-Mao China* (Berkeley: University of California Press, 1992); Susan Shirk, *The Political Logic of Economic Reform in China* (Berkeley: University of California Press, 1993); Carol Lee Hamrin and Suisheng Zhao, eds., *Decision-Making in Deng's China: Perspectives from Insiders* (Armonk, N.Y.: M. E. Sharpe, 1995); and Joseph Fewsmith, *Elite Politics in Contemporary China* (Armonk, N.Y.: M. E. Sharpe, 2001).

39. Nina Halpern, "Making Economic Policy: The Influence of Economists," in U.S. Congress Joint Economic Committee, *China Looks Toward the Year 2000*, vol. 1 (Washington, D.C.: U.S. Government Printing Office, 1986); Nina Halpern, "Information Flows and Policy Coordination in the Chinese Bureaucracy," in Lieberthal and Lampton, *Bureaucracy, Politics, and Decision Making in Post-Mao China*, pp. 125–148, Carol Lee Hamrin, *China and the Challenge of the Future: Changing Political Patterns* (Boulder: Westview Press, 1990); Joseph Fewsmith, *Dilemmas of Reform in China: Political Conflict and Economic Debate* (Armonk, N.Y.: M. E. Sharpe, 1994); Joseph Fewsmith, *China Since Tiananmen: The Politics of Transition* (Cambridge: Cambridge University Press, 2001). Murray Scot Tanner, *The Politics of Lawmaking in China: Institutions, Processes, and Democratic Prospects* (Oxford: Clarendon Press, 1999); Fang Cai, "The Roles of Chinese Economists in Economic Reform," *China Economy Papers*, Australia National University Asia Pacific School, Economics and Management, no. 2 (1998); and Barry Naughton, "China's Economic Think Tanks: Their Changing Role in the 1990s," *China Quarterly*, no. 171 (September 2002), pp. 625–635.

40. Kenneth Lieberthal, *Governing China: From Revolution Through Reform* (New York: W. W. Norton, 1995), p. 181. In the recently issued updated edition of the book, Lieberthal notes the growing political activism of society, but he does not specifically refer to public policy. The text's overwhelming stress is still on state institutions and elites. Kenneth Lieberthal, *Governing China: From Revolution Through Reform, Second Edition* (New York: W. W. Norton, 2004), pp. 199–202, 299–301.

41. David Zweig, *Internationalizing China: Domestic Interests and Global Linkages* (Ithaca, N.Y.: Cornell University Press, 2002); Thomas G. Moore, *China in the World Market: Chinese Industry and International Sources of Reform in the Post-Mao Era* (Cambridge: Cambridge University Press, 2002); and Kun-Chin Lin, "Corpo-

ratizing China: Reinventing State Control for the Market" (Ph.D. diss., University of California, Berkeley, 2003).

42. Tanner is sensitive to the costs incurred because the various models of policy making in China neglect nonstate actors. He writes: "Most models, including those used here, tend to treat political systems as static, and focus more on the statist elements of the policy apparatus than the forces which change state-society relations or expand participation and accountability. This lack of a well-developed theoretical link between studies of policy-making and studies of system transition is as ironic as it is unfortunate, for the link between the two seems fairly natural." Tanner, *The Politics of Lawmaking*, p. 35.

43. Jesse Biddle and Vedat Milor, "Economic Governance in Turkey: Bureaucratic Capacity, Policy Networks, and Business Associations," in Sylvia Maxfield and Ben Ross Schneider, eds., *Business and the State in Developing Countries* (Ithaca, N.Y.: Cornell University Press, 1997), pp. 277–309. In Britain manufacturing companies rely on industry associations more than commercial or financial firms, while nationalized industries are less reliant than private firms on the peak association, the Confederation of British Industry. Mitchell, "The Decentralization of Business in Britain."

44. J. Rogers Hollingsworth, Phillipe Schmitter, and Wolfgang Streeck, eds., *Governing Capitalist Economies: Performance and Control of Economic Sectors* (New York: Oxford University Press, 1994).

45. Franz Traxler and Brigette Unger, "The Dairy Sector," in Hollingsworth, Schmitter, and Streeck, *Governing Capitalist Economies*, pp. 183–214.

46. Wyn Grant, Alberto Martinelli, and William Paterson, "Large Firms as Political Actors: A Comparative Analysis of the Chemical Industry in Britain, Italy and West Germany," *West European Politics*, vol. 12, no. 2 (April 1989), pp. 72–90; and Wyn Grant and William Paterson, "The Chemical Industry: A Study of Internationalization," in Hollingsworth, Schmitter, and Streeck, *Governing Capitalist Economies*, pp. 129–155.

47. Philippe C. Schmitter, "Sectors in Modern Capitalism: Modes of Governance and Variations in Performance," in Renato Brunetta and Carlo Dell'Aringa, eds., *Labour Relations and Economic Performance* (New York: New York University Press, 1990), pp. 3–39; and Dermot McCann, *Small States, Open Markets, and the Organization of Business Interests* (Aldershot, England: Dartmouth Publishing, 1995).

48. Mancur Olson argued that firms in sectors with low concentration have difficulty acting collectively because of the free-rider problem. See his *The Logic of Collective Action: Public Goods and the Theory of Groups* (Cambridge, Mass.: Harvard University Press, 1965). This conclusion has been challenged even by those who accept the significance of economic factors. The above example from Turkey shows that large firms may not want to act collectively if they have individual access to the state. Also see Terry M. Moe, *The Organization of Interests* (Chicago: Chicago University Press, 1980); and Terry M. Moe, "The New Economics of Organization," *American Journal of Political Science*, vol. 28, no. 4 (November 1984), pp. 739–777.

49. Jeffry A. Frieden, *Debt, Development, and Democracy: Modern Political Economy and Latin America, 1965–1985* (Princeton, N.J.: Princeton University Press, 1991); Ronald Rogowski, *Commerce and Coalitions: How Trade Affects Domestic Political Alignments* (Princeton, N.J.: Princeton University Press, 1989); and D. Michael

Shafer, *Winners and Losers: How Sectors Shape the Developmental Prospects of States* (Ithaca, N.Y.: Cornell University Press, 1994).

50. The free-rider problem inhibiting cooperation can be overcome by, among other factors, individuals' commitment to a cause or norms stressing reciprocity, reputation, and trust. Donald P. Green and Ian Shapiro, *Pathologies of Rational Choice Theory: A Critique of Applications in Political Science* (New Haven, Conn.: Yale University Press, 1994); Elinor Ostrom, "A Behavioral Approach to the Rational Choice Theory of Collective Action: Presidential Addres, American Political Science Association, 1997," *American Political Science Review*, vol. 92, no. 1 (March 1998), pp. 1–22.

51. Peter A. Hall and David W. Soskice, eds., *Varieties of Capitalism: The Institutional Foundations of Comparative Advantage* (Oxford: Oxford University Press, 2001); and Mauro F. Guillen, *The Limits of Convergence: Globalization and Organizational Change in Argentina, South Korea, and Spain* (Princeton, N.J.: Princeton University Press, 2001).

52. J. Rogers Hollingsworth and Wolfgang Streeck, "Countries and Sectors: Concluding Remarks on Performance, Convergence and Competitiveness," in Hollingsworth, Schmitter, and Streeck, *Governing Capitalist Economies*, pp. 270–300.

53. Jeffrey A. Hart, *Rival Capitalists: International Competitiveness in the United States, Japan, and Western Europe* (Ithaca, N.Y.: Cornell University Press, 1992); Hollingsworth, Schmitter, and Streeck, *Governing Capitalist Economies*; and Ben Ross Schneider, "Why is Mexican Business so Organized?," *Latin American Research Review*, vol. 37, no. 1 (2002).

54. Andrew Shonfield, *Modern Capitalism: The Changing Balance of Public and Private Power* (London: Oxford University Press, 1965); Peter J. Katzenstein, ed., *Between Power and Plenty: Foreign Economic Policies of Advanced Industrial States* (Madison: University of Wisconsin Press, 1978); and Harmon Zeigler, *Pluralism, Corporatism, and Confucianism: Political Association and Conflict Regulation in the United States, Europe, and Taiwan* (Philadelphia: Temple University Press, 1988).

55. Dickson, *Red Capitalists in China*, p. 22.

56. Karl Fields, "Strong States and Business Organization in Korea and Taiwan," in Sylvia Maxfield and Ben Ross Schneider, *Business and the State in Developing Countries*, pp. 122–151; and Gerald A. McBeath, "The Changing Role of Business Associations in Democratizing Taiwan," *Journal of Contemporary China*, no. 18 (July 1998), pp. 303–320.

57. Herbert Kitschelt et al., "Convergence and Divergence in Advanced Capitalist Democracies," in Herbert Kitschelt et al., eds., *Continuity and Change in Contemporary Capitalism* (Cambridge: Cambridge University Press, 1999), p. 450.

58. Suzanne Berger and Ronald Dore, eds., *National Diversity and Global Capitalism* (Ithaca, N.Y.: Cornell University Press, 1996).

59. Lindblom, *Politics and Markets*. Salamon and Siegfried do systematically compare businesses in different economic contexts, finding that larger firms and less-concentrated and less-profitable sectors influenced the government to grant them lower tax rates. However, while suggestive, the study looks at only one issue area (tax policy) in an advanced industrial democracy (the United States), and it does not consider the potential relevance of variation in patterns of interaction. Most importantly, their study relies strictly on quantitative data on tax rates to

make inferences about influence rather than actually pinpointing industries' attempts to affect government policy. Lester M. Salamon and John J. Siegfried, "Economic Power and Political Influence: The Impact of Industry Structure on Public Policy," *American Political Science Review*, vol. 71, no. 3 (September 1977), pp. 1026–1043.

60. In a review of a book on civil society in China, Chamberlain calls for this type of research: "If market [read 'economic'] forces were more explicitly and effectively addressed in our studies, we might emerge with a keener sense of civil society's absence or presence." Heath B. Chamberlain, "Civil Society with Chinese Characteristics?" *China Journal*, no. 39 (January 1998), p. 80.

61. Segal and Thun investigate how background economic, social, and political factors shape the content and success of local-government sectoral policies. While they make important contributions to the debate about the relationship between political and social institutions and economic performance in individual sectors, their studies are not about how government and businesses interact. Adam Segal and Eric Thun, "Thinking Globally, Acting Locally: Local Governments, Industrial Sectors, and Development in China," *Politics and Society*, vol. 29, no. 4 (December 2001), pp. 557–588; Adam Segal, *Digital Dragon: High-Technology Enterprises in China* (Ithaca, N.Y.: Cornell University Press, 2003).

62. *China Statistical Yearbook 2001* (Beijing: China Statistics Press, 2001), p. 401.

63. A study on business associations in the Czech Republic was conducted only a few years after reforms began, and thus its negative findings are not surprising. The authors found varying levels of autonomy and robustness in associations, but chalked these differences up to differences in leadership quality rather than contrasting economic circumstances. Mitchell Ornstein and Raj M. Desai, "State Power and Interest Group Formation: The Business Lobby in the Czech Republic," *Problems of Post-Communism*, vol. 44, no. 6 (November/December 1997), pp. 43–52.

64. The appendix gives a detailed explanation of how the sectors and firms were selected for this study.

65. There are two possible weaknesses of what has been called the "decision-making approach," in which influence on specific policy decisions is traced. First, the approach only accounts for a narrow form of influence. Some types of industry influence are not directly observed in particular policies but are exhibited in views and behaviors that are widespread in society. Second, obtaining information on business's actual involvement in policy-making is quite challenging even in countries like the United States, not to mention China. However, the value of pinpointing influence, and not just inferring its existence, makes this approach worth attempting.

## Chapter 2. Organizing Business in China

1. On the Mao era, see Harry Harding, *Organizing China: The Problem of Bureaucracy, 1949–1976* (Stanford: Stanford University Press, 1981).

2. China refers to NGOs as "social organizations" (*shehui tuanti*), which include academic societies (*xuehui*), research associations (*yanjiuhui*), industry associations (*hangye xiehui* or *gongye xiehui*), industry guilds (*tongye gonghui*), chambers of commerce (*shanghui*), friendship societies (*lianyihui*), and foundations (*jijinhui*).

The key current regulation is the 1998 *Regulations on the Registration and Regulation of Social Organizations* (*shehui tuanti dengji guanli tiaoli*), which replaced a 1989 law of the same name. The 1989 version, issued October 25, 1989, is contained in Wang Huai'an et al., eds., *Zhonghua renmin gongheguo falu quanshu 2, 1986–1989* (Collection of the laws of the People's Republic of China, vol. 2, 1986–1989), (Beijing: Jilin People's Press, 1990), pp. 884–886. The 1998 version, issued October 25, 1998, is carried in *Fazhi ribao* (Legal daily), November 4, 1998, p. 3. Other regulations are contained in Ministry of Civil Affairs (hereafter MOCA), *Shehui tuanti guanli gongzuo shouce* (Social organizations regulation work handbook), July 1996; and State Economic and Trade Commission (hereafter SETC), *Hangye xiehui gongzuo shouce* (Industry association work handbook), 2002.

3. The specific call to promote industry associations has appeared in numerous Chinese Communist Party and National People's Congress plenum documents, beginning with the November 1993 *Decision of the CCP Central Committee on Some Issues Concerning the Establishment of a Socialist Market Economic Structure*. A selection of citations from key documents and leaders' speeches is contained in Ou Xinqian and Du Jinling, eds., *Zhongguo hangye xiehui: gaige yu tansuo* (Chinese industry associations: reform and exploration) (Beijing: China Commercial Press, April 1999), pp. 1–31.

4. In this book, the term "business associations" includes both chambers of commerce and industry-specific sectoral associations. The terms "industry associations," "trade associations," and "sectoral associations" are used interchangeably.

5. For example, see Han Qiaowen, *WTO 100 wen: hangye xiehui zai zhongguo ru shi houde sikao* (100 questions on WTO: thoughts for industry associations after China joins the WTO) (Shanghai: Shanghai People's Publishing, 2002).

6. Margaret M. Pearson, *China's New Business Elite: The Political Consequences of Economic Reform* (Berkeley: University of California Press, 1997); Gordon White, Jude Howell, and Shang Xiaoyuan, *In Search of Civil Society: Market Reform and Social Change in Contemporary China* (Oxford: Clarendon Press, 1996); and Bruce J. Dickson, *Red Capitalists in China: The Party, Private Entrepreneurs, and Prospects for Political Change* (Cambridge: Cambridge University Press, 2003).

7. "Industry guild" has been another name for "industry association." On the eve of the Communist victory, Beijing had 130, while in 1957 Shanghai still had over 400. Lu Fengtai, ed., *Shehui zhongjie zuzhi yanjiu* (Social intermediary organizations research) (Shanghai: Xuelin Press, 1998); Interview #g25 (see the appendix for an explanation of the interview coding system).

8. In late 1956, the ACFIC had branches in over 90 percent of China's 2,110 counties. Wang Dekuan, "Xin zhongguo shanghuide jianli he fazhan" (The construction and development of new China's chambers of commerce), *Zhongguo gongshang* (China industry and commerce), August 1998, p. 40.

9. The Chinese People's Political Consultative Conference was created in 1949 and serves as an advisory body to demonstrate the alliance of the Chinese Communist Party (CCP) with those beyond its ranks. Its delegates are from thirty-five different "sections" (*jiebie*) of Chinese society, including the ACFIC, the All-China Federation of Women, and the All-China Federation of Trade Unions. The entire membership of the CPPCC meets annually in conjunction with the meetings of the National People's Congress.

10. "Huge Market for Legal Workers," *China Daily*, March 21, 2003 (www. chinadaily.com.cn).

11. For example, see Chen Qingtai, ed., *Shanghui fazhan yu zhidu guifan* (Development and institutional regulation of chambers of commerce) (Beijing: China Economy Press, 1995) pp. 1–4.

12. Because there was no one regulation that governed associations until 1989, White, Howell, and Shang give more credit to local initiative, writing, "In general, local organizations have tended to anticipate their national-level counterparts." White, Howell, and Shang, *In Search of Civil Society*, p. 99, 102. That assessment is accurate in some cases, but parts of the central government have been actively involved in developing associations since the late 1970s.

13. Jonathan Unger, "'Bridges': Private Businesses, the Chinese Government and the Rise of New Associations," *China Quarterly*, no. 147 (September 1996), pp. 795–819; Pearson, *China's New Business Elite*; Christopher Earle Nevitt, "Private Business Associations in China: Evidence of Civil Society or Local State Power?" *China Journal*, no.36 (July 1996), pp. 25–43; and Kenneth W. Foster, "Embedded with State Agencies: Business Associations in Yantai," *China Journal*, no. 47 (January 2002), pp. 41–65.

14. Just after 1949, Yuan worked with Chen Yun, a leading economic policy maker during the Mao era, in Shenyang. After returning to Beijing in 1953, he worked in the Ministry of Heavy Industry and Metallurgy Ministry, and was appointed vice chairman of the State Economic Commission in 1960. In the early 1970s he served as vice director of the State Planning Commission and then in 1978 rejoined the State Economic Commission, becoming its director in 1981. According to Tanner, in the 1980s Yuan was a strong advocate for enterprise managers, even at the expense of party committees. Yuan Baohua, "Bear Firmly in Mind Comrade Chen Yun's Earnest Teachings," *Renmin ribao* (People's daily), July 1, 1996, p. 11; Wolfgang Bartke and Peter Schier, *China's New Party Leadership* (Armonk, N.Y.: M. E. Sharpe, 1985), pp. 236–237; Murray Scot Tanner, *The Politics of Lawmaking in China: Institutions, Processes, and Democratic Prospects* (Oxford: Clarendon Press, 1999), p. 170; Interview #g27. In 1993, the SEC was reorganized and its name changed to the State Economic and Trade Commission (SETC).

15. A more detailed discussion of government policy and efforts to set up sectoral associations can be found in Kenneth W. Foster, "Administrative Restructuring and the Emergence of Sectoral Associations in China" (paper delivered at the Annual Meeting of the Association for Asian Studies, Washington, D.C., April 7, 2002).

16. To complicate matters further, in 1984, the State Economic Commission founded the China Enterprise Directors Association (CEDA, *zhongguo qiyejia xiehui*), also aimed at state-owned enterprises. In 1988 it merged with China Enterprise Management Association (CEMA). Taken together with CEMA's name change in 1999, the existing organization is known by the awkward China Enterprise Confederation–China Enterprise Directors Association (CEC–CEDA).

17. Interview #g27; White, Howell, and Shang, *In Search of Civil Society*, pp. 117, 194–197.

18. Chen Qingtai, *Shanghui fazhan yu zhidu guifan*, pp. 28–30.

19. All data on ACFIC branches and membership are from Interview #g35.

20. In 1989, ACFIC already had 12,877 SOEs and 15,604 collectives as members. Xue Muqiao, "Establish and Develop Non-Governmental Self-Management Organizations in Various Trades," *Renmin ribao*, (People's daily), October 10, 1988, in *Foreign Broadcast Information Service-China Daily Report*, October 18, 1988, pp. 33–35.

21. Private companies register as collectives to avoid the official discrimination directed at their formally private counterparts. Recently, there has been a growing trend for these collectives to "take off their red hats" and re-register as private companies. Ye Bing, *"Haishi 'tuomao' hao"* ("Taking off the hat" is still better), *Zhonghua gongshang shibao* (China business times), April 3, 1999, p. 1.

22. In some cities, the proportion of SOE members is much higher. As of June 1998, 43 percent of the company members of Shanghai's Federation of Industry and Commerce were state-owned or collective enterprises. In Beijing (as of December 1998), the number was 40.3 percent. Interviews #g14, #g25.

23. ACFIC's original charter is in Chen Qingtai, *Shanghui fazhan yu zhidu guifan*, pp. 259–261. The current charter (passed in 1988) is available on its Web site (www.acfic.org.cn). The exemption of all organizations within the CPPCC is made explicit in Article 3 of the 1998 *Regulations on the Registration and Regulation of Social Organizations*.

24. In 1993, ACFIC received approval to be known also as the All-China General Chamber of Industry and Commerce (*zhongguo minjian shanghui*).

25. Entrepreneurs account for the largest proportion, six percent, of the 2,238 deputies in the Tenth CPPCC (2003–2008). In addition to the ACFIC's formally allotted 65 seats, another 91 entrepreneurs who belong to the ACFIC participate in the CPPCC officially representing other social groups. There are also 164 ACFIC members in the Tenth National People's Congress (2003–2008). Besides being a regulator participant in deliberations of economic laws and regulations, the ACFIC has consistently pressed for constitutional amendments granting greater protection to private enterprises. Such amendments were passed in 1999 and 2004. Interviews #g10, #g12, #g14, #g35.

26. This paragraph draws heavily on Unger, "'Bridges': Private Business, the Chinese Government and the Rise of New Associations."

27. At the end of 2001, there were 26 million *getihu* with over 50 million employees. "China Industry: Saving Private Enterprise," *Economist Intelligence Unit-ViewsWire*, April 28, 2003.

28. See Article 5 of the *Provisional Regulations of the People's Republic of China on Private Enterprises*, promulgated by the State Council, June 25, 1988, in *China Laws for Foreign Business* (CCH International), pp. 17, 101–117, 119.

29. In their discussion of rural Chinese social organizations, White, Howell, and Shang do not even mention CTVEA and instead focus on the efforts of local branches of SELA and PEA to organize formally private enterprises. White, Howell, and Shang, *In Search of Civil Society*, pp. 153–183; Interview #g100.

30. In 1993, MOFERT's name was changed to the Ministry of Foreign Trade and Economic Cooperation (MOFTEC), and in 2003 to the Ministry of Commerce (MOC).

31. CAEFI, *China Association of Enterprises with Foreign Investment, 1987–1997*, 1998, p. 61; *Almanac of China's Foreign Economic Relations and Trade, 1998/99* (Beijing: China Economy Press, 1998), p. 57; and Pearson, *China's New Business Elite*, pp. 122–123.

32. "Waiguo shanghui guanli zhanxing guiding" (Temporary regulations on the regulation of foreign chambers of commerce), passed by the State Council on April 28, 1989, issued June 14, 1989, in Wang Huai'an, *Zhonghua renmin gongheguo falu quanshu 2*, pp. 882–883. The regulation says only that "foreign chambers of commerce should be established according to nationality," but officials have interpreted this to mean that each country should have just one chamber of commerce.

33. At its height, there were seven separate U.S. chambers of commerce in China—in Beijing, Shanghai, Shenyang, Wuhan, Chengdu, Guangzhou, and Tianjin. The Wuhan chamber was closed after a visa corruption scandal broke out in 2001, and as of 2003, the Shenyang chamber was not active. Only AmCham Beijing has registered with national authorities. The U.S.-China Business Council, an association with over 250 U.S. company members, has also been registered as a chamber of commerce since 1981. "Wuhan Police Probe Amcham Scandal," *Far Eastern Economic Review*, August 30, 2001, p. 9; Interviews #g17, #g21, #g22, #g36.

34. This figure includes all chambers registered with the China Council for the Promotion of International Trade (CCPIT) as well as unregistered chambers that this researcher discovered in an unsystematic search. However, it does not include the many local chambers of commerce for Taiwanese or Hong Kong businesses that have been created primarily in southeastern China. On the Taiwanese case, see David Ahlstrom, Garry D. Bruton, and Steven S. Y. Lui, "Navigating China's Changing Economy: Strategies for Private Firms," *Business Horizons*, January–February 2000, pp. 11–12.

35. Interview #g22.

36. State Economic and Trade Commission (hereafter SETC), *Woguo gongshang lingyu hangye xiehui gaige yu fazhan zhengce yanjiu* (Policy research on the reform and development of our country's industrial and commercial associations), March 2002; Foster, "Administrative Restructuring."

37. In 1998, the former ministries were restored as lower-level bureaus under the State Economic and Trade Commission. However, in 1999 the gates outside their buildings still had signs for both the bureaus and the general associations (which were in fact the same institutions). Chen Jiagui, ed., *Zhongguo gongye fazhan baogao–zhidu chuangxin, zuzhi bianqian yu zhengce tiaozheng* (China industry development report 1998: institutional innovation, organizational changes and policy adjustments) (Beijing: Economic Management Publishing, 1998), pp. 148–150.

38. The bureaus that were replaced with associations were those for domestic trade, coal, machinery, metallurgy, petroleum and chemicals, light industry, textiles, construction materials, and nonferrous metals. "SETC Eliminates Nine Industrial Bureaus," *ChinaOnline*, February 26, 2001, www.chinaonline.com.

39. It is not known if they were closed for political reasons or because they were not performing well, though the latter is the more likely possibility. White, Howell, and Shang, *In Search of Civil Society*, p. 205. Shi Zuoting, "Guanyu peiyu he fazhan gongshang xiehui ruogan wentide sikao" (Thoughts on some problems on nurturing and developing industrial and commercial associations), *Zhongguo jingmao daokan* (China economy and trade reporter), July 30, 1999, pp. 12–13; SETC, *Hangye xiehui gongzuo shouce*, pp. 419–420.

40. SETC, *Hangye xiehui gongzuo shouce*, p. 259.

41. The eleven national guilds are in the following industries: meat curing, aquatic products, jewelry, textiles and garments, furniture, metals, residential real es-

tate, cosmetics, automobile parts, curios, and tourism. Nine hundred eighty guilds are affiliated with township Federations of Industry and Commerce, 2,045 with county FICs, 611 with city FICs, and 126 with provincial FICs. There were only 888 guilds at the end of 1997. Interview #g35; Wang Dekuan, "Tongye gonghuide jianli he fazhan" (The construction and development of industry guilds), *Zhongguo gongshang* (China industry and commerce), September 1998, p. 40.

42. Chen Lun, "Federation Set Up to Play Role of Regulator," *China Daily*, December 11, 1998, p. 5; Interviews #g15, #g52. In 1994, the government also set up an association for companies in the trading and service sectors, and their more narrowly gauged business associations. Like its industrial counterpart, this association was recast as a federation in 1999. Although its Chinese name properly translates as the China Commercial Federation (*zhongguo shangye lianhehui*), it uses the English name, China General Chamber of Commerce (CGCC).

43. In 1988, it received approval to also be called the China Chamber of International Commerce (*zhongguo guoji shanghui*).

44. "About CCPIT," China Council for the Promotion of International Trade, www.ccpit.org (accessed November 19, 2003).

45. The import-export chambers are machinery and electronics; food and husbandry; textiles; metals, minerals and chemicals; medicine and health products; and light industry and handicrafts. Membership figures for all are not available, but according to their Web sites, as of mid-2003, the China Chamber of Commerce for Metals, Minerals and Chemical Importers and Exporters (www.ccmmc.org.cn) and the China Chamber of Commerce for the Import and Export of Machinery and Electronics Products (www.cccme.org.cn) had two thousand and fifty-one hundred members, respectively.

46. This researcher identified sixteen foreign associations in the capital as of 1999, but the actual number is likely several times higher. By 2002, there were sixty-five foreign business associations in Shanghai, thirty-one of which were American. Yi Fan, "Hangye xiehui jidai chongsu quanwei" (Industry association authority urgently needs remolding), *Wenzhai yu shoucang* (Abstracts and collections) August 28, 2002, www.rongwp.com.

47. The distinction in Chinese is between "departmental regulation" (*bumen guanli*) and "industry regulation" (*hangye guanli*). Zhang Jinsheng and Zhu Jianhong, " '96 hangye guanli luntan kaimu" ('96 industry regulation forum opens), *Renmin ribao* (People's daily), November 19, 1996, p. 2; and Wang Jiqing, "Guanyu hangye xiehuide jianshe wenti" (On the problem of constructing industry associations), *Jingji gongzuo tongxun* (Economic work report), February 28, 1998, pp. 8–9.

48. Sheng Huaren, ed., *Jingmao baipishu: 1998–1999 nian zhongguo jingmao gaige yu fazhan* (Economic and trade white paper: 1998–1999 China economic and trade reform and development) (Beijing: China Economy Press, 1999), p. 105.

49. This sense of rights is discussed in Kristen Parris, "Entrepreneurs and Citizenship in China," *Problems of Post-Communism*, vol. 46, no. 1 (January/February, 1999), pp. 43–61. Parris focuses only on private entrepreneurs; my research found such attitudes to be more widespread.

50. Shen Li, "Si fangmian fuzhi zhongxiao qiye" (Four ways to foster small and medium enterprises), *Zhonghua gongshang shibao* (China business times), April 6, 1999, p. 2; Yu Hui, *Hangye xiehui ji qi zai zhongguode fazhan* (Industry associations and their development in China) (Beijing: Economic Management Press, 2002);

"Xiehui yinggai 'xing' shenme" (What surname should associations have), *Jingji ribao* (Economics daily), January 15, 2002. Interviews revealed a split among officials. Some believe associations should serve both their members and government, while others stress serving only the members. This divided opinion has led to compromise reports that reflect both perspectives and delayed the adoption of new policies on associations. Lu Fengtai, *Shehui zhongjie zuzhi yanjiu*, pp. 37–38; Interviews #g93, #g67, #g68.

51. Interview #g47; Zhang Delin, "Chongfen fahui hangye xiehuide zuoyong" (Fully develop the role of industry associations), *Qiye gaige yu guanli* (Enterprise reform and management), July 1996, pp. 21–24. Also see Liu Li, "Wo guo hangye guanli moshi fenxi" (Analysis of our country's industry regulation model), *Zhongguo gaige* (China reform), February 1999, pp. 18–19.

52. Under the 1989 social organizations regulation, the responsible business department's stated task was to give approval for an association to register with MOCA, and MOCA was then responsible for supervising the association during its lifetime. The 1998 version shifted the supervision duties from MOCA to the responsible business department.

53. When several industrial ministries were downgraded to bureaus of the State Economic and Trade Commission in 1998, authority for over two hundred industry associations switched to the SETC. When the SETC itself was eliminated in 2003, the State-Owned Assets Supervision Administration of China (SASAC) became the "responsible business department" for these associations, the CIEF, and the CGCC. A sign of the SASAC's displeasure at being given this task is that regulatory responsibility was given to a research office within the SASAC. Interviews #g68, #g103.

54. Despite not being allowed to register, foreign industry associations are increasingly condoned by the government agencies with which they need to interact.

55. In April 1994 the State Council issued an order banning government officials at and above the rank of deputy bureau chief (*fujuzhang*) from assuming leadership positions in associations, but it allowed exceptions in special circumstances. Partly because of difficulty implementing the rule, the State Council and Chinese Communist Party Central Committee issued another order in July 1998 lowering the threshold one full administrative rank, to deputy section chief (*fuchuzhang*). MOCA, *Shehui tuanti guanli gongzuo shouce*, p. 34; SETC, *Hangye xiehui gongzuo shouce*, pp. 35–39.

56. Absent a clear definition, officials have interpreted "for profit" to mean that income is divided among an association's staff or members. A December 1989 MOCA notice states that social organizations cannot run companies but can engage in informational activities related to their original mission. A 1995 notice jointly issued by MOCA and SAIC reverses course and permits associations to establish companies that engage in activities related to the associations' missions, further weakening the prohibition against for-profit ventures. MOCA, *Shehui tuanti guanli gongzuo shouce*, pp. 14–18, 54–55; Interview #g45.

57. Also of note, in at least state corporatist countries, corporatism itself was a well-known doctrine expounded by rulers. By contrast, in China the concept is unknown among officials, including those that regulate associations. It also has not received much attention by Chinese scholars. The first book-length treatment of corporatism in China, by Zhang Jing entitled *Fatuanzhuyi* (Corporatism) (Beijing:

China Social Sciences Press) was published in July 1998. It gives an overview of the corporatism literature in the West, including a brief summary of the debate among Western scholars about the existence of corporatism and civil society in China. However, it provides no new research and does not employ the model to analyze China.

58. This view was repeated in numerous interviews and is the same conclusion reached by Pearson, *China's New Business Elite*, p. 122.

59. One potential change in the direction of greater hierarchy occurred in early 2001 when the State Economic and Trade Commission appointed fifteen industry associations, primarily those that had been government bureaus until 1998, to manage on its behalf (*weiguan*) over two hundred more narrowly gauged associations. The fifteen associations officially oversee the other associations' Communist Party affairs, leadership appointments, creation of branches or subassociations, the budget, and foreign-related activities. This policy survived the SETC's elimination and the transfer of authority to the SASAC. However, the regulation states that the associations still do not have subordinate relations. Tentative evidence, discussed in Chapter 3's treatment of the steel industry, suggests continued limits on hierarchical relations. For the text of "Idea on Management of SETC–Regulated Associations," issued January 16, 2001, see SETC, *Shehui tuanti guanli gongzuo shouce*, pp. 73–98.

60. Tony Saich, "Negotiating the State: The Development of Social Organizations in China," *China Quarterly*, no. 161 (March 2000), p. 132.

61. Ibid; White, Howell, and Shang, *In Search of Civil Society*, p. 105. In 2002 the Ministry of Civil Affairs issued a notice permitting national social organizations to establish local branches with approval from their own responsible business departments and the local governments where the new branches would operate. SETC, *Hangye xiehui gongzuo shouce*, pp. 61–62.

62. Private entrepreneurs have complained that this local control inhibits their ability to protect their rights. See Li Jing and Yang Xiaoping, "Feigong jingji huyu qingli guoshi fagui" (Nonpublic economy appeals for sorting outdated laws and regulations), *Zhonghua gongshang shibao* (China business times), March 9, 1999, p. 1.

63. For example, membership in a local branch of the Chinese Association for Enterprises with Foreign Investment used to mean automatic membership in the national organization. However, upon being ordered by MOCA, CAEFI changed its charter so that this is not the case. Interview #g28.

64. The December 1998 MOCA notice defines "identical" social organizations as ones that have the "basically identical" (*jiben xiangtong*) name, nature, purpose, or mission.

65. David L. Wank, "Private Businesses, Bureaucracy, and Political Alliance in a Chinese City," *Australian Journal of Chinese Affairs*, no. 33 (January 1995), pp. 55–71.

66. Companies can circumvent the regulations by affiliating their association not only with another government department but also with the ACFIC, which is why so many associations have registered as industry guilds. Only a small proportion of industry guilds have been able to register with local civil affairs bureaus, but the government has continued to let them operate under ACFIC supervision. Interview #g35.

67. The prevalence of an overlap "problem" among associations has increas-

ingly been lamented by Chinese officials. That trend probably explains why the government has moved from an outright ban on identical associations to, in the 1998 regulations, merely suggesting that when an association already exists, an identical one "need not be founded" (*meiyou biyao chengli*). Wang Jiqing, "Hangye xiehui shanghui jianshede guanjian" (The key to the construction of industry associations and chambers of commerce), *Zhongguo jingmao daokan* (China economy and trade reporter), October 30, 1998, pp. 21–22; Shi Zuoting, "Guanyu peiyu he fazhan gongshang xiehui ruogan wentide sikao"; and Sheng Huaren, *Jingmao baipishu*, p. 107.

68. Others have also noted enterprises in one province joining associations in another, something this researcher documented as well. White, Howell, and Shang, *In Search of Civil Society*, p. 137; Interview #g14.

69. Perhaps holding the record, one northeast Chinese state-owned enterprise has joined 214 industry associations, societies, and foundations. SETC, *Woguo gongshang lingyu hangye xiehui gaige yu fazhan zhengce yanjiu*, p. 45.

70. These findings on business associations concord with recent trends in associations for noncommercial groups. Such associations are increasingly financially independent and face less state intrusion in their activities, and there are multiple associations engaged on the same issue in the same locality. Jude Howell, "New Directions in Civil Society: Organizing around Marginalized Interests," in Jude Howell, ed., *Governance in China* (Lanham, Md.: Rowman and Littlefield, 2004), pp. 143–171.

71. This distinction between China and commonly recognized corporatist states in Europe and Latin America is not an artifact of the academic literature on those countries devoting little attention to alternative avenues of government-business interaction besides associations. Associations in those countries occupy a more central role in mediating government and business than in China. One exception may be Brazil. Schmitter concluded that the associations were not important for government control or industry influence, yet he still labeled Brazil corporatist. Philippe C. Schmitter, *Interest Conflict and Political Change in Brazil* (Stanford: Stanford University Press, 1971), pp. 361–367.

72. Chen Yanni, "Legal Sector Opening Wider," *China Daily*, February 21, 1998; *China Statistical Yearbook 2002* (Beijing: China Statistics Press, 2002), p. 791; Paul Nash, "Do Foreign Law Firms Pose Real Threat?" *China Daily Business Weekly*, February 25, 2003.

73. Hill and Knowlton, the first foreign public relations firm in China, opened an office in 1985. In 1997, there were twelve public relations firms with offices in Beijing who were members of the local American Chamber of Commerce. By 2003, their ranks had doubled. James B. Strenski and Kung Yue, "China: The World's Next Public Relations Superpower," *Public Relations Quarterly*, vol. 43, no. 2 (Summer 1998), pp. 24–26; " Xinhua News Service, "Beijing Holds International Public Relations Meeting," October 15, 1996, in *World News Connection* database, wnc.dialog.com, inserted October 17, 1996. Wang Yong, "WTO Accession to Challenge PR Firms," *China Daily*, November 22, 1999; *American Chamber of Commerce, People's Republic of China-Beijing, 1997–1998 Membership Directory*, p. 237; *American Chamber of Commerce, People's Republic of China, 2003–2004 Membership Directory*, p. 299.

74. For a detailed analysis of the evolving legal profession in China, see Ethan

Michelson, "Unhooking From the State: Chinese Lawyers in Transition" (Ph.D. diss., University of Chicago, 2003).

75. Interviews #s65, #g13, #g19, #g83, #g98, #g99.

76. Barry Naughton, *Growing Out of the Plan: Chinese Economic Reform, 1978–1993* (Cambridge: Cambridge University Press, 1995), pp. 26–55.

77. Barry Naughton, "China's Experience with Guidance Planning," *Journal of Comparative Economics*, vol. 14, no. 4 (December 1990), pp. 743–767.

78. The low priority of associations within the government bureaucracy is a common complaint among those officials responsible for associations. Interview #g45; Sheng Huaren, *Jingmao baipishu*, p. 107; and Shi Zuoting, "Jiakuai fazhan wanshan guanli cujin zhengfu zhineng zhuanbian" (Speed up development, perfect regulation, promote the transformation of government functions), *Zhongguo jingmao daokan* (China economy and trade reporter) March 15, 1999, pp. 14–15.

79. Interviews #g56, #g60.

80. Ed Hewett wrote that in the Soviet Union enterprises and the government engaged in a "ritualized battle for resources" and that enterprises regularly persuaded ministries to adjust their targets. Leitzel argued that planners' lack of information ensured that output targets "became the object of an intense bargaining game between planners and firms and ministries." See Ed A. Hewett, *Reforming the Soviet Economy: Equality Versus Efficiency* (Washington, D.C.: Brookings Institution, 1988), pp. 189–190; Jim Leitzel, *Russian Economic Reform* (London: Routledge, 1995), pp. 21–25.

81. Lobbying attention may shift as more businesspeople become deputies to the National People's Congress, which may prompt the NPC as an institution, as well as individual members, to give greater care to business's needs and preferences through legislation, hearings, and oversight of the other branches of the government. In the Ninth NPC (1998–2003), 430 of the 2,979 deputies (14.4 percent) were businesspeople from state-owned and private companies. In the current Tenth NPC (2003–2008), that figure has risen to 633 of the 2,984 deputies (21.2 percent); that includes the 164 deputies (5.5 percent) who are members of the All-China Federation of Industry and Commerce, and thus, are most likely from privately owned firms. Cai Dingjian, *Zhongguo renmin daibiao dahui zhidu, disiban* (The institution of the Chinese people's congress, fourth edition) (Beijing: Law Press, 2003), p. 221; Interview #g35.

82. The NPC and State Council regularly hold separate meetings with relevant government agencies, experts, and affected sectors when drafting legislation. Interviews #g40, #g44, #g55, #g61, #g79, #g97. Also see Liu Guangcai, "Zuohao difang renda gongzuo qiantan" (Superficial exploration of doing good local people's congress work), *Fazhi ribao* (Legal daily), March 11, 1999, p. 7.

83. Some of the first hearings were held over rates for tap water, telephone service, railways, and taxis and laws regulating foreign chambers of commerce and industry associations. Since 2001, there have been at least four hundred hearings around the country on the setting of prices for specific goods and services. Shen Xiaojie, "Dianxin zifei sheji xin biaozhun" (Telecom fees establish new standard), *Zhonghua gongshang shibao* (China business times), February 8, 1999, p. 2; Frank Ching, "Seeds of Change," *Far Eastern Economic Review*, September 30, 1999, p. 22; Interviews #g17, #g56, #g66. The Legislative Law suggests that the national and local congresses obtain the opinions of "various sides" to an issue during the drafting of legislation by holding "discussion meetings" (*zuotanhui*), "demonstration meetings" (*lunzhenghui*),

and "hearings" (*tingzhenghui*). Text of the law, issued on March 15, 2000, is available on the Xinhua New Agency's Web site, www.xinhuanet.com/legal/flfg.htm.

84. Interviews #g99, #s52.

85. Tanner, *The Politics of Lawmaking in China*, pp. 51–71; Randall Peerenboom, *China's Long March Toward Rule of Law* (Cambridge: Cambridge University Press, 2002), p. 188. Interview #g53.

86. Interview #g32.

87. Interviews #g6, #g38.

88. Joe Studwell. *The China Dream: The Quest for the Last Great Untapped Market on Earth* (New York: Atlantic Monthly Press, 2002), pp. 102–121.

89. Interview #s48.

90. On the roots of the norm of shared interests, see Peter Ferdinand, "Interest Groups and Chinese Politics," in David S. G. Goodman, ed., *Groups and Politics in the People's Republic of China* (Armonk, N.Y.: M. E. Sharpe, 1984), pp. 10–25.

91. "The word 'lobbyist' was first used in Britain to refer to journalists who stood in lobbies at the House of Commons, waiting to interview newsmakers. Its initial modern usage in America came in 1829. According to essayist H. L. Mencken, privilege seekers in New York's capital, Albany, were referred to as lobby-agents. Three years later, the term was abbreviated to 'lobbyist' and was heard frequently in Washington, mostly as an expression of disdain." Jeffrey H. Birnbaum, *The Lobbyists: How Influence Peddlers Get Their Way in Washington* (New York: Random House, 1992), pp. 8–9. Contemporary dictionaries from the PRC translate *youshui* as "go canvassing" or "go about selling an idea" and *yuanwai huodong* as "activities outside the courtyard." Dictionaries from Taiwan translate *youshui* as "to lobby," "to canvass," or "to drum up support." *Youshui* originally meant "wandering persuader," a reference to philosophers and others who traveled among the Warring States (475–221 B.C.) offering their ideas and advice to rulers in exchange for their patronage. I thank Bob Eno for helping me understand the etymology of the Chinese term.

92. Lu Fengtai, *Shehui zhongjie zuzhi yanjiu*, pp. 102–106; Ou Xinqian and Du Jinling, eds., *Guowai hangye xiehui ziliao xuan* (Selected materials on foreign industry associations) (Beijing: China Commercial Press, 1999).

93. One source suggested that it is important to show a ministry how making a decision favorable to the industry could immediately benefit that agency. Interviews #g19, #g38, #g99. Scott Seligman, "How to Get Things Done in China," *Asian Wall Street Journal Weekly Edition*, April 19–25, 1999, p. 25. Foreigners that lobby in China typically say they are involved in "public affairs" (*gonggong shiwu*) work.

94. Interviews #g44, #g61. For a recent discussion of how interest groups affect local politics, see Cheng Hao, Huang Weiping, and Wang Yongcheng, "Zhongguo shehui liyi jituan janjiu" (Research on interest groups in Chinese society), *Zhanlue yu guanli* (Strategy and Management), no. 59, July 2003, pp. 63–74.

95. Interview #g47.

96. Sam Loewenberg, "The Brussels Hustle: For American Businesses, Lobbying The European Union Has Become a Priority," *Legal Times*, March 8, 1999, pp. 1, 4–5, 17; Clive S. Thomas, ed., *Research Guide to U.S. and International Interest Groups* (Westport, Conn.: Praeger, 2004).

97. Kenneth Lieberthal, *Governing China: From Revolution Through Reform, Second Edition* (New York: W.W. Norton, 2004), pp. 192–197.

98. By mid-2003, there were over seventy-eight hundred government Web

sites, triple the number from three years before. "People's Republic of China Market Access Memorandum of Understanding," October 10, 1992, and "People's Republic of China," in U.S. Trade Representative, *2000 National Trade Estimate Report on Foreign Trade Barriers*, available on the USTR Web site, www.ustr.gov; "Internet Brings Life Revolution," *China Daily*, November 12, 2003; "Data on China's IT Industry," *AsiaPort Daily News*, May 10, 2000, p. 3; China Internet Network Information Center, "Zhongguo hulian wangluo fazhan zhuangkuang tongji baogao" (China Internet development situation statistical report), July 2003, www. cnnic.cn.

99. These include draft texts of laws on land management, village elections, and financial securities. In October 2000, the State Development and Planning Commission also authorized summaries of the draft of the tenth five-year plan to be published and available for public comment. Florence I-Cheng Ng, "Public Given a Say on Economic Blueprint," *South China Morning Post*, October 25, 2000.

100. Guo Yali, "Law to Secure Open Government," *China Daily*, May 15, 2001.

101. During hearings on telecommunications fees in December 1998, those attending were repeatedly told not to reveal the substance of the discussions to others. Details of the meeting and the subsequent policy changes emerged in the spring of 1999. "Youdian tiaojia tingzhcnghuishang shuolexie shenma?" (What was said at the hearing on adjusting the price of telecommunications?), and Shen Xiaojie and Zheng Nan, "Xiangxin weilai" (Trust the future), *Nanfang zhoumo* (Southern weekender), April 30, 1999, p. 8.

102. Annual surveys by Transparency International (www.transparency.org) find that China consistently ranks as being perceived to be one of the most corrupt countries in the world. Also see Richard Levy, "Corruption in Popular Culture," in Perry Link, Richard P. Madsen, and Paul G. Pickowicz, eds., *Popular China: Unofficial Culture in a Globalizing Society* (Lanham, MD: Rowman and Littlefield, 2002), pp. 39–56.

103. Xiaobo Lu, *Cadres and Corruption: The Organizational Involution of the Chinese Communist Party* (Stanford: Stanford University Press, 2000).

104. Wank's study on clientelism in Xiamen is a good example. David L. Wank, *Commodifying Communism: Business, Trust, and Politics in a Chinese City* (Cambridge: Cambridge University Press, 1999).

105. This explanation differs from that of Guthrie, who stresses the higher a firm is in the administrative hierarchy, the less dependent it is on connections. The argument here is that the impediments to clientelism on national policy apply equally to firms regardless of their ownership form or administrative rank. Doug Guthrie, *Dragon in a Three-Piece Suit: The Emergence of Capitalism in China* (Princeton, N.J.: Princeton University Press, 1999), pp. 175–197.

106. In a typical case, a multinational corporation used one of these firms to arrange a meeting with a Beijing vice mayor, who they persuaded to allow them to construct a building with more floors than had been originally approved by a municipal agency. Some of these firms are owned by foreigners but employ former Chinese officials. Interviews #g11, #g19, #g30.

107. During a 1999 interview, the company claimed it had influenced the contents of over two dozen national laws and regulations, but it did not want to publicly disclose the specific changes it affected or the clients it represented. Interview #g19.

108. Mayhew, who coined the phrase, notes that elections are only one of multiple mechanisms that make government responsive to outside influence. Besides lobbying legislators, industry also successfully lobbies executive-branch departments and agencies, most of whose staff are unelected civil servants, hence eliminating elections as a direct source of influence on their behavior. David R. Mayhew, *Congress: The Electoral Connection* (New Haven, Conn.: Yale University Press, 1974); and David R. Mayhew, "Observations on *Congress: The Electoral Connection* A Quarter Century After Writing It," *PS: Political Science and Politics*, vol. 34, no. 2 (June 2001), pp. 251–252.

109. The phrase is from Charles E. Lindblom, *Politics and Markets: The World's Political Economic Systems* (New York: Basic Books, 1977), pp. 170–188. Interview #g38.

110. For a wide-ranging discussion of *guanxi*, see Thomas Gold, Doug Guthrie, and David Wank, eds., *Social Connections in China: Institutions, Culture, and the Changing Nature of* Guanxi (Cambridge: Cambridge University Press, 2002).

111. One well-experienced foreign businessman maintains that connections increasingly mean "being well informed and having some personal rapport. That is very different from saying [you] 'can pull strings with people in office,'" which is what it used to mean." Catherine Gelb, "First Hand," *China Business Review*, vol. 30, no. 2 (March/April 2003), pp. 65–69.

112. Others have shown have how connections promote civility and efficient foreign investment. Ming-Cheng M. Lo and Eileen M. Otis, "*Guanxi* Civility: Processes, Potentials, and Contingencies," *Politics and Society*, vol. 31, no. 1 (March 2003), pp. 131–162; Hongying Wang, *Weak State, Strong Networks* (Oxford: Oxford University Press, 2002).

## Chapter 3. The Steel Industry: Walking on One Leg

1. Steel is still one of China's largest industries, ranking fourth in 2001, behind electronics and telecommunications equipment, chemical materials and products, and transport equipment. *China Statistical Yearbook 2002* (hereafter *China 2002*) (Beijing: China Statistics Press, 2002), pp. 429–431.

2. In 2001, China's produced 18 percent of the world's crude steel, up from 13 percent in 1996, the first year it was world's largest producer. *China Statistical Yearbook 2001* (hereafter *China 2001*) (Beijing: China Statistics Press, 2001), pp. 424, 453; *China Statistical Abstract 2003* (Beijing: China Statistics Press, 2003), p. 128; International Iron and Steel Institute, *Steel Statistical Yearbook 2002* (Brussels: 2002), pp. 10–12.

3. Shougang in 1995 accounted for 27 percent of Beijing's industrial output, 22 percent of its sales revenue, and 41 percent of its profits and taxes. The situation in smaller urban areas can be even more dramatic. The Yonggang Group, a steel factory created on the edge of Jiangsu province's Zhangjiagang city in the mid-1980s, employs most of its township's adult residents. Li Ning, "Shougang Group Established," *Beijing Review*, December 9–15, 1996, p. 21.

4. In this spirit, Steinfeld entitles his chapter on Anshan Iron and Steel "The Living Museum of Iron and Steel Technology." Edward Steinfeld, *Forging Reform in China: The Fate of State-Owned Industry* (Cambridge: Cambridge University Press, 1998), pp. 81–123.

5. *China 2002*, pp. 432–435, 442–445.

6. Ibid., pp. 432, 442; *China Statistical Yearbook 1998* (Beijing: China Statistics Press, 1998), pp. 444, 448.

7. Interview #m16. See appendix. All interviews involving the steel industry are coded "#m_."

8. In 2001 there were 215 foreign-invested ventures in steel that accounted for 8 percent of the industry's output. *China 2002*, pp. 432, 452.

9. The largest multinationals have representative offices in Beijing, while smaller ones often have a China presence only at their joint-venture factory. In order to focus on the significance of foreign ownership and national policy making, three of my four foreign cases are centered on the representative office and not the production joint venture. The remaining case is of a small, foreign Singaporean firm that has no local presence other than at its joint venture in the western suburbs of Shanghai.

10. In the industry's early period, integrated steel mills began with open-hearth furnaces. Beginning in the 1950s, in most countries open-hearth furnaces were replaced by more efficient basic oxygen furnaces (BOF).

11. Robert W. Crandall, *The U.S. Steel Industry in Recurrent Crisis: Policy Options in a Competitive World* (Washington, D.C.: Brookings Institution, 1981), p. 11.

12. For a comparison of integrated mills and minimills, see William T. Hogan, *Steel in the 21st Century: Competition Forges a New World Order* (New York: Lexington Books, 1994), pp. 74–93, and James B. Burnham, *Changes and Challenges: The Transformation of the U.S. Steel Industry*, Policy Study No. 115 (St. Louis: Washington University Center for the Study of American Business, 1993). Burnham explains (p. 12): "Continuous casting permits raw, molten steel to be poured directly into continuous process equipment which can produce extremely thin slabs, rods, and similar products. This technology eliminates the ingot/thick slab/billet steps required by previous technology, with their heavy capital requirements for rolling and transport facilities, as well as the large energy requirements associated with reheating before each rolling phase."

13. *The Yearbook of the Iron and Steel Industry of China 1998* (hereafter *Steel 1998*) (Beijing: Ministry of Metallurgy Industry, 1998), pp. 73, 88; *China Steel Yearbook 2002* (hereafter *Steel 2002*) (Beijing: China Iron and Steel Association, 2002), p. 99. International Iron and Steel Institute, *Steel Statistical Yearbook 2002*, pp. 21–26.

14. Another source of inefficiency is that domestically excavated iron ore is of low quality, having an iron content of only 34 percent. The result is that Chinese enterprises have to use more coal to burn more iron ore to produce the raw iron that is then turned into steel. Hogan, *Steel in the 21st Century*, p. 44.

15. By 2001, output per firm had risen to forty-eight thousand tons. This change is primarily the result of the closure of many small producers in 2000 and 2001, not greater capacity among the remaining enterprises. *Steel 2002*, p. 85.

16. Takashi Sugimoto, "The Chinese Steel Industry," *Resources Policy*, vol. 19, no. 4 (December 1993), pp. 272.

17. Shi Xiaohong, "Wo guo gangtie gongye chanye zhengce pingxi" (Comment and analysis of our country's iron and steel industrial policy), *Jingji guanli* (Economic management), no. 241 (January 1999), pp. 46–47.

18. China's steel industry produced fifteen tons of raw steel per worker in 1980, thirty-four tons in 1997, and seventy-four tons in 2001. In 1997, Japan was the world's most efficient producer, at 716 tons per worker, followed by South Korea (438

tons), the United States (417 tons), Germany (411 tons), and Brazil (335). Chinese interview sources argue that their ratios are low because their employee figures include non-steel-related workers. While true, data on steel-related employees is available in scattered form for only a few firms, and it is possible that the ratios for other countries includes firms' non-steel-related employees. More importantly, when the productivity ratio is recalculated for those Chinese companies that do provide such figures, they are still inefficient compared to the world leaders. *China 1998*, pp. 432, 469; *China 2002*, pp. 424, 475. Economic Commission for Europe, *The Steel Market in 1998 and Prospects for 1999* (New York: United Nations, 1999), pp. 16, 28, 34, 48, 70.

19. *Steel 2002*, pp. 86, 111–113.

20. Xinhua News Agency, "Steel Production Accelerated to Promote PRC Auto Industry," June 19, 1998, in *World News Connection* database, wnc.dialog.com, inserted June 22, 1998. *Steel 2002*, p. 109; "Shanghai Baoshan Exports 1.8m Tonnes of Steel Products in 2001," *China Intelligence Wire*, January 14, 2002.

21. The number of Baogang's employees rose from 34,000 prior to the merger in 1997 to 112,000 after the merger in 2001, sending its labor productivity rate down from 251 to 169 tons per worker. Sugimoto, "The Chinese Steel Industry," p. 276; *Steel 1998*, pp. 107, 113; *Steel 2002*, pp. 123, 194. Also see Mary Boyd, "Champion in Training: Baosteel," *China Economic Quarterly*, vol. 7, no. 3 (Third Quarter, 2003), pp. 31–33.

22. The top four firm concentration was 29 percent in 1997, showing that Baogang's absorption of other mills did little to ameliorate this situation. *Steel 1998*, pp. 113–114; *Steel 2002*, pp. 85, 100–101, 122–133; *China Iron and Steel Industry Yearbook 1991* (Beijing: Ministry of Metallurgy Industry, 1991).

23. Patricia O'Brien, "Government Systems in Steel: The American and Japanese Experience," in J. Rogers Hollingsworth, Philippe C. Scmitter, and Wolfgang Streeck, eds., *Governing Capitalist Economies: Performance and Control of Economic Sectors* (New York: Oxford University Press, 1994), pp. 43–71; and Mark Tilton, *Restrained Trade: Cartels in Japan's Basic Materials Industries* (Ithaca, N.Y.: Cornell University Press, 1996).

24. Steinfeld, *Forging Reform in China*.

25. Interviews #m7, #m29.

26. Other organizations without any policy relevance are the China Metallurgy Construction Association, the China Metallurgy Education Society, and the China Statistics Society Metallurgy Statistics Sub-Society.

27. Interviews #m32, #m36.

28. Ibid.

29. "SETC Eliminates Nine Industrial Bureaus," *ChinaOnline*, February 26, 2001, www.chinaonline.com.

30. Interview #m33. Text of speeches given at the association's first meeting and its charter are contained in *Zhongguo gangtie gongye xiehui tongxun* (China Iron and Steel Association notice), no. 1 (February 12, 1999).

31. Interview #m41. When CISA began in January 1999, its 102 enterprises produced 87 percent of the country's steel and employed 75 percent of its workers. Neither CISA nor any of the associations over which it has authority have local branches. CISA was not given authority over stainless steel associations or the China Chamber of Commerce of Metals, Minerals and Chemicals Importers and Exporters, which is affiliated with the Ministry of Commerce. Measures giving

CISA this responsibility were issued in 2001 and 2002, and are available in *Steel 2002*, pp. 33–41.

32. The Stainless Steel Department's founding was aided by the fragmented bureaucracy. Its reputed overseer, the Metal Materials Circulation Association, was originally affiliated with the domestic trade bureaucracy, not metallurgy. It is now supervised by the China Materials Circulation and Purchasing Federation (CM-CPF), which itself is regulated by the State-Owned Assets Supervision Administration of China.

33. Interviews #m29, #m36.

34. Stainless steel products account for less than 1 percent of domestic production. Xu Aidong, "China's Rising Star," *Metal Bulletin*, November 18, 2003.

35. Interviews #m36, #m42.

36. Interviews #m3, #m6, #m18.

37. Interview #m13.

38. Interviews #m11, #m23, #m25, #m39.

39. Interview #m14.

40. Interviews #m15, #m17.

41. Interview #m10.

42. Interviews #m19, #m20.

43. Interviews #m4, #m7, #m21.

44. This situation is consistent with findings by Tony Saich, "Negotiating the State: The Development of Social Organizations in China," *China Quarterly*, no. 161 (March 2000), pp. 124–141.

45. Interviews #m7, #m37. Also see U.S. Department of Commerce Department International Trade Administration, *Global Steel Trade: Structural Problems and Future Solutions*, July 2000, p. 146.

46. While Zhou Guanwu was forced into retirement at age seventy-seven, his son, Zhou Beifang, was given a life sentence for corrupt acts related to his running of Shougang Concord, a subsidiary based in Hong Kong. Steinfeld, *Forging Reform in China*, pp. 165–224; Susan L. Shirk, *The Political Logic of Economic Reform in China* (Berkeley: University of California Press, 1993), pp. 242–243; Holman A. Jenkins Jr., "Hong Kong's Market Stops Believing in 'Miracles,'" *Asian Wall Street Journal*, November 6, 1997, p. 10.

47. Matt Miller, "The Hottest Thing in Cold-Rolled Steel," *Business Week*, September 8, 1997.

48. Eight of the board's fourteen members were carry-overs from the original Baogang, including its general manager, Xie Qihua, who is also an alternate member of the Central Committee. And four are from the two companies that Baogang absorbed, Shanghai Metallurgy Group and Meishan Iron and Steel.

49. The equivalent Western aphorism is "Where you sit is where you stand." Interview #m25.

50. Interviews #m18, #m37. Also see Boyd, "Champion in Training."

51. Yonggang Group, "Introduction to Zhangjiagang City's Yonglian Village," mimeo, June 1999. The company is registered as a township-village enterprise (TVE). Recently, it corporatized and gave 70 percent ownership to the village, 25 percent to the company union, and 5 percent to senior managers. Interview #m12. Given that specific individuals own only a minority of the company, this study treats Yonggang as state-owned.

52. Interview #m13. On government-business relations in Zhangjiagang generally, see David Zweig, *Freeing China's Farmers: Rural Restructuring in the Reform Era* (Armonk, N.Y.: M. E. Sharpe, 1997), pp. 307–318.

53. Interview #m13.

54. Interview #m7.

55. Chronologies of government-sponsored meetings, senior officials' investigation trips to enterprises, policy initiatives, and industry trends are contained in the annual editions of the *Yearbook of Iron and Steel Industry of China* (Beijing: Ministry of Metallurgy Industry and the China Iron and Steel Association).

56. Interview #m18.

57. Interview #m7.

58. Interviews #m4, #m7, #m58.

59. Interviews #m10, #m17, #m19.

60. Interviews #m10, #m11, #m15, #m20.

61. Interview #m18.

62. Interview #m19.

63. Steinfeld, *Forging Reform in China*, pp. 187–193.

64. Interview #m13.

65. Interview #m17.

66. Interview #m36.

67. Interview #m4.

68. Interview #m6.

69. Chen Jiagui, ed., *Zhongguo gongye fazhan baogao: zhidu chuangxin, zuzhi bianqian yu zhengce tiaozheng* (China industry development report 1998: institutional innovation, organizational changes and policy adjustments) (Beijing: Economic Management Publishing, 1998), p. 171.

70. Kazuhiko Shimizu, "Steel Fix," *China Trade Report*, June 1995, p. 3; "1998 nian gang shi gaikuang" (The general situation of the 1998 steel market), *Zhongguo yejin* bao (China Metallurgy News), February 27, 1999, p. 5.

71. Lu Zheng, ed., *Zhongguo gongye fazhan baogao 1999: gaobie duanque jingjide zhongguo gongye* (China industry development report 1999: Good-bye to Chinese industry's shortage economy) (Beijing: Economic Management Press, 1999), p. 157.

72. *Price Yearbook of China 1998* (Beijing: Editorial Board of the Price Yearbook, 1998), p. 349.

73. Wang Chuandong, "Anti-dumping Rule on Steel Created," *China Daily*, September 25, 1998, p. 5.

74. Reported profits, which should always be interpreted cautiously because of Chinese accounting methods, fell from RMB 32.7 billion in 1993 to RMB 2.6 billion in 1997. Over the same period, long-term liabilities rose from RMB 71.5 billion to RMB 128.5 billion, while tax receipts fell from RMB 30.5 billion to RMB 19.5 billion. *China Statistical Yearbook 1994* (Beijing: China Statistical Publishing House, 1994), p. 381; *China 1998*, pp. 446–447.

75. In standard usage the term "dumping" (*qingxiao*) refers to a firm's exporting a good at a price lower than in its home market, but in Chinese law, dumping also refers to the domestic sale of goods at below cost.

76. The relevant laws are the 1993 Anti–Unfair Competition Law and the 1998 Price Law. The Chinese text of the former is in Sun Wanzhong, ed., *Zhongguo falu nianjian, zhencangban* (Law yearbook of China, collector's edition) (Beijing:

China Law Yearbook Service, 1998), pp. 265–267. The English and Chinese texts of the Price Law are contained in *China Economic News*, no. 13 (April 6, 1998), pp. 9–13, 24–27. Also see Volker Pasternak, "The Right Price," *China Business Review*, vol. 25, no. 5 (September–October 1998), pp. 40–43.

77. On cartels in Japan, including in the steel industry, see Mark Tilton, *Restrained Trade*; and Mark C. Tilton, "Japanese Steel and Chemical Cartels," *Chemtech*, vol. 29, no. 9 (September 1999), pp. 49–53.

78. This paragraph draws on Scott Kennedy, "The Price of Competition: Pricing Policies and the Struggle to Define China's Economic System," *China Journal*, no. 49 (January 2003), pp. 1–30.

79. From 1992 to 1996 the Ministry of Metallurgy Industry held "price coordination meetings," where companies were expected to share price information. One industry source reported that voluntary prices were set at these meetings, though clearly with no success. Interview #m24. *Yearbook of Iron and Steel Industry of China 1997* (Beijing: Ministry of Metallurgy Industry, 1997), p. 69.

80. Interview #m29; *Steel 1998*, pp. 419–420.

81. Interviews #m7, #m26, #m37.

82. Interviews #m3, #m18, #m37.

83. Interviews #m10, #11, #13, #m19, #m20.

84. So as to not offend the government, even some companies that opposed the price floors signed the pledge. This did not keep them from privately complaining and violating the pledge later. Interview #m37; "Guojia jiwei, guojia yejinju lianhe fabu zhizhi dijia qingxiao gangcai zhanxing guiding" (SPDC, State Metallurgy Bureau jointly issue temporary regulation to stop low-priced dumping of finished steel), *Zhongguo yejin bao* (China metallurgy news), September 27, 1998, p. 1; "35 hu gangtie qiye fachu changyi" (35 steel enterprises issue call: freely resist low-price dumping actions), *Zhongguo yejin bao* (China metallurgy news), September 29, 1998, p. 1; Wang Chuandong, "China's Metallurgy Sector Gets Lower Gains," *China Daily*, October 2, 1998, p. 5.

85. Interview #m32; "Jiu jia tegang qiye qianding buxiugang bangcai zilujia xieyi" (Nine specialty steel enterprises sign stainless steel billet self-discipline price agreement), *Zhongguo yejin bao* (China metallurgy news), October 20, 1998, p. 1; "Quanguo tegang hangye ni dui liuzhong chanpin shixing jiage zilu" (Nation's specialty steel industry plans to implement price self-discipline for six products), *Zhongguo yejin bao* (China metallurgy news), November 21, 1998, p. 5.

86. As in the other cases, firms were divided over the efficacy of cartels; however, supporters and opponents were not distinguished by ownership, size, or efficiency.

87. Interview #g59; and Zhong Guizhao, "Hangye zilu, gongmo fazhan" (Industry self-discipline, collectively seek development," *Zhongguo jingmao daokan* (China economy and trade reporter), January 15, 1999, pp. 29–30. For more on associations in Wenzhou, see Ou Xinqian and Du Jinling, eds., *Zhongguo hangye xiehui: gaige yu tansuo* (Chinese industry associations: reform and exploration) (Beijing: China Commercial Press, 1999), pp. 182–223.

88. A stainless steel association with similar membership composition refused their members' requests to coordinate price cartels on the grounds that they would not work and were antithetical to a market economy. Interview #m36.

89. Shortly after the cartels for construction and section steel were initiated in March 2000, prices did rise sharply but then fell a few months later. But credit for

this initial rise is hard to pinpoint. By that time, growth in overall supply had slowed, exports were up, demand had expanded as a result of greater government investment in infrastructure projects, and traders were hoarding steel in the hopes of sending prices still higher. "China Adjusts Upward Some Finished Steel Prices," China News Service, April 4, 2000; "Luowen, xiancai shichang chaozuo qifen tai nong" (Debar, wire rod market cooked atmosphere too thick), *Sinometal.com*, April 27, 2000, www.sinometal.com; "China Prod Materials Prices Reverse 40 Mnth Downward Spiral," *ChinaOnline*, April 28, 2000, www.chinaonline.com.

90. *Collection of Materials and Statistics on China's Iron and Steel Industry and Steel Policy*, (Beijing: Japan Iron and Steel Federation, October 2002), pp. 29–30.

91. Tilton, *Restrained Trade*, pp. 190–211, finds that a high concentration level is a prerequisite to a successful cartel, but that other factors, including a "high-tech hook," a downstream cartel, and import protection are also helpful.

92. The Sichuan association collected RMB 50,000 deposits from the cartel members. On the first violation, a member would pay a RMB 10,000 fine, RMB 20,000 after the second violation, and RMB 50,000 after the third. Reportedly no firms violated the floors. Interviews #m31, #m37.

93. Since 2001, CISA's "price and materials coordination group" has brought the top ten producers together on a semiannual basis to discuss prices, but it is unclear if coordination efforts have been successful. Interview #m24.

94. U.S. Trade Representative, "People's Republic of China Market Access Memorandum of Understanding," October 10, 1992, available on the USTR Web site, www.ustr.gov.

95. Ian Dickson, "China's Steel Imports: An Outline of Recent Trade Barriers," University of Adelaide Chinese Economies Research Center, Working Paper Series, no. 96/6 (July 1996), p. 23. China later pledged to reduce those tariffs to 6.1 percent upon accession to the WTO. U.S. Commerce Department, *Global Steel Trade*, p. 140.

96. Because of limited information from interview sources, it is unclear what direct influence Chinese steel companies had on these reforms. However, we can expect that they favored keeping the barriers in place as long as possible. Interview #m40; Dickson, "China's Steel Imports."

97. Imports have consistently surpassed government targets. For example, in 1998, imports were 12.4 million tons, far above the government's declared goal of 7 million tons. *Zhongguo yejin bao* (China metallurgy news), February 14, 1999, p. 1.

98. Ian Dickson, "China's Myriad Customs Regimes and Their Implications for Openness (with Reference to Steel Imports)," University of Adelaide Chinese Economies Research Center, Working Paper Series, no. 97/18 (December 1997).

99. According to one report, shipping costs in China are so high that it was cheaper for Guangdong producers to import semifinished steel from Turkey rather than buy it from Shanghai. Chen Yong-hee, "Not So Fast," *China Trade Report*, January 1997, pp. 4–5.

100. Steel trade statistics are from *The Yearbook of Iron and Steel Industry of China* (various years); and the PRC. Ministry of Commerce Web site (www.mofcom.gov.cn/tjzl.shtml), accessed August 27, 2004.

101. "Caizhengbu, guojia shuiwu zongju guanyu tigao metan gangcai shini ji chuanbo chukou tuishuilude tongzhi" (Ministry of finance and state tax bureau notice on raising the export rebate rate for coal, finished steel, cement, and ships),

*Zhonghua renmin gongheguo shuishou fagui gonggao* (PRC tax law and regulations bulletin), June 16, 1998, p. 7; Wang Hua, "Tigao chukou tuishuilu—cujin jingji fazhande xin jucuo" (Raise export rebate rate–new move to promote economic development), *Zhongguo jingmao daokan* (China economy and trade reporter), April 15, 1999, p. 26; "State Raises Export Tax Rebate Rates," *China Daily*, July 21, 1999, p. 5.

102. Zhao Gang and Gao Yu, "Gangshi jiage zouxiang zhanwang" (Forecast trend for steel market prices), *Zhongguo yejin bao* (China metallurgy news), May 22, 1999, p. 1.

103. *Zhongguo jingmao daokan* (China economy and trade reporter), May 31, 1999, p. 47; Cheng Yuan, "Guochan gangcai jinkou gangcai jiaoban" (National steel calls out to imported steel), *Jingji ribao* (Economics daily), July 2, 1999; "Guojia queding 27 jia zhongdian gangtie qiye dingdian shengchan mianshui gangcai" (The state sets 27 key steel enterprises to produce tariff-exempt finished steel); *Guowuyuan fazhan yanjiu zhongxin xinxi wang* (State council development research center information network), July 26, 1999; "Youguan zhuanjia tan jiaru WTO hou waimao zhengce dui gangtie gongyede yingxiang" (Specialists discuss the effect of post-WTO entry trade policy on steel industry), *Sinometal.com*, May 13, 2000, www.sinometal.com.

104. U.S. Commerce Department, *Global Steel Trade*, p. 154.

105. Translations of articles written by Chinese companies published in *Shijie jinshu* (World Metals) are contained in Dickson, "China's Myriad Customs Regimes," pp. 39–43.

106. Interviews #m3, #m10, #m11, #m33. For one example, see "Jiaru WTO hou zhongguo gangtieye fazhan celue" (Development strategy of China's steel industry after joining WTO), *Sinometal.com*, May 21, 2001.

107. The revised version and its implementing regulations are more consistent with the WTO's Antidumping Agreement. The text of the original PRC Anti Dumping and Anti Subsidy Regulations, promulgated on March 25, 1997, is available online at Chinalaw Web (www.qis.net/chinalaw/prclaw53.htm). The texts of the revised *Regulations of the People's Republic of China on Antidumping*, issued November 26, 2001, implemented as of January 1, 2002, and its implementing regulations, are available on the U.S. Department of Commerce's Trade Remedy Compliance Staff Web site (http://ia.ita.doc.gov/trcs/downloads/documents/china/index.html). The WTO's Antidumping Agreement is available from the WTO's Web site (www.wto.org.).

108. The most avid initiator of cases has been China's equally troubled chemical industry. For an analysis of China's antidumping regime, see Scott Kennedy, "Holey Protectionsism!," *China Economic Quarterly*, vol. 8, no. 3 (Third Quarter, 2004), pp. 24–28; Scott Kennedy, "China's Porous Protectionism: The Changing Political Economy of Trade Policy," *Political Science Quarterly* (forthcoming 2005); and Patrick M. Norton and Kermit W. Almstedt, "China Joins the Trade Wars," *China Business Review*, vol. 30, no. 1 (January–February 2003), pp. 22–29, 42.

109. Taiyuan Iron and Steel was the first to complain; it then persuaded Shaanxi Precision Group and Pudong Iron and Steel, the latter of which had a stainless steel joint-venture with Germany's Kruup, to join it. Song Bo, "Wo guo yejin gongye shouli fanqingxiao diaocha zhengshi li'an" (Our country's metallurgy industry's first antidumping investigation formally filed), *Zhongguo yejin bao* (China metallurgy news), March 27, 1999, p. 1.

110. Given that the United States, Canada, Mexico, India, Chile, and others also initiated antidumping actions against one or more of these three countries at the same time, the Chinese actions should not be seen as frivolous. See Thomas R. Howell and Brent L. Bartlett, "The New Crisis in Steel," testimony before the House Committee on Ways and Means Subcommittee on Trade, February 25, 1999, p. 23.

111. Interviews #m7, #m15.

112. Mike Allen and Steven Pearlstein, "Bush Settles on Tariff for Steel Imports," *Washington Post*, March 5, 2002, p. A1; Meng Yan, "Fighting Dumping Charges—Experts," *China Daily*, April 9, 2002; William Kazer, "Baosteel Cries Foul Over Imports," *South China Morning Post*, April 25, 2002; Patrick M. Norton and Kermit W. Almstedt, "China Invokes the WTO 'Escape Clause,'" O'Melveny and Myers LLP Research Report, May 2003; Interviews #m24, #m25, #m38.

113. In the dumping cases, separate tariff rates were announced against individual respondent firms: 0 to 62 percent in the silicon steel case against firms from Russia; 17 to 58 percent in the stainless steel case against firms from South Korea and Japan; and 0 to 55 percent in the case involving Russia, South Korea, Ukraine, Kazakhstan, and Taiwan. In the safeguard case, tariffs and quotas were announced on a product-by-product basis. The text of all case initiations, preliminary decisions, and final decisions is available from the Ministry of Commerce's "China Trade Remedy Information" (www.cacs.gov.cn).

114. For how economic and political factors affect antidumping case decisions in the United States, see Wendy L. Hansen, "The International Trade Commission and the Politics of Protectionism," *American Political Science Review*, vol. 84, no. 1 (March 1990), pp. 21–46; Wendy L. Hansen and Thomas J. Prusa, "The Economics and Politics of Trade Policy: An Empirical Analysis of ITC Decision Making," *Review of International Economics*, vol. 5, no. 2 (1997), pp. 230–245; and Philip A. Mundo, *National Politics in a Global Economy* (Washington, D.C.: Georgetown University Press, 1999), pp. 231–274.

115. The Chinese steel producers countered, to no avail, that foreign equipment had resulted in deaths as well. Interviews #m4, #m7, #m30, #m36, #m25, #m55; Norton and Almstedt, "China Invokes the WTO 'Escape Clause.'"

116. Interview #m29.

117. Interview #m25.

118. Vaclav Smil, *China's Environmental Crisis: An Inquiry into the Limits of National Development* (Armonk, N.Y.: M. E. Sharpe, 1997); Elizabeth C. Economy, *The River Runs Black: The Environmental Challenge to China's Future* (Ithaca, N.Y.: Cornell University Press, 2004).

119. Jie Zhenhua, "Lijing tuzhi, nuli ba huanjing baohu quanmian tuixiang xin shiji" (Rouse yourself, make vigorous efforts to push environmental protection forward into the twenty-first century), *Huanjing baohu* (Environmental protection), no. 258 (April 1999), pp. 3–9.

120. "Shougang: Model in transition," *Business China*, November 25, 1996, pp. 8–9.

121. Abigail R. Jahiel, "The Organization of Environmental Protection in China," *China Quarterly*, no. 156 (December 1998), pp. 757–787; and Michael Palmer, "Environmental Regulation in the People's Republic of China: The Face of Domestic Law," *China Quarterly*, no. 156 (December 1998), pp. 788–808. For

how economic openness has promoted environmental protection institutions, see Sangbum Shin, "From Red to Green: Economic Globalization and Environmental Protection in China" (Ph.D. diss., Indiana University, 2004).

122. "Environmental Management in China: An Overview," *China Environmental Review*, vol. 1, no. 1 (October 1997), p. 12.

123. Foreign steel companies have had no interest or role in environmental policy making because their China operations produce downstream specialty steels in a relatively "green" production process. The worst pollution comes during the smelting of iron and raw steel.

124. Interviews #m44, #m45, #m52, #m54.

125. Interview #m50.

126. Interview #m51.

127. Interview #m49.

128. Interview #m37.

129. Interview #m45.

130. The 1995 version is in Sun Wanzhong, *Zhongguo falu nianjian, zhencangban*, pp. 455–458.

131. Interview #m52.

132. Interviews #m28, #m43, #m45. Anna Brettell, "Environmental Nongovernmental Organizations in the People's Republic of China: Innocents in a Coopted Environmental Movement?" *Journal of Pacific Asia*, vol. 6 (2000), pp. 27–56.

## *Chapter 4. The Consumer Electronics Industry: Sending Mixed Signals*

1. In the PRC, Chinese use the term *jiayong dianqi*, literally "home electronics," for what is conventionally understood elsewhere as "consumer electronics" (*xiaofei dianqi*). Here, the standard non-Chinese term is used in the analysis and in translation of Chinese texts.

2. A Chinese colleague from Shanghai reports that in 2001 Shanghainese wanted to own a cell phone, DVD player or home theater equipment, and a car or house. They would like both a house and car, but reasonably could only expect to afford one or the other. Correspondence with author, June 9, 2001; *China Statistical Yearbook 2002* (Beijing: China Statistics Press, 2002), p. 328. Also see Deborah S. Davis, ed., *The Consumer Revolution in Urban China* (Berkeley: University of California Press, 2000).

3. Zhou Kan, "Shinco, Idall Form Market Alliance to Ensure Shares," *China Daily Business Weekly*, December 5, 1999, p. 8; "Statistics—VCD Players, Sound Systems in Chinese Households," *Asia Pulse*, December 19, 2000.

4. *China Statistical Yearbook 2002*, pp. 424, 432.

5. Huang Jianzhong, "Caise dianshiji shichang" (Color television market), in Ministry of Machine Industry Science and Technology Information Research Academy, ed., *Zhongguo jidian chanpin shichang baogao xilie, diyi ji* (Report series of China machinery product market, vol. 1) (Beijing: Machinery Industry Publishing Service, 1999), pp. 35–71; *China Statistical Yearbook 2002*, p. 474.

6. "Tigao zhiliang guifan shichang zunshou hangye zhengce zhengque yindao xiaofei" (Raise quality, standardize the market, abide by industry policy, correctly guide consumption), press release distributed at the VCD Achieve Quality and Market Standards Conference, October 30, 1997.

7. Sales of VCD players rose from only 20,000 in 1994 to 11 million in 1997,

to over 19 million in 2001. In 1997 VCR sales fell 40 percent. "China Sales of TV, Video Disk Players Fall in '01—Report," *Dow Jones International News*, March 19, 2002; Shi Guoqiang, "Jiguang shipanji shichang" (Laser disc viewing machine market), in Ministry of Machine Industry Science and Technology Information Research Academy, *Zhongguo jidian chanpin shichang baogao xilie, diyi ji*, p. 82; *Zhongguo dianzi bao* (China electronics news), March 31, 1998, p. 12.

8. Huang Jiangzhong, "Caise dianshiji shichang," p. 41.

9. Many makers of TVs and VCD players also produce a wide variety of durable consumer products, from washing machines to air conditioners and from cordless phones to stereo equipment. And while there is not complete overlap, many TV makers also manufacture VCD players. So, while the TV and VCD player markets have distinct characteristics, there are few *pure* TV or VCD player companies.

10. Zhang Zhong, "Guochan yinxiang you wang qudai jinkou chanpin" (Nationally produced audio products have chance to replace imported products), *Jingji ribao* (Economics daily), July 2, 1998, p. 5; *CAA hangye kuaixun* (CAA industry express), no. 124 (April 1999), p. 4.

11. Sino-MR Corporation, "Zhongguo dianshiji shengchan qiye 1997 nian shengchang, xiaoshou, chukou qingkuang" (China television production enterprises' 1997 production, sales and export situation), April 1998; and Sino-MR Corporation, "Jiayong dianqi xiaoshou jiance: 1998 nian niandu baogao (yingdieji)" (Consumer electronics sales monitor: 1998 annual report, video disc players), March 1999. Because Sino-MR's data comes from surveys of large department stores, their data may marginally overstate concentration levels, since lesser brands oftentimes sell in smaller stores. Interview #c14.

12. For more on increasing concentration among consumer electronics product categories, see Lu Zheng, ed., *Zhongguo gongye fazhan baogao 1999: gaobie duanque jingjide zhongguo gongye* (China industry development report 1999: Good-bye to Chinese industry's shortage economy) (Beijing: Economic Management Press, 1999), pp. 239–250.

13. Ibid., pp. 185–189. The immediate cause for deflation in the steel and consumer electronics in China in the 1990s was the same (and both prompted demands for a policy response), but more broadly, steel prices can have wide swings up and down and are connected to spending on infrastructure, not consumer spending patterns as in consumer electronics.

14. *Price Yearbook of China 1998* (Beijing: Price Yearbook Editorial Board, 1998), pp. 364–365.

15. Xinhua News Agency, "VCD Industry Growing Rapidly," March 5, 1998, in *World News Connection* database, wnc.dialog.com, inserted March 8, 1998.

16. Gao Yu, "Shei dou beng xiang longduan" (All needn't want monopoly), *Sanlian shenghuo zhoukan* (Sanlian life weekly), January 30, 1999, p. 23.

17. On Chinese links to international electronics production networks, see Barry Naughton, ed., *The China Circle: Economics and Technology in the PRC, Taiwan, and Hong Kong* (Washington, D.C.: Brookings Institution Press, 1997). On the growing exports of Chinese consumer electronics, see Evan Ramstad and Karby Leggett, "Chinese TV Maker Konka Mounts An Invasion of Crowded U.S. Turf," *Wall Street Journal Interactive Edition*, May 5, 2000 (interactive.wsj.com); "Color TV Exports Reach 10 Million in 2000," *ChinaOnline* January 18, 2001, (www.chinaonline.com).

18. The VCD player market leader, Xinke, straddles ownership boundaries. It

is a collective formally owned by a township in Jiangsu, but the township has no role in management and has not provided funding in many years. It is categorized as an SOE in this study, since the local government formally has a claim on its assets. In the event the company lists on the stock market, the township would likely receive 50 percent of the shares. Interview #c11.

19. In the 1980s, the largest TV makers were Tianjin's Beijing brand, Nanjing's Panda, Shanghai's Feiyue, and Beijing's Mudan.

20. H. Landis Gabel, *Competitive Strategies for Product Standards: The Strategic Use of Compatibility Standards for Competitive Advantage* (London: McGraw-Hill, 1991); Carl Shapiro and Hal R. Varian, "The Art of Standards Wars," *California Management Review*, vol. 41, no. 2 (Winter 1999), pp. 8–25.

21. Although some Chinese universities and research institutes have been trying to develop digital standards for broadcast television, Chinese TV makers are generally satisfied producing for the nondigital market. Interview #c49; Rhonda J. Crane, *The Politics of International Standards: France and the Color TV War* (Norwood, N.J.: Ablex, 1979); and Gabel, *Competitive Strategies.*

22. Associations in corporatism and pluralism differ in four respects. Corporatist associations lack autonomy (they are initiated by the state, affiliated with the government, staffed by bureaucrats, and financed by the government), have compulsory membership, are hierarchically ordered, and have jurisdictional monopolies. The first characteristic applies only to state, not societal, corporatism.

23. As of mid-1999, there were thirty-three industry associations under the purview of the Ministry of Information Industry, of which twenty-six were originally under the former Ministry of Electronics Industry and seven under the Ministry of Post and Telecommunications. Interviews #c40, #c43.

24. The CECC has former officials as its president and honorary president, but neither are involved in its daily affairs.

25. In the earliest years, when the video association was still known as the National TV International Competition Committee, it was headed by a Mudan executive and run out of a Beijing hotel. From 1986 to 1996, although Panda ran the association, it was based in Shanghai, closer to more television producers. Interviews #c7, #c34.

26. Interviews #c32, #c34.

27. Interviews #c3, #c7, #c21.

28. As a sign of desperation, the Ministry of Information Industry recently took over CVA, moving its office back to the ministry in Beijing and appointing a current government official as its secretary-general. Interviews #c36, #c38.

29. The sub-associations are for finished audio products, VCD players, home-theater equipment, electronic games, video machine mechanisms, and magnetic heads. The representative offices are located in Beijing, Guangzhou, Shenzhen, and Hong Kong.

30. Interviews #c32, #c37. The DVD Forum, created in 1995, is an international association led by patent holders of DVD technology. The forum promotes exchange of technology, sets DVD standards, and collects royalties on behalf of DVD-technology patent holders. For more, visit its Web site (www.dvdforum.org).

31. Even the video association leaders praised the audio association as a model for themselves. Interviews #c8, #c11, #c25, #c34, #c41, #c28.

32. Interviews #c33, #c38.

33. Interviews #c3, #c18.

34. China Audio Industry Association, "Old Association, New Vitality," association brochure, 1999.

35. Interviews #c3, #c12, #c17, #c18, #c19, #c21, #c22.

36. Ni retired in 2004. Ni Runfeng, "Changhong zai xiang shenme changhong zai zuo shenme" (What is Changhong thinking, what is Changhong doing?), *Zhongguo jingying bao* (China business), December 1, 1998, p. 8; Zhang Zhong, "Yunxu shibai—yu TCL jituan zongcai li dongsheng yidu tan" (Allow failure: a discussion with TCL president Li Dongsheng), *Zhongguo jingying bao* (China business), February 9, 1999, p. 8.

37. Interview #c7.

38. Interviews #c1, #c19, #c41, #c43.

39. VCD player makers hosted a series of "VCD Phenomenon" meetings, inviting the industry's largest producers and government officials. Wang Xuefeng, "Zhongguo VCD xianxiang xuyao lengjing sisuo" (Need to soberly ponder China VCD phenomenon), *Zhongguo dianzi bao* (China electronics news), March 6, 1998, p. 1.

40. Interviews #c6, #c12, #c16, #c18.

41. Interview #c16.

42. Interviews #c6, #c23.

43. Interviews #c16, #c47.

44. On the broader policy debate and application across sectors, see Scott Kennedy, "The Price of Competition: Pricing Policies and the Struggle to Define China's Economic System," *China Journal*, no. 49 (January 2003), pp. 1–30.

45. The Chinese text of the Anti–Unfair Competition Law is in Sun Wanzhong, ed., *Zhongguo falu nianjian, zhencangban* (Law yearbook of China, collector's edition) (Beijing: China Law Yearbook Service, 1998), pp. 265–267. The English and Chinese texts of the 1998 Price Law are contained in *China Economic News*, no. 13 (April 6, 1998), pp. 9–13, 24–27. Also see Volker Pasternak, "The Right Price," *China Business Review*, vol. 25, no. 5 (September–October 1998), pp. 40–43.

46. Some large state-owned and private companies were consulted during the drafting processes, but their contributions to the final texts were minimal. Interview #g79.

47. *Zhongguo jingmao daokan* (China economic and trade reporter), September 30, 1998, p. 22; Lu Zheng, *Zhongguo gongye fazhan baogao 1999*, pp. 132–133.

48. Interviews #g51, #g62.

49. Text of the regulation and an SDPC spokesperson's explanation is carried in *Zhonghua gongshang shibao* (China business times), December 8, 1998, p. 2.

50. Excerpts of statements from the conference are contained in "Quanmian renshi jiage zilu" (Fully understand price self-discipline), *Zhongguo jingmao daokan* (China economy and trade reporter), December 15, 1998, pp. 18–22.

51. Gordon White, Jude Howell, and Shang Xiaoyuan, *In Search of Civil Society: Market Reform and Social Change in Contemporary China* (Oxford: Clarendon Press, 1996), pp. 149–150. On price wars in a variety of sectors in the 1990s, see Xu Guangjian and Li Huihua, *Jinrongde heidong: zhongguo jingjide kunhuo yu chulu* (The black hole of finance: The Chinese economy's puzzle and way out) (Guangdong: Zhuhai Press, 1998), pp. 5–17.

52. Interviews #c3, #c30, #c41, #c43.

53. Reports challenge Changhong's claim that it hoarded 75 percent of the country's picture tubes, but other companies' reactions indicate Changhong's move did create a shortage. Sun Honggang, "*Caidian jiage zai kang 60 tian?*" (Will color TV prices hold another 60 days?), *Zhongguo jingying bao* (China business), December 15, 1998, p. 1.

54. Interviews #c3, #c7, #c34, #c43; Li Zhiping, "Caidian caiguan suimo fenghui" (Color TV color picture tube year-end summit), *Zhonghua gongshang shibao* (China business times), January 13, 1999, p. 2; Gao Chujian, "Caidian dazhan yi chu ji fa" (Color TV's great war triggered at any moment), *Zhonghua gongshang shibao* (China business times), January 15, 1999, p. 1.

55. Interviews #c8, #c11; Liu Dong, "Guojia jiwei xinxi chanye bu zhiding shishi shixing banfa zhizhi caiguan caidian bu zhengdang jiage jingzheng" (SDPC, MII formulate temporary regulation stopping color picture tube and color TV unfair price competition), *Zhongguo dianzi bao* (China electronics news), April 15, 1999, p. 1; Pang Yicheng, "Caidianye xin yilun jiage dazhan baofa" (Color TV industry, new round of great price wars breaks out), *Zhongguo jingying bao* (China business), April 27, 1999, p. 1.

56. Interviews #c11, #c43; Liu Jian, "Caiguan tingchan cheng dingju" (Color tube stoppage is set), *Zhonghua gongshang shibao* (China business times), May 24, 1999, p. 1; Zhu Yanyan, "Ba da caiguan chang huifu shengchan" (Eight large color tube factories resume production), *Zhonghua gongshang shibao* (China business times), July 16, 1999, p. 1; Zhang Chunwei, "Jiage dazhan xiaoyan sanjin caidian jutou zuo jie lianmeng" (Great price war gunpowder completely scattered, color TV heads formed alliance yesterday), *Chengdu shang bao* (Chengdu commercial news), June 10, 2000; Guo Aibing, "Policymaker: TV Price Floor Illegal," *China Daily*, August 11, 2000.

57. "1997 nian VCD shi da xinwen" (1997 VCD top ten news), *Zhongguo dianzi bao* (China electronics news), January 2, 1998, p. 12; Interviews #c12, #c30.

58. Interviews #c11, #c18, #c29, #c43, #c45.

59. "Growing Pains: China's DVD Market in Price War," *ChinaOnline*, May 9, 2000.

60. "Old Association, New Vitality." CAA's position, though, did not stop its Home Theater Sub-Association from having its members sign a pledge in March 1999 agreeing not to dump their products. *CAA hangye kuaixun* (CAA industry express), no. 123 (March 15, 1999), pp. 1–2.

61. Mark Tilton found that high concentration levels, supplemented by a "high-tech hook" and downstream cartels or import protection, have facilitated the success of Japanese cartels. Mark Tilton, *Restrained Trade: Cartels in Japan's Basic Materials Industries* (Ithaca, N.Y.: Cornell University Press, 1996) pp. 190–211.

62. "1997 nian VCD shi da xinwen."

63. According to one source, in exchange for dropping the tax plan, Zhu Rongji ordered that banks reduce their loans to VCD-player companies, although this would have been very difficult to implement. No companies interviewed for this study suffered a credit squeeze after this episode. Interview #c25.

64. The 1989 consumption tax on TVs raised their price by approximately RMB 500–600. Interview #c32; Huang Jianzhong, "Caise dianshiji shichang," p. 46.

65. Jay Tate, "National Varieties of Standardization," in Peter A. Hall and David Soskice, eds., *Varieties of Capitalism: The Institutional Foundations of Comparative Advantage* (Oxford: Oxford University Press, 2001), pp. 442–473.

66. *"Zhonghua renmin gongheguo biaozhun fa"* (PRC standardization law), issued December 29, 1988, in Sun Wanzhong, *Zhongguo falu nianjian, zhencangban,* pp. 434–435; "Regulations on the Implementation of the PRC Standardization Law," BBC Summary of World Broadcasts, June 20, 1990. For an overview of the system, see Ann Weeks and Dennis Chen, "Navigating China's Standards Regime," *China Business Review,* vol. 30, no. 3 (May–June 2003), pp. 32–38.

67. The International Organization for Standardization (ISO) in 1996 defined a standard as "a document, established *by consensus* and approved by a recognized body, that provides for common and repeated use, rules, guidelines or characteristics for activities or their results, aimed at the achievement of the optimum degree of order in a given context" (my italics); "General Info on Standardization," World Standards Services Network, available online at www.wssn. net/WSSN/gen_inf.html.

68. Interviews #c29, #c35.

69. On the importance of technical standards for information technology and how this has led industry to be more assertive globally, see Liora Salter, "The Standards Regime for Communications and Information Technologies," in A. Clair Cutler, Virginia Haufler, and Tony Porter, eds., *Private Authority and International Affairs* (Buffalo, N.Y.: SUNY Press, 1999), pp. 97–127. Also see Michael Borrus and Stephen S. Cohen, "Building China's Information Technology Industry: Tariff Policy and China's Accession to the World Trade Organization," *Asian Survey,* vol. 38, no. 11 (November, 1998), pp. 1005–1017.

70. Interviews #c4, #c9, #c10, #c17, #c18.

71. The original VCD player had approximately one quarter the resolution quality of a DVD player. CVD resolution was one half that of DVD; SVCD was two thirds that of DVD. A DVD player had a resolution of six hundred lines, that is, the maximum number of lines on a video screen into which the picture can be separated.

72. The two teams were centered on C-Cube and ESS, respectively, two American suppliers of video decompression chips, the component that embodied much of the standard. C-Cube had been the dominant chip supplier to date. CVD Team members wanted to continue the relationship into a new generation product. The SVCD Team members preferred working with ESS, the new market entrant.

73. Zhou Yonggang, "Shei zai caozuo CVD zhi zheng" (Who is manipulating the CVD war?), *Zhonghua gongshang shibao* (China business times), September 2, 1998, p. 5.

74. Interviews #c1, #c45.

75. Interview #c10.

76. Interviews #c12, #c32.

77. Interviews #c16, #c18.

78. Wang Yuling, "Yi bo san zhe" (One wave, three twists), *Jingji ribao* (Economics daily), August 6, 1998, p. 5.

79. Interviews #c1, #c17, #c19, #c25, #c47.

80. Wan Xuefeng, "Lubiaowei toupiao tongguo SVCD biaozhun" (Recording

standards committee votes, passes SVCD standard), *Zhongguo dianzi bao* (China electronics news), August 21, 1998, p. 1; Interviews #c19, #c29.

81. Ministry of Information Industry, *Chaoji VCD xitong jishu guifan* (Technical specifications for the Chaoji VCD system), SJ/T11196–1998, September 28, 1998.

82. Interviews #c32, #c47.

83. Interviews #c10, #c11, #c42, #c48.

84. The committee's composition had not changed much in the previous few years; most company members of the committee were makers of VCRs and audio equipment. Interviews #c29, #c42, #c47; Jiang Taixuan, "Cong CVD de chutai kan hangye fazhan shei zhu chenfu" (From the CVD's emergence see who sinks and floats in the industry's development), *Zhongguo jingmao daokan* (China economy and trade reporter), August 30, 1998, pp. 26, 16; Gao Chujian, "Zhengfu chushou SVCD" (Government comes out with SVCD), *Zhonghua gongshang shibao* (China business times), September 14, 1998, p. 3.

85. The IEC approved the standard a month later at its annual meeting. Interviews #c42, #c44. Chen Ting, "Biaozhun zhiding ying zouxiang shichang" (Setting standard moves toward the market), *Zhongguo jingji shibao* (China economic times), June 29, 1999; Xinhua News Agency, "China Uses Technical Standards to Expand VCD Market," September 8, 2000, available online from the *Factiva* database, global.factiva.com.

86. The association managed to negotiate royalties down from over twenty dollars to approximately fifteen dollars per machine. Interviews #c37, #c28; "Chinese DVD Manufacturers Reached Agreement with 6C," *AsiaPort Daily News*, May 14, 2002; Anthony Kuhn, "China Spins a New Disc," *Far Eastern Economic Review*, vol. 167, no. 8 (February 26, 2004), pp. 34–35.

87. "Nation to Issue EVD Standard," *China Daily*, October 28, 2003; Rattaphol Onsanit, "China Appears Likely to Let Operators Pick 3G Technology," *Dow Jones Newswires*, November 10, 2003; "AVS Standard May Save China US$300m in Royalty Fees," *China Daily*, July 31, 2003.

88. An American company is the lead developer of the decompression chip for the EVD player. The fight for the next generation mobile phone market has pitted three competing standards: CDMA2000, WCDMA, and TD-SCDMA. According to several sources, the supposed "Chinese" option (TD-SCDMA) was originally developed by Siemens of Germany. Moreover, each alternative could benefit both domestic and foreign companies, and proponents of all three alternatives have intensely lobbied the government. Finally, the AVS standards committee, which has benefited from little government interference, has had domestic and foreign member companies, all of whom have voting rights. Interviews #c46, #c27, #c37, #c49, #c50, #c51, #c52, #c53, #c54, #c55; Scott Kennedy, "Holey Protectionism!," *China Economic Quarterly*, vol. 8, no. 3 (Third Quarter, 2004), pp. 24–28. On recent official policy, see Richard P. Suttmeier and Yao Xiangkui, "China's Post-WTO Technology Policy: Standards, Software, and the Changing Nature of Techno-Nationalism," *NBR Special Report*, no. 7 (May 2004).

89. Gao Chujian, "Chaoji SVCD xin biaozhun you yuyin" (Chaoji VCD new standard has reverberations), *Zhonghua gongshang shibao* (China business times), October 26, 1998, p. 3.

## Chapter 5. The Software Industry: Approaching Pluralism

1. "China Sets Up National Software Association," *EDP China Report*, September 19, 1984, p. 308. Except for China Software and Technical Services Corporation (CS&S), all the software companies interviewed for this project were formed, or opened their offices in China, at the earliest in the latter half of the 1980s. IBM, one of the world's largest computer hardware makers and software developers, opened its first office in China in 1979, but it was not until the late 1980s that IBM focused on the software industry. Wang Xiufeng, "Investing in China: IBM Follows Suit," *China Information*, vol. 1, no. 12 (December 1994), p. 15.

2. The sales figure includes RMB 33 billion of products and RMB 40.6 billion of service. The 400,000 employees figure includes technical and nontechnical personnel. In 2001 there were 250,000 software specialists, up from 132,000 in 1998. *2001 Annual Report of China Software Industry* (Beijing: China Software Industry Association, 2002) (hereafter *2001 Software Report*), pp. 51, 54, 61; *China Statistical Yearbook 2002* (Beijing: China Statistics Press, 2002), pp. 117, 577.

3. In 2001, there were 13 computers per 100 urban households. The distribution was heavily tilted toward coastal localities: Beijing (45 per 100 homes), Guangdong (35), Shanghai (38), Tianjin (21), and Zhejiang (20). As of mid-2003, there were 474,000 Web sites in China. The figure of 68 million Internet users involves double counting of people with multiple Internet accounts. *2001 Software Report*, p. 47; *China Statistical Yearbook 2002*, p. 340; China Internet Network Information Center, "Zhongguo hulian wangluo fazhan zhuangkuang tongji baogao" (China Internet development situation statistical report), July 2003, available at www.cnnic.cn.

4. On China's Y2K problem and steps taken to resolve it, see Zhang Qi, "Wo guo jiejue Y2K cunzaide zhuyao wenti ji gongzuo jianyi" (Our country's existing main problems and suggestions for work to solve Y2K), *Zhongguo jisuanji bao* (China infoworld), April 8, 1999, p. B1.

5. In 1998, the United States's 18,000 software firms had 218,000 employees, or 12 employees per firm. Interview #s102 (see appendix for explanation of interview codes).

6. Segal and Thun make the same point about the information technology sector as a whole, contrasting it with the more vertically integrated auto industry. Adam Segal and Eric Thun, "Thinking Globally, Acting Locally: Local Governments, Industrial Sectors, and Development in China," *Politics & Society*, vol. 29, no. 4 (December 2001), p. 564.

7. UFSoft Corporation, "Yingjie xin guanli shidai" (Welcome the new era of management), UFSoft brochure, 1998, p. 4.

8. Steven Mufson, "In China, Professor Leads a High-Tech Revolution," *Washington Post*, June 10, 1998, p. C12. The average age of Kingsoft's employees is even lower, just twenty-five years old. Interview #s48 (see appendix for explanation of interview codes).

9. *2001 Software Report*, p. 56; Interview #s48.

10. Firm-level data from the China Software Industry Association inappropriately combines sales of software and provision of systems integration, yielding a top-four concentration of 22.7 percent. This approach skews the data upward since the top-listed firms are not primarily software producers. *2001 Software Report*, pp. 57–59.

11. Piracy has stifled sales of legal Microsoft software. Although the company does not publicly disclose sales figures for China, CSIA estimates that Microsoft had 4 percent of the software product market in 2001. *2001 Software Report*, p. 57. Sluggish sales have prompted internal dissension over business strategy, which partly accounts for the rapid turnover of managers for its China operations. One former manager wrote about her experience in Wu Shihong, *Nifeng feiyang: weiruan IBM he wo* (Up against the wind: Microsoft, IBM and me) (Beijing: Guangming Press, 1999). Microsoft claims it is losing money in China, but two interview sources from Chinese companies claim Microsoft's China operations are profitable despite piracy. Robyn Meredith, "(Microsoft's) Long March," *Forbes*, February 17, 2003, pp. 78–86; Interviews #s49, #s100.

12. The China Software Industry Association estimates that 60 percent of firms are domestic private, collective (registered to local governments but likely genuinely owned by individuals), or foreign-invested. But given that the smallest software companies are private and less likely to be included in this data, CSIA significantly overstates the proportion of the industry composed of state firms. *2001 Software Report*, p. 26.

13. U.S. Commerce Department International Trade Administration, *U.S. Industry and Trade Outlook '99* (New York: McGraw-Hill, 1999), pp. 28–29.

14. *2001 Software Report*, p. 38. This is just a slight change from 1998, when domestic firms had 30 percent of the market. Yang Fu, "Ruanjianye heshi tiqi yaogan" (When will the software industry straighten its back?), *Caijing*, January 1999, pp. 46–48.

15. Catherine Gelb, "Installing a Software Sector," *China Business Review*, vol. 24, no. 5 (September–October 1997), pp. 28–36.

16. Interview #s22.

17. Associations in corporatism and pluralism differ in four respects. Corporatist associations: (1) lack autonomy (they are initiated by the state, affiliated with the government, staffed by bureaucrats, and financed by the government); (2) have compulsory membership; (3) are hierarchically ordered; and (4) have jurisdictional monopolies. The first criterion only applies to state corporatism.

18. In 1998, MEI was merged with the Ministry of Post and Telecommunications and was renamed the Ministry of Information Industry (MII).

19. To get around this ban, MII received a waiver from the State Council. Interview #c43.

20. Interview #s59.

21. In late 1998, when this study began, regional associations existed in Anhui, Beijing, Dalian, Inner Mongolia, Jiangsu, Ningxia, Shaanxi, Shanghai, Shanxi, Shenyang, Shenzhen, Sichuan, and Tianjin. Since then, software associations have been set up in every province.

22. Interview #s66.

23. Interview #s60.

24. In 1999, CSIA had twenty-four sub-associations. Some closed because of inactivity, leaving fifteen in 2002. Interview #s72.

25. In 2003, USITO also had forty-nine direct corporate members with operations in China. In addition to being a policy advocate, for several years USITO also operated a title verification office. With the cooperation of China's National Copyright Administration, USITO placed the copyright and licensing applications

of domestic software into a registry that foreign companies could then review to see if any of the applications violated their own copyrights.

26. In 1998, there were only five hundred members. Interviews #s59, #s72.

27. A CSIA official said that CSIA lost authority over regional associations in 1992, but regional association officials maintained that they have never been subservient to CSIA. No documents were found that support CSIA's contention of previous leadership.

28. Interview #s66.

29. In addition to BSIA, other local associations that are involved in software issues include Beijing Software Retailers Industry Standards Committee (founded by Federal and other retail stores), the Beijing Experimental Zone (BEZ) Hightech Enterprise Association (run by the municipal government), and the Beijing Information Industry Guild (affiliated with the Beijing municipal Federation of Industry and Commerce).

30. The group, a sub-association of the China Information Industry Chamber of Commerce (*zhongguo xinxi chanye shanghui*), promotes digital products that combine telecommunications, computers and consumer electronics. Bing, "Kuangjia chuding" (Frame initially set), *Zhongguo jisuanji shijie* (China computerworld), July 12, 1999, p. A1.

31. In December 1998, SRS (Stone Rich Sight, *sitony lifang*) merged with a foreign company to become Sina.com, now Sina. Although it still develops Internet software, it has become primarily an Internet content provider. For more on Sina's background, see David Sheff, *China Dawn: The Story of a Technology and Business Revolution* (New York: HarperBusiness, 2002).

32. Interviews #s59, #s68.

33. CSIA-ABM, *Zhongguo ruanjian hangye xiehui caiwu ruanjian fenhui shouce* (CSIA Accounting and Business Management Sub-Association handbook), 1998, p. 2.

34. Interviews #s28, #s67.

35. The text is available from CSIA's Web site (www.csia.org.cn).

36. On the rare occasion a firm seeks the CSIA's help, it does so because CSIA's leaders are former or current officials who can easily contact the bureaucracy. Interview #s68.

37. Interviews #s66, #s70, #s71.

38. When asked if he thought it was a good idea to set up a completely independent software association, one executive dismissed the idea, admonishing, "Don't you know about Falun Gong [the banned spiritual group]? The government is afraid of organizations it cannot control. As soon as there is an organization, there is danger."

39. Interviews #s29, #s57.

40. Interview #s65.

41. Interview #s27.

42. The company's founder is also a member of two local associations for information technology entrepreneurs. Both were described as entirely independent and involved in policy advocacy. Interviews #s44, #s64, #s50.

43. Interviews #s4, #s17, #s44, #s45.

44. Interviews #s34, #s35.

45. Interview #s36. These views conflict with previous research that has found the ACFIC to be more representative than other associations. Jonathan Unger,

"'Bridges': Private Businesses, the Chinese Government and the Rise of New Associations," *China Quarterly*, no. 147 (September 1996), pp. 795–819; Margaret M. Pearson, *China's New Business Elite: The Political Consequences of Economic Reform* (Berkeley: University of California Press, 1997).

46. Interview s#18.

47. Interview #s17.

48. Interview #s11.

49. The sub-association is listed as a CSIA sub-association as of early 2002 but does not appear on a list compiled at the end of 2002. Interviews #s39, #s42, #s72.

50. Depth of interaction is measured along several criteria: (1) companies' attention to policy; (2) the regularity of interaction; (3) the range and rank of officials and departments contacted; (4) the fora of interaction; (5) the range of policy issues; and (6) the degree of company proactiveness.

51. Interviews #s22, #s52.

52. Liu Ren and Zhang Yongjie, *Zhishi yingxiong: yingxiang zhongguancunde 50ge ren* (Knowledge heroes: 50 people that have influenced Zhongguancun) (Beijing: China Social Sciences Press, 1998), pp. 408–418. Also see Dominic Gates, "Microsoft's Man in Beijing," *Industry Standard*, July 17, 2000.

53. Interviews #s6, #s13.

54. The primary exception among the largest firms examined in this study, as of 1999, was Oracle. But its limited interaction with the government has been due to its own preference, not the government's. Oracle has had no government relations division in its China offices, and its management has only occasionally sought out officials. Nor has Oracle made much use of business associations. It is a member of the Beijing Software Industry Association, but it has not been an active participant. Instead, Oracles has relied on its Chinese clients (large companies and government agencies) for policy information. Interview #s43.

55. For example, senior executives from multinational information technology firms made at least twenty-four visits to China in 1998. Liu Haifeng, "'98 dashi kan hao" ('98 general trend looks good), *Zhongguo jisuanji shijie* (China computerworld), January 4, 1999, p. A20.

56. Interview #s22; "Gates Pushes Microsoft In China Trip," *New York Times*, March 23, 1994, p. D3; and Microsoft (China), "Geici zhongguo zhixing shuoguo leilei" (Gates China trip piles up great achievements), www.microsoft.com/china/press (accessed March 10, 1999).

57. Interviews #s20, #s33. Also see Dong Kaihong, "Zhongwen ruanjian zou xiang hefang" (Which direction is Chinese software headed?), *Zhongguo jisuanji shijie* (China computerworld), January 25, 1999, p. A8.

58. MII first hosted a meeting on Linux with experts and large companies in July 1999. See "Linux: fazhan zhongguo ruanjian chanyede qiji" (Linux: a juncture in the development of China's software industry), *Zhongguo jisuanji bao* (China infoworld), July 19, 1999, pp. A2–A4. Some Chinese have seized on reports that a Canadian software firm supposedly found a "NSAKey" in Windows that they hypothesize would permit U.S. government agencies a backdoor into Chinese government networks. Microsoft has flatly denied the charges and stated it still had good relations with the Chinese government. Regardless, the government has been quite sympathetic to these concerns. Chen Chong, the MII official who has overseen software policy, said in mid-2000 that "we don't want one company to mo-

nopolize the software market." By using Linux, he continued, "we can control the security . . . [and] we can control our own destiny." Craig S. Smith, "Fearing Control by Microsoft, China Backs the Linux System," *New York Times,* July 8, 2000, p. B1. A popular book that fed off and stoked these fears is Fang Xingdong and Wang Junxiu, *Qilai—tiaozhan weiruan 'baquan'* (Challenge Microsoft 'hegemony') (Beijing: All-China Federation of Industry and Commerce Press, June 1999). On the weaknesses of Linux, see Charles Bickers, "Latching on to Linux," *Far Eastern Economic Review,* August 31, 2000, p. 34.

59. Interviews #s25, #s36, #s37.

60. Interview #s4.

61. The same view of the party as irrelevant to industry policy was also expressed by an association leader. Interviews #s49, #s52, #s71.

62. Interview #s50.

63. Interview #s54.

64. In 1997, IDG published 285 information industry magazines and newspapers in eighty countries. Li Xiguang, "China's Paper Tiger Hails From Boston," *Washington Post,* November 11, 1995, p. B11. Andrew Tanzer, "The Most Popular Publications in China," *Forbes,* August 25, 1997, p. 48.

65. If the manager was not ethnic Chinese, other Chinese staff help foreign managers interface with domestic businesses and the government. Compared to software firms, more of the foreign steel and consumer electronics firms examined in the study used the latter approach, but this may be a distinction of nationality and not industry, since most of the firms studied in these two sectors were from Asia. Not enough companies were interviewed to allow making a definitive conclusion.

66. Liu Ren and Zhang Yongjie, *Zhishi yingxiong,* pp. 112–122.

67. Interview #s36.

68. An executive from the Internet content provider and software developer Sina said, "It's dangerous to rely too heavily on relationships in volatile power structures . . . There is far more risk today in allying yourself politically with someone in the government, than in just pursuing the private enterprise profit motive." James Ryan, "China.com," *The Industry Standard,* January 15, 1999, www.thestandard.com.

69. Interview #s4.

70. *China Statistical Yearbook 1998* (Beijing: China Statistical Publishing House, 1998), pp. 55, 281.

71. An extended examination of China's taxation system is Donald Brean, ed., *Taxation in Modern China* (New York: Routledge, 1998).

72. Hu Yingnan and Xiao Shifeng, *"Ruanjianye bukan shuifu"* (Software industry cannot endure tax burden), *Zhonghua gongshang shibao* (China business times), January 26, 1999, p. 7.

73. Interviews #s24, #s45, #s66.

74. Interview #s24.

75. The notice also exempted software firm employees from income taxes beginning January 2000. "Zengzhishui cong 17% xiatiao dao 6%" (VAT adjusted down from 17% to 6%), *Zhongguo jisuanji shijie* (China computerworld), August 8, 1999, p. A1.

76. "China Cuts Sales, Business Taxes for Hi-Tech Cos—Report," *Dow Jones International News,* December 6, 1999.

77. Interviews #s79, #s86, #s89.

78. In the March 1999 NPC plenum, Wang Wenjing submitted the resolution "Jianyi zhiding xinxing chanye fuzhi fa" (Suggestions to formulate a law to foster emerging industries). See *Meizhou yongyou* (UFSoft weekly), April 6, 1999.

79. Interviews #s46, #s66, #s69, #s76.

80. The positions of CSIA and the regional associations were also helped by being given the responsibility to certify firms' software as being eligible for the VAT reduction. One observer credits these new powers with the rise in the associations' membership roles, although firms need not join the associations to have their products approved. Interview #s56.

81. Interview #s45.

82. "Beijing Witnesses Influx of High-Tech Ventures," *China Daily*, October 11, 1999.

83. In June 2000, in part due to continued industry pressure, the State Council issued a document providing a wide range of policy incentives to the software industry, which included reducing the VAT to 3 percent. The policy also provided for greater access to capital through creation of a government-financed venture capital mechanism and easier access to stock markets, exemptions and reductions of the income tax and tariffs, direct import-export rights for firms above a certain size, and encouragement of government agencies to purchase domestic software when it and a foreign software are of similar price and quality. Several ministries followed with complementary policies. Interview #s71; PRC State Council, Document No. 18, "State Council Notice on Some Policies to Encourage the Development of the Software and Integrated Circuit Industries," issued June 24, 2000, available on the CSIA Web site (www.csia.org.cn); *2001 Software Report*, pp. 75–76. Also see Tang Zhengyu and Beth Bunnell, "New Software and Integrated Circuit Incentives Bolster Hi-Tech," *China Law and Practice*, vol. 14, no. 7 (September 2000), pp. 44–47.

84. Yang Fu, "When Will the Software Industry Straighten Its Back?" pp. 46–48.

85. This ratio held constant from the mid-1990s to the year 2000. Yan Yan and Jiang Jian, "Zhongguo ruanjian chanye saomiao" (Scanning China's software industry), *Zhonghua gongshang shibao* (China business times), January 12, 1999, p. 7; Kathy Wilhelm, "Tomorrow's IT Powerhouse?" *Far Eastern Economic Review*, June 14, 2001, pp. 36–38.

86. The figure has slightly declined, from 96 percent in 1996 to 92 percent in 2002. "Eighth Annual BSA Global Software Piracy Study," Business Software Alliance, June 2003.

87. In 1997, SRS (now Sina) estimated that three hundred thousand copies of its Internet software had been illegally downloaded, while only ten thousand copies had been purchased in stores. Connie Ling, "The Asian-Language Blues," *Asian Wall Street Journal Weekly Edition*, April 14, 1997, p. 12. In 1999, Kingsoft estimated that there were several million copies of its word processing software, WPS, installed on Chinese computers, but the company had only sold forty thousand copies. Interview #s19.

88. Interview #s18.

89. Susan K. Sell, *Private Power, Public Law: The Globalization of Intellectual Property Rights* (Cambridge: Cambridge University Press, 2003).

90. Andrew C. Mertha, *The Politics of Piracy: Intellectual Property in Contemporary China* (Ithaca, N.Y.: Cornell University Press, forthcoming 2005).

91. BSA offered suggestions about an association, but the initiative came from Chinese firms and a local intellectual property rights lawyer. By 2003 CSA had eighteen members, including at least one foreign company, Microsoft. Interviews #s65, #s47, #s75.

92. *Economics Daily* ran a series, "Xiang daoban liang hongdeng" (Shine a red light against pirates) over a four-week period that included articles by CSA, its members, and the BSA. See *Jingji ribao* (Economics daily), November 21, 1998, p. 6; November 28, 1998, p. 8; December 5, 1998, p. 8; and December 12, 1998, p. 8.

93. Interview #s63.

94. Interview #s65.

95. On UFSoft, see Qiao Hai, "The Yongyou Group Establishes an IPR Protection System," *Guoji maoyi wenti* (International trade news), February 26, 1996, p. 2, in *Foreign Broadcast Information Service—China Daily Reports,* April 4, 1996, pp. 45–46.

96. Legend, which changed its name to Lenovo in 2004, is China's leading computer company. *Meizhou yongyou* (UFSoft weekly), April 6, 1999.

97. Lana Wang, "Programmer Ready to Repel Big Competitors," *South China Morning Post International Weekly,* January 3, 1998, p. Business 8.

98. Many Chinese believe that Microsoft's public commitment to fighting piracy is disingenuous, partly because of ambiguous comments Bill Gates made in mid-1998 while speaking to students at the University of Washington: "Although about three million computers get sold every year in China, people don't pay for the software. Someday they will, though. And as long as they're going to steal it, we want them to steal ours. They'll get sort of addicted, and then we'll somehow figure out how to collect sometime in the next decade." Brent Schlender, "The Bill and Warren Show," *Fortune,* July 20, 1998, p. 54.

99. Xiao Wei, "Microsoft Offers Help to Colleges," *China Daily Business Weekly,* November 29, 1998, p. 6; and Interview #s12.

100. Microsoft Corporation, "Piracy and Counter-Piracy: A Long Struggle Over the Fate of the Software Industry," Microsoft media briefing background materials, November 1998.

101. Mike Laris, "In China, Challenging The Pirates," *Washington Post,* January 3, 1994, p. F13; "Microsoft Wins Its First Software Copyright Case in China," *ChinaOnline,* February 24, 1999 (www.chinaonline.com); "Software Developers to Put Pirates in Court," *China Daily Business Weekly,* June 27, 1999, p. 5; and "Court Rules in Favor of Microsoft, Adobe in Shanghai Software Piracy Case," *ChinaOnline,* April 26, 2001 (www.chinaonline.com).

102. Interview #s29.

103. The drafting group for both was headed by the National Copyright Administration and included legal scholars and officials from the Ministry of Information Industry and the State Administration of Industry and Commerce. After the initial drafting, the Copyright Law was revised and issued by the National People's Congress. The State Council provided a coordinating role for both laws and issued the software regulations itself. For the original texts: National People's Congress, "Zhuzuoquan fa" (Copyright law), issued September 7, 1990, in Sun Wanzhong, ed., *Zhongguo falu nianjian, zhencangban* (Law yearbook of China, collector's edition) (Beijing: China Law Yearbook Service, 1998), pp. 167–172; State Council, "Jisuanji ruanjian baohu tiaoli" (Computer software protection regulations), issued June 4, 1991, in Wang Huai'an et al., eds., *Zhonghua renmin gongheguo*

*falu quanshu 1990–1992* (PRC law compendium, 1990–1992) (Jilin: Jilin People's Press, 1993), pp. 724–728. For the revised texts: "PRC, Copyright Law (Revised)," issued October 27, 2001, *China Law and Practice*, vol. 15, no. 10 (December 2001/January 2002), pp. 53–70; State Council, "Jisuanji ruanjian baohu tiaoli" (Computer software protection regulations), issued December 20, 2001, available on the Xinhua News Agency's Web site (www.xinhuanet.com/lewgal/flfg.htm).

104. The NCA reportedly wanted to eliminate the regulation to conform to international practice, in which software programs are classified as literary works and do not require separate legislation. Interview #s97.

105. Said one government official about CSA's efforts, if it "did not represent software firms, the loss by firms would be quite large." Interviews #s78, #s83.

106. This last element has proven most controversial because it goes beyond the requirements of TRIPS, which limits liability to commercial end users. Some Chinese legal specialists have criticized the government for bending too much to the demands of industry, particularly Microsoft. In October 2002 the Supreme People's Court issued an interpretation of the two laws. It reaffirmed the liability of commercial users of pirated software, but observers disagree whether the court invalidated the liability of private end users. Interviews #s52, #s99, #s101. For a sophisticated critique of a strict intellectual property rights regime, see Shou Bu, Fang Xingdong, and Wang Junxiu, eds., *Wo huyu* (I appeal) (Jilin: Jilin People's Press, 2002).

107. The NPC's Standing Committee momentarily deadlocked over Article 43 of the original Copyright Law, which permitted government media to broadcast or print copyrighted materials without permission or royalty payment to the copyright holder as long as the materials were not used for profit. NCA's initial revised draft deleted Article 43 because it clearly violates international agreements, but the State Council Legislative Affairs Office reinserted the language when the draft moved to their office, because of lobbying from news agencies and the Communist Party's Propaganda Department. A former head of the NCA is a Standing Committee member, and when the Standing Committee began its deliberations, he and another member (a famous songwriter) vociferously criticized the article and persuaded other members to join them in blocking it. Unable to reach a compromise, the State Council withdrew the draft and sent it back to the NCA for revisions. The offending article was eventually removed. Interviews #s45, #s46, #s70, #s96, #g53. Also see "State Council Asks Parliament to Consider Copyright Law Amendment," Xinhua News Agency, December 26, 2000.

108. Interviews #s83, #s96.

109. Ministry of Finance, "Kuaiji diansuanhua guanli banfa" (Measures on the regulation of accounting computerization), and "Shangpinhua kuiji jisuan ruanjian pingshen guize" (Rules for the approval of commercialized accounting computer software), both issued June 30, 1994. The initial rules were reinforced with Ministry of Finance, "Kuaiji diansuanhua gongzuo guifan" (Accounting computerization working guidelines), issued June 10, 1996. These documents, originally posted on ABM's Web site, are available from the author.

110. These charges were made by a government official and domestic firms, but foreign companies faced even greater discrimination. Although several applied, only one foreign firm, DacEasy, had its software approved by the ministry. A representative from one foreign company reported that the Ministry of Finance de-

nied the appraisal system even existed. Interviews #s34, #s35, #s36, #s43, #s67, #s89.

111. UFSoft Corporation, "Yingjie xin guanli shidai" (Welcome the new management era), 1998, p. 4. Xu reportedly received a car from UFSoft. Interviews #s35, #s36, #s89.

112. Despite his lost utility as a patron, UFSoft eventually hired Xu to help with business development. He also remained a leader of ABM. Interview #s74.

113. Matt Pottinger, "China Considers Rule Favoring Local Firms in Software Purchases," *Wall Street Journal*, March 7, 2003; Interviews #s49, #s50, #s52, #s72, #s100.

## Chapter 6. Conclusion: China's Political Economies

1. A stress on economic factors is found in Wyn Grant, Albert Martinelli, and William Paterson, "Large Firms as Political Actors: A Comparative Analysis of the Chemical Industries in Britain, Italy and West Germany," *West European Politics*, vol. 12, no. 2 (April 1989), pp. 72–90; and Dermot McCann, *Small States, Open Markets, and the Organization of Business Interests* (Aldershot, England: Dartmouth Publishing, 1995). A collection of both views are found in J. Rogers Hollingsworth, Phillipe Schmitter, and Wolfgang Streeck, eds., *Governing Capitalist Economies: Performance and Control of Economic Sectors* (New York: Oxford University Press, 1994); and Sylvia Maxfield and Ben Ross Schneider, eds., *Business and the State in Developing Countries* (Ithaca, N.Y.: Cornell University Press, 1997).

2. On steel, see Patricia O'Brien, "Governance Systems in Steel: The American and Japanese Experience," in Hollingsworth, Schmitter, and Streeck, *Governing Capitalist Economies*, pp. 43–71; Mark Tilton, *Restrained Trade: Cartels in Japan's Basic Materials Industries* (Ithaca, N.Y.: Cornell University Press, 1996); and the Web site of the American Iron and Steel Institute (www.steel.org). On consumer electronics, see Alan Cawson, "Sectoral Governance in Consumer Electronics in Britain and France," in *Governing Capitalist Economies*, pp. 215–243.

3. America's software industry displays both a multitude of active trade associations as well as direct lobbying by leading firms. For a typical article on Microsoft, see Joel Brinkley, "Awaiting Verdict, Microsoft Starts Lobbying Campaign," *New York Times*, November 1, 1999, p. C6.

4. Tony Saich found the same strategy in social organizations more generally. See his "Negotiating the State: The Development of Social Organizations in China," *China Quarterly*, no. 161 (March 2000), pp. 124–141.

5. For more on the decline of the Chinese Communist Party's role in economic policy making, see Murray Scot Tanner, *The Politics of Lawmaking in China: Institutions, Processes, and Democratic Prospects* (Oxford: Clarendon Press, 1999).

6. Later in the chapter, the discussion considers the possibility that there is variation in political circumstances within China that has caused some of the variation found in government-business relations.

7. This fact does not dilute the utility of employing these frameworks. Since they have been the dominant lenses through which China and other countries' government-business relations have been analyzed, drawing on them has permitted comparison with earlier research on China and other cases. In addition, to invent an alternative framework for my analysis would have been necessarily ad hoc and

arbitrary. As noted in the introduction, the frameworks were meant to be starting points of analysis, not end points.

8. There may be an intent to move the steel industry toward a state corporatist order, but this plan has yet to be realized. Nor does state corporatism capture the continued significance of direct government-business interaction beyond the sector's associations.

9. Internationalization and other economic factors have been used to explain the decline of corporatism globally. Philippe C. Schmitter, "Sectors in Modern Capitalism: Modes of Governance and Variations in Performance," in Renato Brunetta and Carlo Dell'Aringa, eds., *Labour Relations and Economic Performance* (New York: New York University Press, 1990), pp. 3–39; McCann, *Small States, Open Markets, and the Organization of Business Interests;* Markus M. L. Crepaz, "An Institutional Dinosour: Austrian Corporatism in the Post-industrial Age," *West European Politics,* vol. 18, no. 4 (October 1995), pp. 64–88; Leif Lewin, "The Rise and Decline of Corporatism: The Case of Sweden," *European Journal of Political Research,* vol. 26, no. 1 (July 1994), pp. 59–79; Gerald A. McBeath, "The Changing Role of Business Associations in Democratizing Taiwan," *Journal of Contemporary China,* no. 18 (July 1998), pp. 303–320; Wolfgang Streeck and Philippe C. Schmitter, "From National Corporatism to Transnational Pluralism: Organized Interests in the Single European Market," *Politics and Society,* vol. 19, no. 2 (June 1991), pp. 133–164; Howard Wiarda, "Dismantling Corporatism: The Problem of Modernization in Latin America," *World Affairs,* vol. 156, no. 4 (Spring 1994), pp. 199–203.

10. No two sectors are economically identical. Although the proportion of output contributed by state-owned enterprises is similar (72 percent in steel, 67 percent in autos), foreign-invested firms account for a larger portion of output in autos (31 percent) than steel (8 percent). *China Statistical Yearbook 2002* (Beijing: China Statistics Press, 2002), pp. 432, 442, 452. Also see Eric Harwit, *China's Automobile Industry: Policies, Problems, and Prospects* (Armonk, N.Y.: M. E. Sharpe, 1997); and Eric Thun, *Changing Lanes in China: Foreign Direct Investment, Local Governments, and Auto Sector Development* (Cambridge: Cambridge University Press, forthcoming).

11. Interview #g5 (see appendix for an explanation of interview codes).

12. Interview #g37. Also see the CMRA's Web site (www.cmra.org.cn).

13. Not all cases are unambiguous, showing that both economic and political factors shape government-business interaction. The Internet content provider (ICP) industry has a significant number of private and foreign-invested firms. In April 1999, in an attempt to self-regulate themselves and interact with officialdom, eight ICPs established the China Internet Content Providers United Development High-Level Conference (*zhongguo ICP lianhe fazhan gaoceng huiyi*). Originally unregistered, in January 2000 the group became affiliated with the China Information Economic Society as the society's Internet Enterprise Department. The group, which has grown to thirty-four companies, has held monthly meetings since its founding. For its first two years, officials were regularly invited to discuss policy issues related to the development of the Internet. But in June 2001, the government launched the Internet Society of China (ISC), which most major Internet companies have since joined. Although the Internet Enterprise Department remains open, its original role as a channel for policy dialogue has diminished. However, ISC has not been active, meeting only once per year. To fill the void, some foreign-

invested Internet companies joined the American Chamber of Commerce in Beijing and participate in the chamber's IT/Telecommunications Forum. But Internet companies primarily lobby directly. The major ICPs have hired former Communist Party and government officials to assist them in this effort. As in software, private and foreign ICPs have as in-depth contact with officialdom as their state-owned counterparts. Despite the limits on associations, lobbying has resulted in ICPs being allowed to reprint more news stories and expand their business beyond what authorities originally preferred. Interviews #s40, #s41, #s48, #s55, #s56; Zhao Lei, "Wangluo neirong shang da jiemeng" (Internet content providers' great alliance), *Zhonghua gongshang shibao* (China business times), April 14, 1999, p. 12. For more information on ISC, see its Web site (www.isc.org.cn).

14. State Economic and Trade Commission (hereafter SETC), *Hangye xiehui gongzuo shouce* (Industry association work handbook), 2002, pp. 419–454.

15. Chen Shengyong and Wei Zhongqing, "Minjian shanghui yu siying qiyezhu jiecengde zhengzhi canyu" (Private business associations and the political participation of the private entrepreneur class), *Zhejiang shehui kexue* (Zhejiang social sciences), September 2003, pp. 19–26; Li Fan, "Minyinghua zhutui zhongguo hangye xiehui" (Privatization helps China's associations), *Guoji jinrong shibao* (International financial times), September 12, 2002, p. 2. The same sources of regional variation were also found by Gordon White, Jude Howell, and Shang Xiaoyuan, *In Search of Civil Society: Market Reform and Social Change in Contemporary China* (Oxford: Clarendon Press, 1996).

16. Schmitter, "Sectors in Modern Capitalism"; Hollingsworth, Schmitter, and Streeck, *Governing Capitalist Economies;* Maxfield and Schneider, *Business and the State in Developing Countries;* White, Howell, and Shang, *In Search of Civil Society;* Jonathan Unger and Anita Chan, "Corporatism in China: A Developmental State in an East Asian Context," in Barrett L. McCormick and Jonathan Unger, eds., *China After Socialism: In the Footsteps of Eastern Europe or East Asia?* (Armonk, N.Y.: M. E. Sharpe, 1996), pp. 95–129; and Margaret M. Pearson, *China's New Business Elite: The Political Consequences of Economic Reform* (Berkeley: University of California Press, 1997).

17. Interview #c45.

18. One official writes: "Of course in the transitional period, the government will not support [read "control"] all industry associations, but should grasp key ones and walk on two legs: provide support to important industries, and except for special needs let enterprises start and voluntarily form them according to law generally without support . . . I am afraid that a minority of important industry associations will have to maintain an 'official color' for a certain period." Wang Jiqing, "Guanyu hangye xiehuide jianshe wenti" (On the problem of constructing industry associations), *Jingji gongzuo tongxun* (Economic work report), February 28, 1998, pp. 8–9. Similar arguments are put forward by Shi Zuoting, "Guanyu peiyu he fazhan gongshang xiehui ruogan wentide sikao" (Thoughts on some problems on nurturing and developing industrial and commercial associations), *Zhongguo jingmao daokan* (China economic and trade reporter), July 30, 1999, pp. 12–13; and Liu Li, "Wo guo hangye guanli moshi fenxi" (Analysis of our country's industry regulation model), *Zhongguo gaige* (China reform), February 1999, pp. 18–19.

19. Shi Zuoting, "Guanyu peiyu he fazhan gongshang xiehui ruogan wentide sikao."

20. Zysman stresses how such technology differences, embodied in the oil and steel industries on the one hand and the consumer electronics industry on the other, affect government-business relations in France and explain why the French state has more successfully promoted the first two industries than the latter. John Zysman, *Political Strategies for Industrial Order: State, Market, and Industry in France* (Berkeley: University of California Press, 1977). The current study does not dispute the importance of technological differences, but argues that other economic factors are equally important in shaping government-business relations.

21. Works that have found corporatist state-society relations include Pearson, *China's New Business Elite;* White, Howell, and Shang, *In Search of Civil Society;* and Unger and Chan, "Corporatism in China."

22. Those who stress clientelism include David L. Wank, *Commodifying Communism: Business, Trust, and Politics in a Chinese City* (Cambridge: Cambridge University Press, 1999); David Zweig, "Undemocratic Capitalism: China and the Limits of Economism," *National Interest,* no. 56 (Summer 1999), pp. 63–72; and He Qinglian, *Xiandaihuade xianjing: dangdai zhongguode jingji shehui wenti* (The pitfalls of modernization: The economic and social problems of contemporary China) (Beijing: China Today Press, 1998).

23. It is possible that interview sources hid from me their roles as government patrons or business clients. To overcome this problem, I interviewed multiple companies, including competitors, and well informed outside observers who had nothing to gain from hiding clientelist practices. As cited earlier, those interviews did yield some possible examples of patronage. It is also possible that national public-policy lobbying is so new that patron-client ties have yet to be firmly established. This study's findings suggest, though, that it will be difficult to establish effective and enduring patron-client ties on public policy.

24. For more on the declining utility of connections in business, see Doug Guthrie, *Dragon in a Three-Piece Suit: The Emergence of Capitalism in China* (Princeton, N.J.: Princeton University Press, 1999), pp. 175–197; and Bruce J. Dickson, *Red Capitalists in China: The Party, Private Entrepreneurs, and Prospects for Political Change* (Cambridge: Cambridge University Press, 2003).

25. Wank's research concerns relations between small merchants and local Xiamen officials, while Pearson interviewed Chinese managers of foreign joint ventures primarily located along China's coast outside Beijing. In both types of cases, relations between the two sides were driven toward firm-specific issues. Small merchants are the least likely type of firm to be interested in public policy, and they are the most vulnerable to official exploitation, making patronage a tempting strategy to remain in business. Chinese managers of joint ventures are likely responsible for the day-to-day aspects of their business, while broader strategic decisions about the foreign partners' views of Chinese government policy are made by their foreign partners on site or, more likely, at the foreign company's offices in Beijing, Shanghai, or Hong Kong.

26. Schmitter, "Sectors in Modern Capitalism"; McCann, *Small States, Open Markets, and the Organization of Business Interests;* Crepaz, "An Institutional Dinosaur"; Lewin, "The Rise and Decline of Corporatism"; McBeath, "The Changing Role of Business Associations in Democratizing Taiwan"; Streeck and Schmitter, "From National Corporatism to Transnational Pluralism": Wiarda, "Dismantling Corporatism"; Neil J. Mitchell, "The Decentralization of Business in Britain," *Journal of Politics,* vol. 52, no. 2 (May 1990), pp. 622–637; and David Vo-

gel, "Government-Industry Relations in the United States: an Overview," in Stephen Wilks and Maurice Wright, eds., *Comparative Government-Industry Relations* (Oxford: Clarendon Press, 1987), pp. 91–116.

27. David Strand, "Protest in Beijing: Civil Society and Public Sphere in China," *Problems of Communism*, vol. 39, no. 3 (May–June 1990), pp. 1–19; Thomas B. Gold, "Urban Private Business and Social Change," in Deborah Davis and Ezra Vogel, eds., *Chinese Society on the Eve of Tiananmen: The Impact of Reform* (Cambridge, Mass.: Council on East Asian Studies, 1990), pp. 157–78; and Gordon White, *Riding the Tiger: The Politics of Economic Reform in Post-Mao China* (Stanford: Stanford University Press, 1993), pp. 198–232.

28. Victor Nee, "A Theory of Market Transition: From Redistribution to Markets in State Socialism," *American Sociological Review*, vol.54, no. 5 (October 1989), pp. 663–81; and Andrew Walder, "Markets and Inequality in Transition Economies: Toward Testable Theories," *American Journal of Sociology*, vol. 101, no. 4 (January 1996), pp. 1060–1073.

29. White, Howell, and Shang, *In Search of Civil Society*; Pearson, *China's New Business Elite*.

30. Daniel Kelliher, *Peasant Power in China: The Era of Rural Reforms, 1979–1989* (New Haven, Conn.: Yale University Press, 1992); Kevin J. O'Brien and Lianjiang Li, "The Politics of Lodging Complaints in Rural China," *China Quarterly*, no. 143 (September 1995), pp. 756–783; Merle Goldman and Roderick MacFarquhar, eds., *The Paradox of China's Post-Mao Reforms* (Cambridge, Mass.: Harvard University Press, 1999); Elizabeth J. Perry and Mark Selden, eds., *Chinese Society: Change, Conflict and Resistance, Second Edition* (London: Routledge, 2003).

31. Minxin Pei, "Citizens v. Mandarins: Administrative Litigation in China," *China Quarterly*, no. 152 (December 1997), pp. 832–862; Kristen Parris, "Entrepreneurs and Citizenship in China," *Problems of Post-Communism*, vol. 46, no. 1 (January/February 1999), pp. 43–61.

32. The Chinese description of this dynamic is legendary: "Those above have policies, those below have counter measures" (*shangmian you zhengce, xiamian you duice*). Originally applied to the national and local government, respectively, "above" and "below" have also been descriptions of the state and society, respectively.

33. Saich reports how two social groups directly influenced national policies for family planning and protection of rural habitats. See Tony Saich, *Governance and Politics of China, Second Edition* (Hampshire, England: Palgrave Macmillan, 2004), pp. 190–192.

34. Since business involvement is still a contentious issue, it makes sense to view business lobbying in China as what O'Brien terms "boundary-spanning contention" that straddles protest and institutionalized participation. Though not specifically referring to China, O'Brien categorizes lobbying as a fully accepted form of political activity. Kevin J. O'Brien, "Neither Transgressive nor Contained: Boundary-Spanning Contention in China," *Mobilization: An International Journal*, vol. 8, no. 1 (February 2003), pp. 51–64.

35. This version of Chinese policy making, known as fragmented authoritarianism, was introduced by Kenneth Lieberthal and Michel Oksenberg, *Policymaking in China: Leaders, Structures, and Processes* (Princeton, N.J.: Princeton University Press, 1988).

36. Tanner, *The Politics of Lawmaking in China*. The original "garbage can"

model from which Tanner borrows posits that actors in the political process do not necessarily act according to their revealed self-interest but according to widely accepted norms of behavior. In China, those norms are no longer fully accepted. James G. March and Johan P. Olsen, *Rediscovering Institutions: The Organizational Basis of Politics* (New York: The Free Press, 1989).

37. Gordon C. Chang, *The Coming Collapse of China* (New York: Random House, 2001); Bruce Gilley, *China's Democratic Future: How It Will Happen and Where It Will Lead* (New York: Columbia University Press, 2004).

38. Such an incrementalist path to democratization is consistent with Tanner's view of the potential implications for the growing power of the National People's Congress. Tanner, *The Politics of Lawmaking in Post-Mao China*, pp. 231–252. On Wang Wenjing, see Xinhua News Agency, "NPC Deputy Appeals for Self-Employed Businessmen's Easy Access to Local Elections," March 11, 2003, in *Factiva* database, global.factiva.com (accessed August 29 2004).

39. Since I did not consistently ask sources about democratization (interviews focused on more concrete, immediate issues), I cannot make any firm conclusions about the relative support for democracy versus continued Chinese Communist Party rule among businesspeople. For a study that more systematically addresses this question as well as the party's response, see Bruce J. Dickson, *Red Capitalists in China: The Party, Private Entrepreneurs, and Prospects for Political Change* (Cambridge: Cambridge University Press, 2003). Also see An Chen, "Capitalist Development, Entrepreneurial Class, and Democratization in China," *Political Science Quarterly*, vol. 117, no. 3 (Fall 2002), pp. 401–422; and Margaret M. Pearson, "Entrepreneurs and Democratization in China's Foreign Sector," in Victoria E. Bonnell and Thomas B. Gold, eds., *The New Entrepreneurs of Europe and Asia: Patterns of Business Development in Russia, Eastern Europe and China* (Armonk, N.Y.: M. E. Sharpe, 2002), pp. 130–155.

40. The classic statement on the importance of elites in the democratization process is Dankwart A. Rustow, "Transitions to Democracy: Toward a Dynamic Model," *Comparative Politics*, vol. 2, no. 3 (April 1970), pp. 337–363. For a defense of this position as applied to East Asia, see Edward Friedman, *The Politics of Democratization: Generalizing East Asian Experiences* (Boulder, Colo.: Westview, 1994).

41. Stephen Handelman, *Comrade Criminal: Russia's New Mafiya* (New Haven: Yale University Press, 1995). Another example of how democracy has left economically entrenched interests with disproportionate political power is the Philippines. Paul D. Hutchcroft, *Booty Capitalism: The Politics of Banking in the Philippines* (Ithaca: Cornell University Press, 1998).

42. Consistent with this view, Anne Thurston has found that one of the key ingredients making for fairer village elections in China is a low concentration of wealth (and political power) in villages. Anne F. Thurston, *Muddling Toward Democracy: Political Change in Grassroots China*, United States Institute of Peace Peaceworks, no. 23 (August 1998).

43. For comparative data on China's income inequality, see World Bank, "World Development Indicators Online," devdata.worldbank.org/dataonline. For different interpretations of the significance of growing inequality on popular political attitudes in China, see Martin K. Whyte, Jie Chen, Edward Friedman, and Youngmin Zhou, "China's Credibility Gap: Public Opinion and Instability in China," Woodrow Wilson International Center for Scholars, *Asia Program Special*

*Report*, no. 104 (August 2002). On the importance of income equality for democratization in East Asia, see Gerald L. Curtis, "A 'Recipe' for Democratic Development," *Journal of Democracy*, vol. 8, no. 3 ( July 1997), pp. 139–145.

44. Interviews #g15, #g52, #s70, #s87.

45. Interviews #g17, #g47, #c31, #c32, #c33, Zhang Delin, "Chongfen fahui hangye xiehuide zuoyong" (Fully develop the role of industry associations), *Qiye gaige yu guanli* (Enterprise reform and management), July 1996, pp. 21–24. Lu Fengtai, ed., *Shehui zhongjie zuzhi yanjiu* (Social intermediary organizations research) (Shanghai: Xuelin Press, 1998).

46. On the policy toward and condition of Wenzhou's associations, see Ou Xinqian and Du Jinling, eds., *Zhongguo hangye xiehui: gaige yu tansuo* (Chinese industry associations: reform and exploration) (Beijing: China Commercial Press, April 1999), pp. 182–223. On the city's financial groups, see Kellee S. Tsai, *Back-Alley Banking: Private Entrepreneurs in China* (Ithaca, N.Y.: Cornell University Press, 2002), pp. 120–165. For Shanghai's 2002 regulations, see SETC, *Hangye xiehui gongzuo shouce*, pp. 144–156.

47. Interviews #g65, #g67.

48. Nicholas Lardy, *China's Unfinished Economic Revolution* (Washington, D.C.: Brookings Institution Press, 1998).

49. Edward Steinfeld, *Forging Reform in China: The Fate of State-Owned Industry* (Cambridge: Cambridge University Press, 1998).

*Appendix: Case Selection and Interviews*

1. In the year 2000, agriculture accounted for exactly 50 percent of employed labor (down from 83.5 percent in 1952 and 70.5 percent in 1978), compared to 22.5 percent in industry and 27.5 percent in services. *China Statistical Yearbook 2001* (Beijing: China Statistics Press, 2001), pp. 50, 108.

2. Doug Guthrie, *Dragon in a Three-Piece Suit: The Emergence of Capitalism in China* (Princeton, N.J.: Princeton University Press, 1999).

# Index

ABM. *See* Accounting and Business Management Sub-Association

Accounting and Business Management Sub-Association (ABM), 138–139, 140, 141, 142, 150, 156–157, 165, 170

Action-response model of state-society relations, 177–178

Adobe, 141

Agreement on Trade-Related Aspects of Intellectual Property Rights (TRIPS), 152, 154

Agriculture, 128, 190–191

Air pollution in steel industry, 89

All-China Federation of Industry and Commerce (ACFIC), 9, 10, 27, 30–32, 35, 37, 39, 41–42, 44, 69–70, 108–109, 136, 141, 183; as distinguished from other associations, 31–32; members of, 31, 40; political background of, 31–32

American Chamber of Commerce, 33, 70, 137, 142

American Iron and Steel Institute, 162

Angang Steel. *See* Anshan Iron and Steel

Anhui, 98

Anshan Iron and Steel, 57, 61, 80, 87

Anti-Unfair Competition Law (1993), 111

Associations, 4, 7, 13–16, 164–165, 175, 176; affiliation with responsible business department, 38–39, 40; based on members' ownership form, 29, 38; based on product type, 29, 38; in consumer electronics industry, 97, 101, 102–106; financial resources for, 39–40; hierarchy among, 41; independence of, 37; limited autonomy of, 36–40; monopolies of interest of, 43–44; national-level, 41–42; relationship between economic characteristics and development of, 169; in software industry, 134–142, 158–159; staffing for, 39; steel-related, 58; as transmission belts, 7, 37; as voluntary, 40

Association system: mapping China's, 28–36; restructuring, 181–182

Atmosphere Anti-Pollution Law, 91

Audio-visual coding standard (AVS), 125

Automobile industry, 168

Autonomy, inverted-U shaped relationship between influence and, 70, 139–140, 163

Baogang. *See* Baoshan Iron and Steel

Baoshan Iron and Steel, 22, 62, 64, 68, 71, 72, 73, 81, 85, 86, 87, 90

Basic Oxygen Furnace (BOF), 61

Beidaihe, 25

Beijing, 1, 49, 50, 131, 192

Beijing Electronics Information Industry Office, 135

Beijing Number 1 Computer Factory, 142